The Good Book

The Good Book
the true story of Y'ALL

by
James Dean Jay Byrd
and
Steven Cheslik-DeMeyer

Published by The Lucky Green Dress Company, P.O. Box 24903, Nashville, Tennessee 37202-4903.

Library of Congress Cataloguing-in-Publication Data
Byrd, James Dean Jay, 1967-
The good book : the true story of Y'all / by James Dean Jay Byrd and Steven Cheslik-DeMeyer
p. cm.
ISBN 0-9672542-0-5 (alk. paper)
1. Y'all (Musical group) 2. Country musicians — United States Biography. I. Cheslik-DeMeyer, Steven. II. Title.
ML421.Y35B97 1999
782.421642'092'2 — dc21
[B] 99-37120
CIP

Manufactured in the United States of America

For Alison White

Contents

Foreword and Acknowledgments

In the summer of 1994, a group of women we'd never seen before walked up to us on the street in New York City. One of them handed us a $20 bill and said, "That's for *The Next Big Thing*." (*The Next Big Thing* was our second self-released recording. At the time, we were asking fans to buy the CD ahead of time to raise money to press it.) Jay said, "Thanks!" but as she started to walk away, he hollered after her, "Wait — how will I know who it's for?" The woman shot back, "I'm Laurie. I'm a friend of Satan's!"

Now, before you start to think we sold our souls for fame and fortune, let us explain. A few months earlier, we had gone to a very non-traditional Easter party hosted by Alison Colby (not the Miss Alison to whom this book is dedicated). We were invited to the party by mutual friends of ours and Alison's, Lizzy Yoder and Mark Bellncula. Lizzy and Mark used to produce a monthly cable cooking show in New York called "Lick the Spoon." Lizzy was the host. She would cook vegetarian dishes in her tiny Lower East Side kitchen, and, with the help of "blue screen" technology, she had musical guests. Mark was the director and camera man. They called us because they'd seen one of the posters we put up all over town advertising our ongoing cabaret show, "An Evening of Stories & Songs with Y'ALL." Our posters used to always say, "Y'ALL — white trash country gospel" and the white trash part caught Lizzy's eye because she was planning a white trash episode of "Lick the Spoon." She asked us to be that episode's musical guest. That was our first taste of television.

When we arrived at the Easter party, since we didn't know anyone there except Lizzy and Mark, we ended up standing in the middle of the living room of the small apartment and turning in a circle to face each person as they introduced themselves to us. Lizzy and Mark were the second-to-the-last two people we turned to, and since we knew them already, as a joke, Lizzy said, "I'm the Easter Bunny!" Not to be outdone, Mark said, "And I'm Jesus." The next and last person, someone we didn't know, without missing a beat said, "And I'm Satan." Everybody laughed, and the nickname kind of stuck. Her real name is Christine Murray.

Christine became a fan and a good friend and the regular "proprietress" of the Y'ALL Country Store, selling our merchandise for us at shows. We always introduced her from the stage as "Satan." It always got a laugh, but I sometimes wonder what our parents and other people must've thought when they heard that on recordings of our performances!

So that's how we met Laurie the literary agent. Laurie was a friend of Christine (Satan), and Christine was a friend of Alison Colby, and Alison Colby was a friend of Lizzy and Mark.

Christine brought Laurie to a few of our shows. She liked Jay's stories, and she told Christine to tell us that we ought to write a book. We didn't know anything about Laurie at the time. But Christine mentioned it more than once, and so Laurie's name was fresh in our minds when we saw the article in the business section of *The New York Post* about her and some other big-time New York literary agents. Laurie was in the article because she had gotten unheard of advances for two first-time authors: the man who wrote *The Bridges of Madison County*, and the man who wrote *The Christmas Box.*

So, we got to thinking a book might be a very good idea indeed! We met Laurie at her office, and the three of us talked about what kind of a book we would write. At the time, we were selling a homemade spiral-bound book we wrote called *The Y'ALL Singin' Cookbook.* It had recipes, music, illustrations, and some of the stories from our first cabaret show. We were making them one at a time at Kinko's and losing lots of money on them, but we loved the book. We thought we'd like to do a nice hard cover version of it. But Laurie thought we should write our autobiography. Actually, she kind of tricked us into it, dangling the carrot just out of our reach, saying "Give me the first chapter, that's all you have to do. I'll send it around and see if anybody's interested." Once we'd done that, she said, "This is good, now just give me the first hundred pages." We did that, and she said, "Okay, keep going." And before any of us knew what we'd done — about a year and a half later — we'd written a book!

Now, to back up a little, we have to admit our initial thought was that Laurie would get us a huge advance and we'd finish writing *The Good Book* in some exotic island vacation spot. Her initial thought was probably more along the lines of she'd be able to interest one of those big publishers whose names she had in her little black book in yet another novel by yet another unknown author (or two-man team) once we'd written the whole thing.

The big publishers read it, three or four of 'em anyway, and they all told Laurie they liked it, but they didn't know what to do with it. As it turned out, the publishing industry was taking a swing in a different direction since *The Bridges of Madison County.* Apparently, all they're looking for anymore is "tried and true."

Well, Laurie knew about all our plans — our TV variety show idea, our upcoming recordings, a nationwide tour — and she decided that before she got too many refusals, she would put *The Good Book* on a back burner until we got a little more famous. We understood and trusted her decision, but boy were we disappointed! After all, we were hoping *The Good Book* would *make* us famous. Besides that, we thought it was a really *good book*, if we can brag a little. We worked hard on it, and it broke our hearts to think it wasn't gonna be published. So we decided to publish it ourselves. (We've never been ones to wait around for somebody else to do things for us.)

And that's where you come in, dear reader. We'd like to start by acknowledging *you*! All y'all who believe in Y'ALL enough to buy this book with your own money. We'll show them, won't we?!

Now, on to naming names...A great big thank you goes to Martha Nicholson Steele, our Editor and Production Manager, who took our manuscript and turned it into a real-live book. Thank you to Joan Giroux for her thoughtful and thorough proofreading, and Joe and Mary Murphy for putting our songs down on paper for us.

The following kind and charitable souls are to be particularly acknowledged for buying their copies of *The Good Book* in advance, to help us raise the money to print it. Thank you (in alphabetical order) Larry Allen & Jeff Wilson, Sheila Allen, Michelle Bennett, Suzanne Bradbeer, Marie Byrd & JD Douthitt, Trey Casimir, Cousin John Chaneski, Scott & Sharon Cheslik, Kay Soforenko, Gaynor Coté & Barry Talesnick, Chrisanne Eastwood & Debbie Malkin, Melissa

Edmands, Kevin Heald, Lori Kagan, Stephen Keever & Greg Giovanni, Annette Kudrak, James Latzel, John Mahoney, Donna Mellen, Joyce Oliveira, Renée Olson, Julie Preston, Thomas Tegan, Peggy Register, Carol Rice & Donald Maglio II, Curtis Robertson, Aunt Dottie & Uncle Herman Saatkamp, Kim-Bob Scown, Susan R. Smith, Michael Taylor, Margaret Tobin, Flora White, Sherri Wilcauskas, and Agnes & Charles Young.

✪✪✪

Since this book represents a culmination of seven years of telling stories and singing songs on stage, we want to try to acknowledge all the people who made it possible for us to keep doing that. Some of these folks we don't see much of anymore, but all of 'em certainly had a hand in making our career happen. Here they are (in somewhat chronological order). Blair and Flamingo East, columnist J.R. Taylor, promoter Tony Mariano, Miss Alison White, Colette Black at Upstairs at Rose's Turn, photographer Michael Wakefield, Ellie Covan and Dixon Place, Tim Maner & the CowGirl Chorus, Kristin Marting, Barbara Busackino, Randy Rollison — and everybody at HERE; columnist Michael Musto, artist Dan Roth, the Singin' Pine Trees, Monica "Li'l Mo" Passin, Tom Meltzer, Anthony Erice, Mark Russell at PS 122, Shelby, John, Joe — and everybody at Happy Endings; Michael DeSalvo & Nick Orth, Piper and Two Boots, photographer Kim Hanson, Russ Gage & Billy Ehret, Stephen Keever, Steve Wilson — and everybody at Borders Books/Philadelphia; Micheline at CB's 313 Gallery, the Rhythm Ranchers (our first back-up band), Chris Young at Comedy Central, Mike "Slo-Mo" Brenner & "Uncle Al" Hewitt — and all of the Low Road; Phyllis Barney and the North American Folk Alliance, mentor Jeri Goldstein, Keith, Robert, Michaela, Kathy — and everybody at WXPN-FM/Philadelphia; Laura Cantrell at WFMU-FM, Matt Winters at WKCR, Phil Shapiro — and DJs everywhere who have played our music, Ken and ABC Cafe/Ithaca, publicist Richard Flohil & Krista, photographer Catherine McGann, and Brian Schneider. Also, Nashvillians Chet Flippo, Tom Roland, Bob Bailey-Lemansky, Billy Block, Katy K, Charles Earle, Steve Key, Mack Hill — and everybody at Radio Cafe; Bob Meador & Jo Walker-Meador, Fats Kaplin & Kristi Rose, Darith Bowlin, and the Music City Slickers.

Furthermore, we can't imagine life without "Cousin Rob" Meador. But enough about *him*!

There are many, many, *many* people who helped us over various hurdles along the way; those who need particular acknowledgment include Liz Banks, Robert Harvey, Indigo, Michael Melford, Bill Resnick, Vito Sclafani, and Brad Wilson.

We both want to acknowledge the support, encouragement and love we get from our families and each other every day.

✪✪✪

These people (and many of those mentioned previously) sponsored our first three recordings. We can't thank them enough: (In alphabetical order) Karen Abraham, Julie Alexander, Meredith Allen, Margaret Amabile, Stephen Amico, Grant Anderson, Julie Arch, Jeff Baron & Gary Carlisle, David B. Bean, Bill Beard, Marcie Beaucoup, Tom Blankin, Deborah Block, Judy Boxley, David N. Brown, Hilary Bulman, Yogi Butler, Ruth Callahan, Christine Campbell, Paul Cardoza, Trey Casimir, Kevin Cathcart, Michael Cheslik, Lenore Cheslik, Michael Coons, Martin Cross, Tad Davis & Susan Vosburgh, Rod de Jong, Johnny De La Cruz, Melinda Di Maio, Diane & Bill, Mitch & Alesia Donner, Billy Dove, Ashka Dymel &

Bobby Davis, Gretchen Elkin & Beth Hassrick, Dina Emerson & Will Pomerantz, Evan, Amy Fix, Martin J. Flowers, Jason Folkman, Tommy Frenna, Kimberly Gambino & Hannes Dekassian, Abigail Gampel, Noah & Francesca Gans-Pfister, Alex Giardino, Teri Gil, Ilsa Gilbert, Jeanne Gilliland, Tim Goecke, David Goldberg & Stephen Bitti, J. Greco & R. Katz, Emma Griffin, Ed Hart & Valary Oleinik, Martin Stone Hennessee, Kathy Hill, Jonathan Horowitz, Peggy Horrocks & Daniel Begun, David Jon Houck, Annette Houlihan-Verdolino, Andrew Jacobs, Donna Jewell, John & Allan, Jonathan & Janet & Isis, David-Lloyd Jones, Avner Kam, John Kelly, Loren Kidd, Grant King, Margarita Kurtz, Rob Klengler, Jeffrey Kubis, Miss Kelly Kuvo, L Cafe, Larry Langham, Gale Lavinder, Lisa Lerner, Don Lindgren, R. LoGiudice, Adam Lowenbein, Amelia Lynne, Maria Maggenti, Philip Mahin, Camryn Manheim, Vickie Marchand & Craig Schlanger, Dan Martin & Michael Biello, Jo Marz, Deborah Massa, Ms. Anna C. Mathis, Kevin McDermott, Byrd McDonald, Mikiodo, Pat Morgan, Stephen Nisbet, Perry Ojeda, Andrew Onody, D. Ruth Oppenheimer, Kate Ostrow, Patti Palen & Robin Hackett, Alyson Palmer, Nancy Paule, Jan-Peter Pedross, Joelle Pezely, Reverend & Mrs. Bruce Phillips, Mark Randall, Bubba Retting, Joe Richvalsky, David Robinson, Glen M. Santiago & John Hoge, David Saradin, Bev Schneider, Gerard Schneider & Tina Trimble, Steven R. Schreibman, Suzanne Schuckel, Heather Scott, Jessica Shatan, Katsuho Shimoharu, Carl Skutsch, Elizabeth Smullens, Snork, Naomi Sokoloff, Lillian Stack & Chester, Amy Stiff, Mark Tadlock, Kaadi Taylor, Polly Tessler, Camden Toy, Jeffery & Mikey Tran-Browne, Frank Trocchia, Alexander Turoff, Stephanie Urdang, The Vespa Family, Laura Vogel, Richard vonFoerster & Don Schumacher, Elizabeth Vredenburgh, Fletcher Vredenburgh, Lauren Webster, Mark Wellen, Sue White, Dr. Darin G. Wiggins, John Williams, Jim-Bob Williams, John Wind & Kirk Kirkpatrick,

Carter Allen Winkle, Maxine Yablonsky & Alan, Clint & Richard Sarno-Young, Basia Zak, and Francine Zerfas & Royston Coppenger.

✪✪✪

We're sure there are lots of others we *should've* mentioned. We didn't mean to leave any of you out, and we'll happily hand-write your name in these acknowledgments and print it in later editions of *The Good Book* if you just ask us to, because you have surely made life after the Epilogue special!

But most of all, thank you to our many fans all over the world. We wrote this because of you; we hope you like it.

James Dean Jay Byrd & Steven Cheslik-DeMeyer
July 1999

Prologue

1 In the beginning, there was a town. [2]And the town was called Circleville. [3]The town was situated in a state called Ohio. [4]And in the town there was a field and a sky. [5]And the field and the sky were separated by a highway. [6]And the highway was wide. [7]Two lanes in both directions. [8]And the highway was called U.S. Highway 22.

2 The field was made of rich soil. [2]And in the soil seeds had been planted. [3]And from the seeds vines had grown. [4]And they were tangled and thick and close to the earth. [5]In the autumn the vines would bear fruit. [6]And the fruit would be called pump-kin. [7]And the harvest of the pump-kin would cause great joy among the people of the town of Circleville. [8]And a festival of the pump-kin would ensue. [9]Many things would be crafted from the pump-kin. [10]Pies and cakes and cookies. [11]Soups, salads and stuffings. [12]Punches, ciders, cocktails. [13]Knick-knacks, doll clothes, jewelry and costumes. [14]And ribbons and prizes would be given to the best of each of these things. [15]And to the second and the third best of each of these things. [16]And it would be good. [17]But that would not be until the autumn.

3 Beside the field ran a creek. [2]And the creek was wide but it was not deep. [3]It was not home to any livestock. [4]It was used mostly as a drainage creek for the field. [5]And it was good.

4 The highway ran across the path of the creek. [2]The highway was therefore made to ride up and over the creek. [3]And it was good because never should the creek rise to meet the highway. [4]And it did not. [5]Though the creek did rise when the rain came down. [6]And on this day the rain did come down.

5 It was the twenty-fourth day in the month of May in the year 1992. [2]Traveling north was a young man who was without hair and who wore a dress. [3]And the dress was green. [4]And the dress sparkled in the light for it was dotted with rhinestones. [5]The young man had received the dress from his uncle who told him the dress would bring the young man luck. [6]This because the dress had brought the elder man much luck. [7]It was therefore known as the Lucky Green Dress. [8]And it was good because it fit the young man well and in it the young man felt good and lucky. [9]And so he was.

6 Traveling east was a young man who was dressed in the style of his father. [2]And of his father's father. [3]And these garments were suited for working in a cornfield. [4]And they were sturdy and therefore good traveling clothes. [5]And as the young man traveling east arrived in the town known as Circleville he noticed a storm on the horizon. [6]And the storm was traveling fast. [7]And the storm carried with it many clouds that were dark and pregnant with much rain. [8]And it was not good. [9]But the young man saw the overpass fashioned in the highway, and he saw the creek beneath it. [10]And that was good. [11]For that was where he would bed down for the duration of the storm.

7 The young man traveling east arrived beneath the highway and next to the wide and shallow creek without getting wet from the storm. [2]No sooner did he arrive, though, than the sky opened up and the rain came down. [3]And the rain came down long and hard and heavy. [4]For three days and three nights, it did rain.

8 As the young man traveling east readied for himself a comfortable bed beneath the overpass, the young man traveling north arrived in the town known as Circleville. [2]And as the rain came down, the young man traveling north

found himself lost in the midst of the pump-kin field. [3]And the young pump-kin vines were very strong. [4]And they tangled around his boots. [5]And his boot heels sank into the rich earth that nurtured the pump-kin vines. [6]And he knew not where he was. [7]And he knew not where he was going. [8]And he was sore afraid. [9]And he stood where he was without moving.

9 Lo, the sky was dark, and the air about it, yet the Lucky Green Dress sparkled still. [2]And its sparkle was bright. [3]And the sparkle caught the eye of the young man traveling east who was now secure beneath the highway overpass. [4]And the young man traveling east felt a foreboding. [5]And he sensed trouble. [6]He tried to ease his weary mind, weary from his foot travels. [7]But he was not successful. [8]He took the sparkle that he saw in the field to be a sign. [9]And he knew what he must do. [10]But just as he had prepared himself to enter the storm, a flash of lightning appeared. [11]And its brightness blinded him briefly. [12]And shortly thereafter the crack of thunder sounded. [13]And its quickness and its volume made him know that the lightning had struck close by. [14]And it was not good. [15]And he was sore afraid.

10 With the cracking of the thunder, the young man traveling north let out a scream. [2]And in his mind he wondered if the Lucky Green Dress was so lucky after all. [3]The scream of the young man traveling north made its way to the ear of the young man traveling east. [4]And the young man traveling east knew that the scream was that of a person. [5]And he knew that the sparkle was coming from the same person. [6]And he knew what he must do. [7]And he knew that he must hasten to do so, because the person in the field seemed truly to be in distress. [8]And it was so.

11 The young man trav-
eling east entered the
storm. [2]And his boots
were filled with water. [3]But it
mattered not. [4]The young man
traveling north never saw the
young man traveling east. [5]He
saw only the hand that appeared
in front of him. [6]And he heard
a voice. [7]And the voice was the
voice of the young man travel-
ing east. [8]And he saith, "Come
and go with me." [9]And the
young man traveling north rec-
ognized the voice, though he
had never before heard the other
young man speak. [10]And he rec-
ognized the words that were be-
ing spoken. [11]And he was com-
forted in his distress. [12]He took
the hand that was offered him.
[13]And it was strong. [14]And it
pulled him out of the rich soil
where his boots had become
stuck. [15]And as he was freed
from the soggy earth, the earth
sucked up the rain and the air.
[16]And from the sucking up of
the rain and the air came forth
a sound. [17]And the sound was a
funny sound. [18]And it brought
forth laughter from the bellies
of the two young men.

12 The young man trav-
eling north held tight
to the hand of the
young man traveling east. [2]And
they ran with haste. [3]Even
though they could see one an-
other not. [4]And soon they
found themselves beneath the
highway overpass. [5]And they
were very wet. [6]But the ground
beneath the overpass was dry.
[7]And it was good.

13 For the first time the
two young men
looked upon the face
of the other. [2]The young man
traveling east said that his name
was Steven. [3]The young man
traveling north said that his
name was Jay Byrd. [4]Immedi-
ately, the two young men felt a
familiarity with one another
they had never before experi-
enced. [5]And their hearts were
glad. [6]And as they spoke one
with the other, a seed was
planted. [7]And from that seed a
great kinship grew. [8]And it grew
rapidly. [9]And it grew and it

grew. [10]And it still grows to this
day.

14 Lo and behold, there
were scraps of wood
and twigs and dried
leaves beneath the overpass.
[2]And the two young men gath-
ered up the kindling. [3]Steven
had experience and was able to
build a fire there. [4]And as their
clothes dried the two young
men became closer and more fa-
miliar one with the other. [5]And
their hearts were glad and beat
rapidly. [6]They shared with one
another stories from their lives.
[7]And out of their stories they
were inspired to write songs.
[8]And they did so together. [9]And
the songs were sweet and funny.
[10]And they were good.

15 That night the two
young men slept close
together. [2]Their arms
were wrapped tightly around
one another. [3]And they both
dreamed of the other through-
out the night. [4]And the dreams
were good.

16 On the morning of
the fourth day, the
storm ceased. [2]The
two young men began to make
plans together. [3]They spoke of
their travels. [4]And though they
had traveled separately before,
they decided they would travel
together now. [5]And the joining
of their travels, one to the north
and one to the east, now sent
them traveling to the northeast.

17 In not more than two
months time, the two
young men found
themselves in a very big city.
[2]Where Jay Byrd had come
from, the city was known as the
Big Apple Pie. [3]It was indeed
big but was not much like pie
or apples. [4]And they were sore
afraid. [5]But they were also very
excited. [6]And they decided to
make their home together there
in the Big Apple Pie. [7]And they
continued to write songs to-
gether. [8]And they sang their
songs for the many people there
in the city. [9]And they told the
people their story. [10] And the
people in the city loved their

story. 11 And they loved their
songs. 12 And they cherished the
two young men and came to
know them as Y'ALL. 13 And it
was good. 14 It was very, very
good.

18 Several years later, the
two young men
known as Y'ALL
wrote a book that told their
story. 2 And it was a good book.

Part One

In the Beginning

Are You On The Top 40 Of Your Lord?

Moses led his people to the edge of the sea,
Prayed, "Dear Lord, please help me set my people free";
Raised his staff into the sky, the sea, it opened far and wide,
Moses is on the Top 40 of the Lord, Lordy, Lordy.

David had no weapons for to go to war,
Goliath had him knockin' up on Heaven's door;
Dave threw a stone into the sky, hit the giant right between the eyes,
David is on the Top 40 of the Lord, Lordy, Lordy.

Genesis, Exodus and Leviticus
Have many wonderful messages to teach us;
If we pray and pray and pray and read the Good Book every day,
We too can be on the Top 40 of the Lord, Lordy, Lordy.

Chapter One

Okey-Dokey, Texas

I was born in Okey-Dokey; Texas, which is the southeast point of the equilateral triangle created by it, Houston, and Galveston. I left when I was twenty-four, led by a vision. Like they talk about in the Bible a lot. The reason I use the Bible as my example is because my Daddy's a preacher. Some folks might question that. He never graduated from Bible college. He had a run-in with some of his teachers about the way he proposed to teach the gospel. So he quit Bible college.

The Bible college was in Waxahachie, Texas, decidedly northeast Texas. After Daddy quit, he and my Momma packed up the Rambler station wagon and drove back to Goose Creek, which was where most of their family lived. Most of them except for Daddy's parents. *They* were farmers in Big Squaw, which is about halfway between Goose Creek and Waxahachie. Daddy and Momma met when they were teenagers and both of them were counselors at a summer camp in Nacogdoches. As soon as they were old enough to get a license, they married and moved to Waxahachie.

While they were there, their first daughter Rose Anne was born. Barely a year later, they'd returned to Goose Creek and Deana was born. Rose Anne had been named after my Momma (Rose Marie), so Deana was named after Daddy. His name is Roy Dean so her name is Dean-a. I was supposed to be born in Goose Creek, too. So everybody thought. But I ended up getting born in a storage closet at the Okey-Dokey VFW Hall. It was October 1967. Daddy had entered an amateur preaching contest. There wasn't any sign of me when he sent in his entry form. (Perhaps the excitement of his being accepted into the competition is the reason I'm here today!) They couldn't have timed it any better, though, because Momma went into labor just as Daddy was supposed to begin his shortened-for-competition half-hour sermon.

He considered pulling out of the competition, considering that I was already two weeks late, but Momma wouldn't let him. He even tried to get her to stay at home. But she refused. So the five of us went, Rose Anne and Deana, Momma, me in Momma's belly, and Daddy with a million things on his mind.

Daddy was scheduled to go on second. The first preacher up was a young man, a farmer who called himself Brother Jones. Momma always insists he called himself "Brother" so nobody would mistake him for their child! He was short in stature and had features that certainly conjure up images of youth. Bright copper hair and penny-sized freckles. Also, he wore a brand new pair of overalls and a borrowed suit coat. He must've figured that if preaching didn't work out, he could always return to farming. And why put out all that money for a whole suit when he might not have an occasion to wear it again?

Brother Jones's sermon was shorter than any of the other contestants' because page three of his five-page sermon disappeared somewhere (and he didn't even try to fill in the blanks to make for a smooth transition). As he preached, Momma paced back and forth in front of a row of metal folding chairs rubbing her belly and breathing in rhythm in the makeshift backstage of the Hall. It was also a makeshift office and a makeshift kitchen, according to the event taking place. Rose Anne and Deana sat prim and proper in two folding chairs, wearing their matching green leaf print dresses that Momma had made out of some old tablecloth fabric, with orange velvet ribbons as belts and in their hair. Daddy stood over the industrial sink at the least-occupied end of the room, practicing his preaching gestures.

The rest of the backstage room was packed with the members of the Austin Angels Halleluia Heaven-Bound Gospel Choir. They had kindly fit the Okey-Dokey amateur preaching competition into their busy traveling schedule in exchange for a meal and the floor of the VFW Hall where they would sleep that night.

The mayor's wife, Edna Joy, was the organizer of the event, and she believed the inclusion of the choir gave the competition a little more respectability. At this point in time, Okey-Dokey, Texas, was still trying to live down its tarnished reputation from 1959 when the former preacher emptied out the Okey-Dokey First Baptist Church safe and then tried to cover up his crime by burning the church down.

Most of the residents of Okey-Dokey moved away immediately after that incident. Many of the rest moved out in the years following. In 1967 there were only forty or fifty people living in Okey-Dokey. Frank Joy was the only one who had any political leanings whatsoever, and he was easily elected mayor of the small town. His first act as mayor was to build the VFW Hall. His father had died in WWII and his grandfather in WWI, so he thought it was a good idea. The VFW Hall was built on the land where First Baptist had stood.

Although none of the remaining townspeople of Okey-Dokey were church-goers, many folks in the neighboring communities (Goose Creek, Highland, and others) thought it somewhat sacrilegious to not replace the church. Edna Joy's family lived in one of those neighboring communities. She wasn't about to let her family, which she never got along with in the first place, call her sacrilegious for something her husband did. She didn't get along with *him* much either. But she did put on a good show.

She organized a good event as well. She was the one who came up with the idea for the preaching contest. She called all the newspapers in towns as far away as Austin, Texas, and Lake Charles, Louisiana, and put classified ads about the competition in them. She hand-selected the five competitors from the more than fifty entries she got, basing her decisions on the essays they wrote and the way their names fell off her tongue: Brother Jones, Roy Dean Byrd, Eldon Lee, Mackenzie "Mac" Donaldson, and Jerry Jim Johnson. Then she contacted the leader of the Austin Angels

Halleluia Heaven-Bound Gospel Choir and made arrangements to have them come by and sing between each of the five preachers who would be competing. She also arranged for food to be cooked to feed the choir.

✪✪✪

The drive from Goose Creek to Okey-Dokey is about forty-five minutes on the main road. In 1967 there was a shortcut that took between seven and ten minutes off that time. Children who were fortunate enough to ride this shortcut called it the Bumpity-Bump Road for obvious reasons. Daddy and Momma knew about the Bumpity-Bump Road — and many other shortcuts around Goose Creek — because they always seemed to be pressed for time, what with two small children and one on the way. Since Momma had gotten toward the late part of her pregnancy, Daddy never took the Bumpity-Bump Road with her in the car. On this night, though, Rose Anne thought she would help her Momma out but in the process got her hair caught in her dress zipper and it took a good ten minutes to get it loose. This was one night when they simply could not be late. Preaching had been Daddy's lifelong dream. So it was decided that they would have to take the Bumpity-Bump Road to get to the competition on time.

The Rambler station wagon had been Daddy's pride and joy when he bought it. He'd worked as many as three jobs at a time to save up the money for it. But the trips to and from Waxahachie took their toll on the Rambler. The main problem was the shocks. They were, as they say, shot. So, between the bad shocks and the Bumpity-Bump Road, I found myself in a pretty ready position to be born.

Momma had already practiced twice before so she knew what she was doing. But she didn't want Daddy to know what was going on since he had so many things on his mind this night, the most exciting night of his life. Even though Daddy had experienced the miracle of childbirth twice before, he never got used to it. He always cried. At first, while Momma did all the birthing work, he cried because he couldn't help her. And then when each of the girls was born, he cried for another hour. Tears of joy. His crying was a bit hard on Momma, though — and Rose Anne and Deana were both born in hospitals. She wanted to delay his reaction as long as possible because she wasn't sure if she'd make it to a hospital this time.

Because of the swift delivery of Brother Jones's sermon (which left a confused look on the faces of the members of the congregation), the choir wasn't quite ready to go on for their first performance of the evening. There was a great hustling and bustling in the backstage area of the VFW Hall. Momma was bumped around in the excitement as fifteen people tossed their arms into maroon satin choir robes and did a few hasty la-la-la-la-la warm-up scales. Daddy was oblivious to it all. He was slicing the air over the industrial sink with his left arm, touching on several points in silence. The choir made their way onto the stage and started with a song that probably sounded something like "Are You On The Top 40 Of Your Lord?" I like to think so, anyway. But one choir member stayed behind. She had a big cream-colored pile of hair topping off her round coffee-colored face, and she introduced herself as "Ont Pearl" (pronounced "ont" as opposed to our traditional "ant" or "aint"). She ushered Momma to the storage closet off the backstage area and halfway down the hall that leads to the bathroom. As they disappeared around the corner, Daddy had a feeling something was happening and turned around. Aunt Pearl popped her head back into the room and said, "Sister Marie's gonna have your baby boy, Brother Roy!"

Daddy went speechless, so Momma says — although nobody else has ever seen such a thing. A boy? They had no idea. He figured Aunt Pearl was guessing. Or maybe she had secret powers! He looked at Rose Anne and Deana sitting so quietly in their chairs with their perfect little matching outfits which they were so proud of. Aunt Pearl seemed to read his mind. "Don't worry about them, Brother Roy, they'll be fine. You just go out there and preach your sermon. Do it for Ont Pearl!"

Daddy went out on the stage. He went out there for Aunt Pearl. But he didn't preach. The congregation was pretty worked up over the gospel choir and they applauded long and hard when Edna Joy introduced Daddy and left the pulpit to him. He stood there after the applause died down. Just stood there and looked out over the more than a hundred people who'd gathered there for this competition — more people than had ever been in the VFW Hall. He was smiling on the inside. He was beaming. But on the outside he looked a little pale. His smile was more like a grimace. Edna Joy considered that she may have made a mistake by inviting this man into the competition. She returned to the pulpit, pushed herself (all four feet seven inches) in front of the six-foot two-inch man and announced him again. The congregation applauded again, but not quite as vigorously. They had given it their all before with no reward, so their applause was more out of politeness this time. Daddy cleared his throat but the tears had already started to flow as he said, "I want y'all to know how happy I am to be a part of this wonderful event. I don't know how many people actually entered the competition, but I feel lucky to have been selected." Edna Joy quickly reported from her seat right in front of the stage that there had been more than fifty entries. "More than fifty? Well, then, I am *very* fortunate to have been selected. But I won't be able to preach. Not tonight. Not right now. Don't get me wrong. Preachin' is important to me. Very important. It's one of the most important things in my life. In fact it's prob'ly the *most* important thing to me, after my family. It is. Yes, preachin' is *the* most important thing in my life after my family. And that's the reason I'm standin' here sayin' this now." He completely broke down. "Right now my wife is behind me, somewhere, makin' a family." Nobody understood what he was saying. So he got control of himself and clarified. "My wife is havin' a baby boy!"

The congregation applauded wildly. They were still applauding as Daddy passed weeping through the backstage area, past the choir members and on through to the hallway. The applause continued as Edna Joy stood up and said, "How's about some more from that choir?!" And it continued as choir members hurriedly zipped up their robes again and returned to the stage. The applause had finally died down when Daddy figured out which of the many doors in the hallway opened to the storage closet where Momma and Aunt Pearl and I were. Momma says it was actually a very cozy storage closet. There was a cot in it and Aunt Pearl had made it up with the dark green tablecloths she found on the shelves. As Daddy entered, Aunt Pearl was leaving, to check in on the girls. She pointed Daddy to an overturned mop bucket where he sat down, looked at Momma and me, and sobbed. Momma laughed.

✪✪✪

A couple hours later, Aunt Pearl brought my sisters into the storage closet to meet me, and she told Daddy that he oughta get out there 'cause it was gonna be his time to preach soon. And no sooner had he arrived than the choir let out a multifaceted "Aaay-maaan!"

Edna Joy grabbed Daddy and said, "What perfect timin', Brother Roy! Everybody else is done. Are ya ready now?"

"I sure am!" He hugged her and kissed her wetly on the cheek near her lips. When she approached the makeshift pulpit, Edna's knees were a little weak and she announced Daddy as "the proud father of free babies — I mean *three* babies," and everybody giggled, and most of them thought my Momma had had triplets.

Unlike Brother Jones, Daddy doesn't write notes and read from them and call that a sermon. He studies a story from the Bible and goes on about it. And on and on. His competition sermon was about the Tower of Babel. Daddy likes the Old Testament a lot. None of the congregation had much familiarity with the Old Testament so Daddy easily kept their interest with the story of the Tower of Babel.

What it says is that way back in the time of Noah and his

sons, everybody was getting their lives together after the big forty-day flood. Somebody said, "Hey, why don't we build ourselves a city inside a big tall tower and just hide away in there, and that way we won't have to worry about floods anymore. And we'll be safe because we won't have to change anything about ourselves or grow or anything like that." But the Lord had other plans for these folks, so the Scripture says. The Lord spread them all over the face of the Earth so they couldn't easily visit each other a lot. After a time, they couldn't even understand exactly what each other was saying anymore because their languages had changed. And they grew in different directions and did things in different ways in their different parts of the world. And they all became more interesting because of it.

So, Daddy says, the story of the Tower of Babel tells us that we must work to understand and appreciate each other's differentness. Not try to get everybody to be just the same. That's not the way the Lord wants it. And it's just not very interesting. We're all individuals, Daddy says, no matter if we come from Africa or Asia or Galveston or Goose Creek, or right next door. We're all valuable and worthy people.

Now, some folks think the story of the Tower of Babel is about the wrath of God; others say it promotes segregation. Daddy says the parables in the Bible aren't there to teach us fear. They speak of the goodness in us individually and as a human race. He says that's why they call the Bible "The Good Book."

Well, folks'd never heard talk like that before. And it struck a chord in them. And even though it was after midnight by the time Daddy finished his sermon, nobody left. Even though many in the congregation had come from towns outside of Okey-Dokey, and even though they had to get up the next morning and work, nobody left. Edna Joy sat on the edge of the stage, happy tears welling up in her eyes brought on by the success of the event she'd organized (and maybe a little bit because of the unexpected smooch). Since they were from so many different towns, the folks in the congregation introduced themselves by name and hometown and chatted with each other in a friendly manner 'til it was time to announce the winner of the amateur preaching contest. Then they were very silent.

Nobody was surprised that my Daddy was the winner. Still, when his name was announced, the electricity in the room ignited them and their applause exploded through the walls of the VFW Hall. It was such an explosion that one of the young children in the congregation who had long since fallen asleep was startled into an upright position and cried 'til the applause died down. It was such an explosion that the choir director was startled from *his* sleep in the driver's seat of the choir bus out in the parking lot and he stumbled into the VFW Hall pulling on his choir robe in a daze, thinking it was time to sing yet again.

But the winner was nowhere to be found. As soon as he'd said his final Amen, Daddy had gone backstage for Aunt Pearl, who was sitting in one of the folding chairs where Rose Anne and Deana had been at the beginning of the evening. She stood to meet him and led him out to the Rambler station wagon and drove him to the hospital in Houston to his family.

When Aunt Pearl delivered Daddy there, she hugged the girls (asleep in the next hospital bed), kissed me on the forehead and walked out of the room. At the door she stopped and said, "Brother Roy, you've got a message. It's a good message. You need to get that message around. Do it for Ont Pearl!" And then she disappeared.

Daddy suddenly realized he hadn't thanked Aunt Pearl. He says not even five seconds passed before he jumped up from the chair next to Momma's bed and ran to the door, but she had disappeared down the long corridor. At the nurses' station they must've confused Daddy for a mental patient because they told him there was no lady in a choir robe and to go back to bed. On his way back to Momma's room, he came up with my name: James Dean Jay Byrd. James from my Momma's granddaddy, Henry James Davis, Dean from his own name, and Jay because *his* Momma's, my Mamaw's favorite bird was the jaybird. When he told Momma, she laughed. But she didn't tell him to change it.

Daddy scooped up the girls and took them home.

The next morning, he called Edna Joy, and over high school girl gushes of congratulations, she said she'd happily contact the choir director when they arrived in Galveston that afternoon and help Daddy get in touch with the choir member who called herself Aunt Pearl. But when she called, the choir director told her that neither the name nor the description fit anybody who wore the Austin Angels Halleluia Heaven-Bound Gospel Choir choir robe. And because of this, Daddy is convinced that Aunt Pearl was an angel.

✪✪✪

Brother Roy's name and reputation spread all over the state of Texas and into parts of Louisiana and Arkansas. He was offered lots of preaching jobs. And along with the offers came gifts of money. The letters accompanying the gifts explained that they'd taken up an offering for the wonderful young preacher from Goose Creek, Texas, who was at the beginning of his career. They also said things like: "If you currently happen to be looking for a congregation of your own, this is the place to be."

Daddy wrote Thank You notes to every one of the churches that sent gifts but told them that, after a lot of consideration, we (the Byrd family) had decided that it would be a better choice for us to travel all around Texas and preach out of a tent, revival style, instead of confining ourselves to one church. For some reason, this news didn't sit too well with some of the churches that had sent congratulations to Daddy. One of them even mentioned that Daddy should be thankful that, considering the situation (the fact that he hadn't received a college degree and wasn't really an ordained minister), a church such as the one mentioned would make such an offer. Daddy wrote back and said that he was indeed very thankful. Most of the other churches simply didn't respond.

One of the first things Daddy did with the gift money he received was to put new shocks on the Rambler. He took us kids out for one last ride on the Bumpity-Bump Road before he took it to the shop, though. I don't remember the ride, but Deana enjoyed it so much her laughter caused her to lose control of her bladder. And because of that, up until they were twelve or thirteen, whenever Rose Anne really wanted to push Deana's button she'd call her "*Pee*-na."

Another chunk of the money went to purchase the actual tent for the revivals. Daddy bought the plain, off-white and yellow-striped canvas structure from a group of sideshow performers in Galveston. An old U-Haul trailer came with the package. The group had covered the box-on-wheels with a painting of garish carnival faces, but Daddy didn't even leave Galveston before having the trailer painted back to its original orange. When he got home, he stenciled BYRD and the outline of a peace dove on both sides of the trailer.

For the next thirteen years, we traveled all up and down the East Texas Coast holding revival meetings in the tent. We might still be traveling if it weren't for Uncle Joe, my Daddy's brother. You see, a very wealthy Louisiana businessman by the name of Richard Jackson kinda fell out of the sky on top of my Daddy's brother and gave him the funds to start up a three-acre trailerpark in Okey-Dokey. Apparently, Richard Jackson's family owned most of the land in Okey-Dokey, and they were getting antsy to use it or get rid of it (something to do with taxes). Richard Jackson's aunt had had awnings put on her house by Uncle Joe, and that's how he found Uncle Joe.

He arrived at Uncle Joe's doorstep in Goose Creek, Texas, with the plans for the trailerpark and lots of money. He told Uncle Joe his intention was to set up a place for his aging mother to call home, since he traveled a lot with his business. The smell of cash may have swayed Uncle Joe a little, but what really sold him on the idea was old Mrs. Jackson, Richard's mother, who was sitting out in the back seat of Richard Jackson's Cadillac Coupe de Ville. The moment they laid eyes on each other, Uncle Joe and old Mrs. Jackson became instant friends and they remained friends those final six years of her life. The one thing they had most in common, believe it or not, was their taste in clothes.

Prior to the deal with Richard Jackson, Uncle Joe's aluminum carport, awning and patio cover business could barely be called profitable. Though he and Aunt Nicki were poor, they were a happy couple, as far as everybody could tell. Still, he wanted to be more successful, if not for himself, for Aunt Nicki. Uncle Joe's a good and honest and traditional man.

It seemed that with the arrival of Richard Jackson, his luck was turning around. His connections in the aluminum industry proved very fortunate, too. He was able to purchase the entire park's worth of trailerhomes at about half the cost of the quote originally given to Richard Jackson. But once the trailerhomes were bought, Richard was nowhere to be found. He'd flown to Japan for business and left Uncle Joe with a joint bank account full of money.

Uncle Joe brought in the landscapers who dug up the ground, stirred it around, and turned it into a well-groomed grass-plugged three acres of natural-looking hills (even though Okey-Dokey isn't naturally very hilly). And then for an entire week, eighteen-wheelers filled the Okey-Dokey air with black smoke and the smell of diesel fuel as they pulled monstrous aluminum homes down the soft paved roads of the trailerpark. Each of the roads was marked with short little signs. The main road was named Freedom Boulevard; it loops through the three acres like a big horseshoe. All the other roads branch off from Freedom Boulevard: Happy Lane, Sunny Circle, Heav'nly Hill, etc. Uncle Joe named all the roads himself. At the main entrance of the trailerpark stands the last piece of construction added, a modest sign of painted aluminum framed in natural-looking wood (which means it has bits of bark still on it):

Freedom Acres Mobile Home Park

There are thirty trailerhomes in Freedom Acres — a little less than half of them double-wides, a little more than half normal size. Uncle Joe had one of the manicured hills built up taller than all the others at the farthest spot from the main entrance. On it was placed the best of all the trailerhomes, a top-of-the-line double-wide deluxe model "2000," or something like that. Anyway, on the front end of it, just above the little point of picket fence that camouflages the pulling hitch, Uncle Joe had "Nicki 2000" professionally painted in very fancy letters below the garden boxes. It's faded but still there today.

Aunt Nicki had stayed away from Okey-Dokey during the construction of the trailerpark, so Uncle Joe was very excited when it was time to take her on the little trip he'd planned for months and months. It's probably important to say here that Uncle Joe wears dresses. Up until this point, he only had one dress, a chartreuse green dress with lace overlay and white rhinestones. He calls it the Lucky Green Dress. Back then he only wore it at home. But on this day he put the Lucky Green Dress on to take Aunt Nicki to Okey-Dokey to see Freedom Acres. (It'll all make sense soon enough.) Aunt Nicki wore pants.

Hardly a word was spoken the entire forty-five minute drive from their modest house in Goose Creek to Freedom Acres in Okey-Dokey. At one point Aunt Nicki looked at Uncle Joe in his dress and said, "What if you git a speedin' ticket in that thang?" Uncle Joe promised he wouldn't speed. And then Aunt Nicki looked back at him and said, "Oh, honey, the shoulder seam is frayed again. And I just fixed it." (Aunt Nicki works out of her home as a seamstress.)

Uncle Joe pulled onto Freedom Boulevard and stopped. Multicolored aluminum as far as the eye could see. All of the colors natural and very tastefully chosen, nothing outside of the realm of tan, green, brown or blue. Uncle Joe pointed to the tallest hill off in the distance with the sun about to set behind the sparkling new trailerhome on it. "There she is, the S.S. Nicki 2000!" He looked at Aunt Nicki, his face beaming, but she looked a little sick.

"Joseph, honey, I'm sorry, but I just can't do it." It was something she'd been planning to say for some time.

Of course, when everybody thought back on it, trying to figure out *why* Aunt Nicki divorced Uncle Joe, they assumed it was because of the dresses. But that's not so. She'd tell you herself if you asked her. Aunt Nicki simply couldn't fathom living in a trailerhome, even if she was the first lady of a trailerpark *empire.* She hadn't told Uncle Joe her feelings sooner because she knew how much it all meant to him and she didn't want him to stop following his dream just because she didn't have the same dream.

Uncle Joe's a very sensitive man, and he was devastated. He couldn't figure out how they'd come to the crossroads of their relationship all of a sudden. Weren't trailerhomes just a step away from carports, awnings and patio covers? Aunt Nicki felt like it was a step in the wrong direction.

✪✪✪

If Richard Jackson hadn't called Uncle Joe, I think I'd probably be telling a different story right now. I don't think Uncle Joe would've been able to continue with the Freedom Acres trailerpark. But Richard Jackson did call, and his call changed everything. Richard was still in Japan, and he had no plans to leave anytime soon. He said, "You got a mother, Joseph?"

"Yes."

"You got a sister?"

"No."

"Well, you do now! That old woman drives me crazy! She's yours! You can have the business, too!" Uncle Joe wasn't able to get a word in edgewise about all the money he'd saved on the purchase of the trailerhomes before he heard a dial tone. And then sure enough, a week later, all the papers arrived in the mail naming Uncle Joe sole owner of the business and sole signatory of the bank account. That piece of mail made Uncle Joe richer than any Byrd had ever been. He buried himself in his work and when he finally came up for air claimed he was over the pain of being left by Aunt Nicki, though I don't think he'll ever really get over her.

He felt sorry for old Mrs. Jackson, the way her son treated her, so he gave her the Nicki 2000. He didn't really think he needed the four bedrooms of a double-wide anyway since he was a bachelor again; and he was glad he made that decision once he discovered how much stuff old Mrs. Jackson had accumulated in her seventy-eight years. Uncle Joe moved into one of the smaller models, right next door to old Mrs. Jackson so he could keep an eye out for her, and because he really liked her.

After the two of them were settled, Uncle Joe notified all of his family in Goose Creek that he'd sell them trailerhomes at cost. The family came in droves. In fact, everybody except Uncle Joe's Aunt Alice and her second husband Artie Bean (who, by the way, is Aunt Nicki's second cousin) moved to Okey-Dokey. Then, with some of the money left in the bank account, Uncle Joe bought a closed-down gas station just off Interstate-10 and turned it into Okey-Dokey Mobile Madness, a trailerhome sales lot.

✪✪✪

Over the years, Uncle Joe has set up and sold lots of trailerparks in Okey-Dokey, Texas: Golden Pebbles, Country Estate, Okey-Dokey's Affordable Luxury, the Place, just to name a few. Some of them are really nice, some are not so nice. Golden Pebbles kinda straddles the line between nice and not-so-nice. There's a huge fountain at the main entrance in which all of the pebbles in it have literally been painted gold! Even though it's the oldest trailerpark in Okey-Dokey, Texas, I think Freedom Acres is still the nicest of them all. That probably has something to do with the fact that just about everybody who lives there is my kinfolk!

✪✪✪

Now, I wanna back up a little bit to the subject of Richard Jackson. Some folks may think Richard Jackson pawned his mother off on Uncle Joe because Uncle Joe is kind of an oddball. And maybe he did. Uncle Joe *is* kind of an oddball. After all, he wears dresses. When Richard Jackson arrived unannounced at Uncle Joe's front door in Goose Creek, Uncle Joe opened the door without thinking. There was no way for him to cover up the dress he was wearing, so he pretended there was nothing unusual about it the whole time Richard Jackson was selling him on the trailerpark idea. And Richard Jackson pretended along with him. Of course, that may've been because Richard Jackson had more sinister plans on his mind. Who knows? Regardless, Uncle Joe credits the business deal that came out of that day to the fact that he was wearing a dress. That's why he started calling it the Lucky Green Dress. Apparently old Mrs. Jackson was pretty eccentric herself, because about a month after they were neighbors, she and Uncle Joe got drunk on cooking sherry and Uncle Joe divulged his "hobby" to her and the next thing you know, *she* had on the Lucky Green Dress and he was trying on everything in her closet.

Richard Jackson must've spent countless guilt-dollars trying to cover up his feelings about his mother. By the time he disappeared to Japan, she was pretty well set; her closet was full of expensive dresses and her bank account was full of money. She's probably the richest person who ever lived in a trailerhome, followed by Uncle Joe.

The two of them ran around like high school girlfriends, rarely separated those six years. They even took to gallivanting around in matching dresses during the last two years when she was in her wheelchair. Nobody in Freedom Acres ever said anything about them. And whenever they ventured out beyond the trailerpark or the Mobile Madness sales lot, they never seemed to notice all the stares and pointing and occasional picture-taking going on.

I don't remember old Mrs. Jackson too well. I just remember

that she was so old I was scared of her. There weren't any physical peculiarities about her. She didn't talk much, except one-on-one. Usually the only person she talked to was Uncle Joe. And the Lord. Uncle Joe took old Mrs. Jackson to church in Goose Creek every Sunday morning (there still wasn't a church in Okey-Dokey at this point).

It was actually because of her death that we stopped doing the East Texas Tent Revival Circuit. We were all very tired of it. All of us except Daddy. Each new day seemed to make him happier than the previous one, but it became harder and harder for us kids to live with. We were teenagers and, other than each another, our only friends were spread out over about a hundred thousand square miles, from Corpus Christi to Texarkana.

The decision to stop traveling came suddenly in the fall of 1981. During our summer break in July, I'd gone to stay with Daddy's parents, my Mamaw and Papaw. When I returned, the decision had been made. We would be moving into the Nicki 2000. Uncle Joe had made all the arrangements and had in fact been secretly planning it since before old Mrs. Jackson died, with her blessings.

The first thought on Momma's mind was that stopping would make Daddy very sad. But Uncle Joe had even thought that part through. He purchased a piece of land and planned to build a church on it. Before he met old Mrs. Jackson, Uncle Joe wasn't a church-goer, but one of the things he got from his friendship with her was a love for the Bible and a keen ear for gospel music. He wanted a place where he could sing in the church choir and not have to drive twenty miles to get there, and not have to put on a suit and tie to do it. He knew that if any church was gonna let him worship in a dress, it'd most likely be my Daddy's church! (And since old Mrs. Jackson had died, he'd acquired lots of new dresses!)

Daddy refused the aluminum church that Uncle Joe proposed to build him. He said, "For thirteen years I've been preachin' in a tent. I'm a tent revivalist. Can't change that now!" So they set up the tent revival permanently on a beautifully landscaped slope of land completely encircled by tall pines (just a hop, skip and a jump from the VFW Hall where I was born). And everybody was happy for quite some time.

Chapter Two

Kornflake, Indiana

About a thousand miles north-northeast of Okey-Dokey, Texas, is the Museum of Corn. It was created in 1948 by the Kornflake Historical Society of Kornflake, Indiana, and is located in the tiny Kornflake Town Meeting Hall & Court House. The "museum" is really just two six foot long, four foot high, two-and-a-half foot deep display cases on opposite walls in the hallway leading to the bathrooms. If Steven hadn't said, "This is it!" when he took me there at Christmas in 1993, I wouldn't have even known it was a museum.

One of the exhibits in the glass cases is "The 12 Stages of Corn." The first eleven stages lie in the bottom of jars of some kind of cloudy liquid with unmistakable labels on them: STAGE 1, STAGE 2, STAGE 3, etc., referring to the different stages in their formation at which they were arrested, from seedling to bursting kernels on a fat ear. I'm sure the colors were at one time bright yellows and greens and golden, but over the years, they've all become albino, the only color a gray cloud hovering around the ears about a quarter-inch thick. STAGES 9, 10 and 11 look very similar, except that the husk is peeled back a little farther from one to the next, like an agricultural striptease. The twelfth stage of corn is a dinner plate piled high with kernels, with a fork sticking out (probably a fork, although the tines are buried in the mound), the whole thing dunked into a block of resin or something clearish like that. It's not as appetizing as I'm sure it's supposed to be.

Other "pickled" items include:

a) A pitiful-looking ear of corn from the first white man's harvest (no date given);

b) A "Siamese Ear," sliced across the girth to reveal a perfect figure "8";

c) "The Heart," an ear sliced down the middle to reveal a hole in the shape of a perfect Valentine heart ("probably created by a bug," it says, but impressive still);

d) "The One Kernel Ear," a particularly disturbing ear of corn that looks like it might've been stuffed into a sheath of pus. If it were the yellow color it's probably supposed to be, it might look like a giant yellow roach-type bug or something (yuck!);

e) etc.

On the walls above the glass cases are plaques with snippets of vital (if somewhat dated) information about the history of Kornflake, Indiana:

- The name of the town was originally Corn Lake. A lack of literacy among the folks who first lived there — and the fact that there isn't (or isn't any *longer*) a lake in the town — is what brought about the current spelling.
- Its center is exactly 250 miles north of the center of Nashville, Tennessee.
- There are more acres of corn per capita in this town than in any other town in the United States of America.
- There were originally a couple dozen corn farms in Kornflake, but buyouts and mergers brought them to the current six by the early 60s. Two of the farms are rather large (500 or more acres each), three are smaller (200–300 acres), and the sixth one is tiny (50 acres). (I think the point they were making is that there isn't much room for people in this town.)

✪✪✪

Steven's mother grew up in Gallop, Indiana, forty-five minutes southwest of Kornflake. Of course, she wasn't called "Steven's mother" when she was growing up; she was called "Sharon." 'Cause that was her name: Sharon Cheslik.

She always tells Steven how dull her childhood was, but I find it a little hard to believe that growing up in a house made entirely of glass could be all that dull. Y'see, Steven's mother's mother and father worked at the glass company in Guenther, Indiana, one town over, and they were always bringing home loads of free glass that they'd gotten at work — the "slightly imperfect" glass that the company couldn't sell. So her mother and father spent all their time knocking holes in the walls of their house and putting windows in them just because they could! Sharon says she felt like she lived in an aquarium.

Steven's father, Scott DeMeyer, grew up in Mission City, Minnesota, but he didn't spend much time there. Like *his* father, Scott was a roamer, a traveling man. A lot like Steven turned out to be. But I'm getting way ahead of myself here — Steven's mother and father haven't even met in the story yet! Let me back up a few years.

Let's go back to Sharon, back in Gallop, Indiana, all alone and bored. Steven says she was bored with *everything* when she was growing up. She even thought the grass in Gallop was the dullest color of green. And when the sun passed over Gallop, it was dulled by the big invisible dull dome that sat on top of the town. (Okay, so there wasn't really any dome of dullness over Gallop, but I want you to understand the magnitude of the boredom Sharon experienced as a child. It's very important to the story.)

All the boys in Gallop, Indiana, were dull, too — dull as minnows in a pond — and only four of them were anywhere near her age. Sharon knew this because she dated all four of them at least once. Elmo Smith, the one boy she dated the most, was the son of the foreman of the Guenther Glass Company, or the GGC as they called it. He was always trying to impress Sharon by telling her, "Someday, every grain of sand in Gallop, Indiana, will have to go through *my* hand." (And Elmo was the least boring of the bunch!) Y'see, Gallop, Indiana, is where the Guenther Glass Company got all their sand to make glass. Apparently, many, many years ago, Gallop, Indiana, was all lakes, but they dried up. So, basically, Sharon grew up in an aquarium in the middle of a dried-up lake bed. You might think she'd be embarrassed having to walk around in a house that everybody could see right through, but nobody lived close enough to be looking in. So, I think we're all beginning to grasp the very potent level of dullness in Sharon's childhood, aren't we?

Sharon's older brother, Carroll, apparently felt the same way about Gallop, Indiana, as she did, because after he graduated from high school, he stayed on with his job at the glass factory just long enough to buy a used Honda motorcycle and get out of town. If Carroll were a fish, he'd be a salmon, 'cause he swam upstream. He almost escaped, too, but as he was waiting to cross the Canadian border, his bike broke down and he couldn't get it started again.

So Carroll was sitting on his smoldering motorcycle outside one of those convenience stores right there on the border — one of them with all the signs in French *and* English that sells perfume and beer and fine crystal trinkets and boxes of candy and other stuff — just sitting there thinking about what he was gonna do (and kinda feeling a little sorry for himself) when a guy on a fancy Harley-Davidson motorcycle pulled up and parked next to him. Carroll said, "Nice bike."

"Thanks. Need help?" Carroll said he did, and the guy got to work on the Honda with hardly another word.

Carroll went into the store and bought a couple of beers and a couple of Canadian-American hotdogs, and when he returned with them, the guy with the Harley was shaking his head as he looked at the Honda engine. Carroll had to ask him a hundred questions but finally got outta him that the Honda needed a doomaflicky that he didn't have with him but could get at the motorcycle shop where he worked — back in Mission City, Minnesota. That's right, the Good Samaritan was Steven's future father, Scott DeMeyer!

Carroll and Scott pushed their bikes to Mission City (it was only an hour away on foot), and on the way, Scott said that he was planning a cross-country bike ride. He was gonna make a big "X" across America: down to Florida, over to California, up and over to Maine and then maybe up into Canada again. Carroll asked Scott if he went to Canada much and Scott said, "Only when I'm hunting." But he didn't hunt for geese or caribou or anything exotic like that; he hunted for his father. "He ends up around Thunder Bay a lot."

That was about all Scott told Carroll about his father that day. He doesn't talk much to *anybody* about his father, and Steven never really knew his Grandpa DeMeyer, so he couldn't get it from the horse's mouth, so to speak. Over the years, though, stories surfaced about Grandpa DeMeyer, and Steven was inspired to write a song about him.

Carroll asked Scott if he could join him on his cross-country journey and Scott said, "Not on *that* bike!"

Six months later, Carroll put a down payment on a Harley-Davidson, and he and Scott took off from Mission City together. On the first day out, though, Carroll realized they were heading in the direction of Gallop, Indiana. It'd been about a year since he'd been there, and it was real close to his sister's birthday, so he thought he oughta stop by and say howdy.

Their timing was perfect. They arrived at the Cheslik home on September 1, 1960, Sharon's seventeenth birthday. Sharon was in the kitchen trying to convince her mother that white was definitely *not* her favorite kind of cake when she heard the sputtering of two Harley-Davidsons coming up the dirt road that ended at their house.

Now, I don't know if all Harley-Davidson motorcycles sound the same, but once, when I was about six or seven years old, we were traveling with the tent revival just south of Texarkana when a gang of Harley-Davidsons passed our little Rambler station wagon and the U-Haul on the highway. It sounded like there were hundreds of them, but it was probably more like ten or fifteen. I tell you what, the racket those motorcycles made terrified all of us, except Daddy. Momma and Rose Anne and Deana and I jumped onto the floorboards and covered our eyes and ears. Momma said it sounded like they were cussing at us. She must've been talking about the motorcycles and not the bikers 'cause you couldn't have heard a marching band over those engines. Daddy tried to calm us all down. He said, "Don't be afraid; they're friendly!" like we'd discovered alien life forms or something. He even said they gave him a thumbs-up sign. From the looks of them, I think Daddy misunderstood their sign language. We were just thankful they didn't kill us!

Well, thanks to that little flashback, I was a bit concerned when Steven first told me his father was a biker. But Sharon sure wasn't threatened by the sound of the two motorcycles as they got closer and closer to her house. Of course, all that dullness she was forced to endure probably caused her to do things that other folks might not do. She ran out of the kitchen toward whatever it was, and her eyes locked with Scott's. He was the most exciting thing she'd seen in all her life, all the way down to the piece of cigarette paper stuck to his bottom lip. Carroll hugged his sister but she kept her eyes planted on Scott over her brother's shoulder.

Carroll laughed and said, "Have you two met?"

Scott and Sharon said "Hi" simultaneously. Carroll shook his head and went into the house. Scott and Sharon talked and talked. Well, Sharon did most of the talking; to this day, Scott's not much of a talker. He *is* a good listener though.

Carroll found his mother in the kitchen reading a tin of cocoa. She hugged him and they went together to find his father, who was in the extra bedroom framing a newly-installed window. His father asked Carroll what he thought about them adding on a back porch, completely enclosed by glass. His mother said, "My plants need more light." Carroll thought it was a fine idea. But he found out they weren't asking because they cherished his thoughts so much as they needed his help hauling the glass home from the GGC. They'd be able to pick up the glass in three days. (Steven grew up calling his Grandma and Grandpa Cheslik's back porch the Circus Room, because the glass they used for the walls was so warped, everything outside was all distorted and funny-looking.)

When Carroll told Scott that he needed to stay in Gallop for a few days to help with some new windows, Sharon just said, "Oh *god*!" and Scott asked her where they could possibly put another window in that house. At that moment, Sharon fell in love with Scott; he had fallen in love with her the moment he saw her running out of the house. Of course, you knew they were gonna fall in love sooner or later — or else Steven wouldn't be here to tell me the story that I'm telling you!

Scott and Sharon were inseparable those next three days, Sharon talking and Scott listening. But, unfortunately, the story gets sad before it gets happy again. After the glass was hauled to the house, Scott still wanted to go on his cross-country journey. He told Sharon that he had to get the roaming out of his system before he settled down. He said he believed that's why his father was so unhappy, because he didn't do his roaming *before* he settled down.

Sharon begged to be able to go with Scott and Carroll, but she was the only one who thought it was a good idea, seeing as how she had just turned seventeen and still had two years of high school to go (Scott was twenty-three). So Sharon was stuck in Gallop. She protested by getting a job at a curtain company, right down the road from the glass factory.

✪✪✪

Sharon's high school was called Our Mother of Piety High. It's in Terre Haute, Indiana, which is about thirty miles east of Gallop. It's a Catholic school, in case you don't know. I didn't know. What I do know is that it didn't give Sharon the stimulation she needed as a teenager. They wore boring uniforms and their teachers were strict nuns, just like you see in the movies. The best thing going for Our Mother of Piety High was that it was a coed school. But that was good and bad for Sharon, too, because it was the same school Elmo Smith went to, and he had a really hard time understanding that Sharon was in love with somebody who was traveling cross-country on a motorcycle. He thought she was just saying that to have an excuse to dump him. Even when she showed Elmo the postcards Scott sent her, he accused her of writing them herself, just to break his heart.

✪✪✪

One day in October, while Sharon was reading a love letter Scott wrote to her (as opposed to the usual postcards), she accidentally stepped up onto the wrong school bus and discovered Kornflake, Indiana. Nobody noticed her mistake because all the kids looked alike in their uniforms.

When the bus driver realized his last passenger was an accidental stowaway, he told Sharon he'd turn onto the highway to take the quick route back, but she convinced him that she had taken this bus on purpose, that she'd come here (wherever she was) to visit a relative.

When she stepped off the bus, the first thing Sharon saw was corn. Corn was everywhere. Of course, she'd never been here before, but she knew it must be Kornflake — *everybody* knows that Kornflake has more corn than people. Nothing but corn as far as the eye could see. Corn, corn, corn. She was a little worried that she might have a hard time finding civilization in all this corn, but she certainly wasn't bored!

She started walking and the first farm she came to was a rundown farmhouse and barn with nothing growing in the fields. On the front gate, hidden mostly by weeds, was a faded For Sale sign. Sharon climbed over the gate and walked up to the farmhouse. It was two stories tall. When she looked up at it, the sun-fried wood seemed to go on forever. It was too dark inside for her to see anything through the windows, and the doors were all locked, so she just stood back and looked at it.

The barn was similar to the house, except that it had no windows. Sharon laughed to herself thinking what her parents would do about *that*! It was gray, too, like the house and like the fields around them. She kinda felt sorry for the farm; it looked abandoned, too. But there was nothing she could do about it so she climbed back over the front gate and headed on down the road.

It was dusk before she came to another farm. But boy, oh boy, what a farm it was! Floodlights had been planted in the ground all the way around the farmhouse and barn, and just as Sharon looked toward the farmhouse from the road, somebody inside decided it was time to switch the lights on. *Pow!* Sharon's heart jumped up into her throat and slid back down slowly, but didn't make it all the way back to her chest the whole evening.

The house and barn looked like they'd been made out of humongous patchwork quilts. And in a sense, they had. Sections of walls had been taken from old farmhouses and barns, and they were all put together to create these two buildings. No two sections were exactly the same size or texture, and they all had been painted bright colors — white, purple, green, red, etc. — and designs were painted on them: flowers, squiggly marks, ears of corn, farm animals, stuff like that. One patch of farmhouse wall had words painted on it at eye-level. Sharon moved closer to read it.

Thayer-famous:
Patchwork Quilts
Corn Husk Dolls & Toys
Various & Sundry Crafts
and Popcorn!

Sharon read the sign over and over, her mouth hanging open. Suddenly, a sharp voice called out from an unseen open door on the other side of the light. "Who's that?"

Sharon walked toward the voice unafraid; she introduced herself and said, "I took the wrong bus!"

The man that went with the gruff voice was tall and round; his belly extended way out in front of him and his skin was thick and tanned. He was Mr. Thayer. He invited Sharon in and called her father and convinced him that she should stay the night and catch the bus to school from there in the morning.

As Mr. Thayer talked on the phone, Sharon sat in a chair pulled out from the dinner table, which was in the middle of being set. She smelled fresh-baked cornbread and realized how hungry she was. In the living room, a radio was on. Old-time country music drifted into the kitchen. It was the first music like that that Sharon had ever heard and she liked it. A high-pitched straining voice sang along with the song, a little ahead of the singer on the radio. The woman that went with the old lady voice was short and round with Lucy-red hair. She was Mrs. Thayer. Her lips were painted a vibrant red and her hand-crocheted apron was another shade of red. Her dress was blue with a happy yellow flower print. The splash of colors seemed to enter the room before she did.

As soon as she saw Sharon, she said, "Hello, dear!" in a sing-songy voice that was caught up in the tune on the radio. She put another plate on the table and continued to sing key words of the song, unsuccessfully trying to keep quiet while Mr. Thayer was on the phone.

Mr. Thayer sat the phone in its cradle and said, "There!" Mrs. Thayer set trivets on the table and big, bright bowls of food on them. She told Sharon they had a granddaughter at Piety; she recognized the uniform. But Mr. Thayer told her that their granddaughter had graduated five years ago. Mrs. Thayer stopped, thought about it, and laughed at herself. Mr. Thayer joined in, and then so did Sharon.

Before much time had passed, Sharon was calling the Thayers Pop and Grandma. They insisted. They didn't get much company (other than the folks who stopped in to buy crafts) and they were tickled by Sharon. Sharon was likewise tickled by them; she didn't have any grandparents, and Pop and Grandma Thayer suited her just fine.

Over dinner, all three of them talked non-stop and laughed as they fought for control of the conversation. Pop and Grandma Thayer told Sharon all about the life of farmers and how they met and fell in love; Sharon in turn told them about life without Scott and his travels and how they met and fell in love. She avoided talking about Gallop, Indiana, as much as possible.

Later, the three of them sat in the beautiful stone living room over a platter of cookies that nearly covered the whole coffee table and they talked 'til way past all of their usual bedtimes. Grandma Thayer said it was a *sin* that Sharon had never made a corn husk doll and told her, "Come Thanksgiving, I sure could use a little helper for the holiday season!"

Sharon couldn't sleep that night. Partly from excitement and partly because the bed the Thayers put her in was so soft she couldn't lay straight. She propped herself up and wrote a long letter to Scott and told him where the letter he'd sent had ended her up. She told him about the little farm next to the Thayer's and wrote, "Maybe someday we can be as happy as them."

✪✪✪

After Thanksgiving, Sharon quit her job at the curtain company and worked as much as Grandma Thayer would let her, which was a lot. She made corn husk dolls like there was no tomorrow. She also learned quilt-making and baking and canning and "various and sundry crafts," like the sign on the front of the house said (these included bookmarks, padded frilly photo album and frame covers, cozies for extra toilet paper rolls and stuff like that). Grandma Thayer always had the local radio station playing while they worked and she'd sing along in her little old lady voice. Soon, Sharon was singing along, too. Sharon learned lots of country songs and was particularly fond of the female singers, especially Loretta Lynn.

When she stayed overnight (which was often) Sharon would ask Pop Thayer over the dinner table all kinds of questions about farming, saying that it was important for her to know as much as possible about it, because someday she believed she and Scott would be married, and they just might decide to become farmers. "Maybe we'll even buy the little farm next to yours, and then we can be neighbors forever!" The Thayers thought that was a real good idea.

Sharon had to send the letters she wrote to Scott in bundles, whenever he was in a town long enough to give her an address, but he sent her postcards from every little gas station and diner he stopped at. She taped a map of the United States on the wall in her bedroom and tacked the postcards around it near their points of departure. By the time Scott returned, Sharon's bedroom wall looked like a snapshot gallery.

✪✪✪

The morning of Saturday, September 1, 1961, Grandma Thayer was up with the sun and in the kitchen preparing a feast for the birthday barn dance they had planned for Sharon for that night. Two roasts were in the oven, and lots of other things were bubbling and steaming and scenting the air all around the house. As Grandma Thayer prepared the five bowls of colored frosting for the Raspberry-Stuffed Chocolate Birthday Cake, Pop entered the kitchen.

"Ma, I got a young man here says he aims to buy the old Tilson Farm next door."

Grandma Thayer looked up. She knew it was Scott DeMeyer the moment she laid eyes on him. "Well, I'll be!" They'd heard so much about each other, they felt like instant family.

Pop asked Grandma if she knew what time they expected Sharon and the others. Sharon was bringing her parents and they would be there about four or five, and the other folks would be coming sometime around six. Pop said, "That just might give us enough time."

Pop and Scott disappeared for the rest of the afternoon; they went to Terre Haute to visit the son of the late Farmer Tilson to see about the farm. Pop said he would co-sign for the purchase and Scott put his Harley-Davidson up as collateral. He intended to surprise Sharon with the purchase for her birthday (as if being there wasn't surprise enough).

Scott and Pop were still gone when Sharon and her parents arrived at the Thayer Farm. Grandma Thayer didn't say a word about the surprise, though she thought it would be the *end* of her! She gave the Chesliks a tour of the farmhouse and showed them some of the crafts their daughter had made with her own hands. They were very impressed and somewhat surprised. Sharon's mother held up a frilly, quilted photo album cozy and said, "Our Sharon made *this*?" Sharon just rolled her eyes.

As the sun set, thirty some-odd people descended upon the Thayer barn, mostly long-time friends and relatives. A banquet table was set up against one wall in the barn and covered with a handmade patchwork tablecloth, and then all the food Grandma Thayer had made was placed on it in a decorative array. Sharon's huge patchwork-style birthday cake sat up on a pedestal in the middle of it all. Eighteen handmade light brown candles were placed at perfect intervals around the top rim of the cake. Then three rows of black string with knots tied in them were draped from candle to candle. It looked just like a little barbed-wire fence guarding the decoration inside: SHARON CHESLIK, written in block letters of cream cheese a half-inch thick. Her first name formed the top half of a circle and her last name formed the bottom half. In the center, the number "18" was written with powdered sugar-dusted raspberries. Sharon stood at the banquet table with her parents gawking at the cake, afraid to touch *anything*.

At the farthest wall from the double-door entrance to the barn, a small stage had been set up. Pop's cousin Clem Thayer and his band put chairs in a semicircle on the stage and sat in them. They took their instruments out of their cases, a fiddle, a banjo, a jaw harp and a bass fiddle, and tuned them together. "Pling-pling-pling!" (All except the jaw harp.)

Suddenly, Pop appeared and made his way to the stage. His looming presence caused a hush to fall over the barn. "Some of y'all know the little lady whose eighteenth birthday we're celebrating tonight, and some of ya don't. Well, regardless, Ma's made enough food for *all* of ya!" Everybody cheered. "But before the dance gets started, there's a little surprise we've been cooking up for the birthday gal."

Scott took his cue and appeared in the doorway of the barn. Pop pointed at Scott, and Sharon turned around, not knowing what to expect. A whole collection of reactions registered on her face before the scream made it to her mouth. She ran and jumped on Scott and they almost fell over.

Only a handful of folks at the barn dance had ever even heard of Scott DeMeyer, so their interest was limited. This included the band. As soon as Pop stepped off the stage, Cousin Clem counted off, "One, two, three, four," and the night was underway.

✪✪✪

After the birthday cake was cut and eaten, Scott walked Sharon out to his motorcycle. He told her that he had a birthday present for her and motioned to the Harley. Sharon said, "I don't know how to drive a motorcycle!"

He told her to get *on* the bike, then he blindfolded her, lit a cigarette and drove slowly up the road to the little farm he'd secretly bought that day. When they got there, he told her to stay put. She was so excited, she had no idea where she was. Scott pulled the For Sale sign off of the gate and put it in her hands. As soon as she felt the splintery old wood, she knew what it was. She threw off her blindfold. *"What?"*

"I think we just bought the farm. That is if you still wanna get married."

(I don't think I have to tell you what Sharon said!)

✪✪✪

Nine months later, the day after Sharon's high school graduation, she and Scott joined their names together and became Mr. and Mrs. Cheslik-DeMeyer. The ceremony was held on Saturday, June 1, at Our Mother of Piety Catholic Church in Terre Haute, Indiana. Father Thiele — the same priest who baptized Sharon — married them. Scott hadn't gone to church much in his life, but he told Father Thiele they'd be at mass every Sunday from then on.

They spent their honeymoon on the newly christened Cheslik-DeMeyer Farm. Scott's wedding gift to Sharon was a pretty-much-completed bedroom and bathroom upstairs and a pretty-much-completed kitchen downstairs. The rest of the farmhouse sat in shadows. Sharon's wedding gift to Scott was a $100 tab at the Shaw-Tuck Hardware & General Store (across the square from the Kornflake Town Meeting Hall & Court House, and the Museum of Corn).

They started work on their farm the next morning by drawing a big chart with

THINGS TO DO / DO DATE / DONE

written on it and tacking it to the wall of their dark and musty living room. If everything went as planned, they'd finish the farmhouse in two years, the barn in the third year and have a functioning farm by the end of the fourth.

But everything *didn't* go as planned. Quite the opposite. (I'm sorry to have to be the one to remind you that this is life, and in life, things go up and down quite a bit.) Just four months after their short honeymoon, Sharon was pregnant. Though they loved the idea of having a family, it was on the very bottom of the Things To Do chart — and it was just written there as a little joke between them:

"Fifth year, have 100 kids!!!"

Scott Cheslik-DeMeyer, Jr., was born on August 18, 1962.

On August 19, work on the farm continued, as much as it could. The baby himself didn't delay construction of the farm, it was all the other jobs Scott and Sharon took to pay for everything that kept them so busy. Scott had gotten a job at the glass factory with his father-in-law shortly after Sharon's birthday, and shortly after Junior's birth, he started working part-time with Pop on the Thayer Farm in the evenings. Sharon worked with Grandma Thayer on the crafts throughout her pregnancy and barely paused to have the baby before she was back again (even though Grandma Thayer told her she could take as much time as she needed). This left them Saturdays and Sunday evenings to work on the farm. Sunday mornings were reserved for mass. It was a hectic schedule, but it was worth it for the results they knew they'd soon have.

They knew they definitely didn't want to have any more kids before the Cheslik-DeMeyer Farm was up and running. Grandma Thayer kept telling Sharon she oughta get some birth control pills, and tried to inspire her by calling up the radio station every day and requesting Loretta Lynn's song "The Pill" (the one where she sings she's gonna throw out her old maternity dress and buy some fancy new clothes now that she's got the birth control pill). But the Catholic Church didn't approve, and Sharon had never gone against the Church and she couldn't bring herself to do it now.

Sharon and Scott took the matter to Father Thiele. Unfortunately, all he had to offer them was lots of warm smiles and some dubious advice. With sweat beads on his forehead, the priest told Sharon and Scott how to apply the Rhythm Method. He said, "What you have to concern yourselves with the most...is the matter of...continence...during the woman's...ovulation period."

He seemed relieved when Sharon told him they knew all about the Rhythm Method and that they were already *applying* it. "But it's not working for us."

To that, Father Thiele said, "Well, then, just be faithful and all things shall come to pass as directed by God," or something priestly like that.

Sharon and Scott remained faithful, and they went to mass every Sunday morning, and they watched deadlines pass on the Things To Do chart as Father Thiele and his parishioners watched the Cheslik-DeMeyer family grow. It seemed like all they had to do was pass a hammer and Sharon got pregnant again! Jack was born on July 23, 1963; Louis was born on September 1, 1964 (his mother's twenty-second birthday); Edward was born on July 31, 1965; and Michael was born on February 11, 1967.

After each birth, Sharon and Scott went to Father Thiele, each time a little more desperate. But each time, the best and only advice the priest could give them was to be faithful and to practice the Rhythm Method. They couldn't figure out which part of his advice they weren't doing right.

Sharon said, "Maybe there's something wrong with us. Or maybe there's something wrong with the Rhythm Method. We can't stop having babies!"

The priest said that he'd pray for them, the Rhythm Method, *and* the babies.

✪✪✪

As much as I don't like to say it, Steven was the straw that broke the camel's back on the Cheslik-DeMeyer Farm. His mother discovered that she was pregnant with him in the blazing heat wave of August 1967, just six months after Mike was born. When she told Scott, they both knew what had to be done. Scott put a layer of hay on the bed of the beat-up old tricolored Chevy/Ford truck the Thayers had loaned them. The three older boys — five, four, and three years old — climbed into the middle of the "hayride" in the truck bed, then Sharon and Scott got in the front with the two younger boys and Steven on the way, and they went to see Father Thiele.

Always before when they had met with the priest, Scott kept their boys wrangled as best as they could as Sharon pleaded for help. But this time, he let the boys loose. And as the four of them clambered about, chewing the corners of furniture, climbing the walls of books and playing with the communion silver, Scott stood up and said, "Look, Father, we're overwhelmed here. We don't need prayers, we need help!"

The priest was distracted; he ran about moving this boy and that, pulling them off of his nice things. All the while, he kept insisting that God had plans for them *and* that God has laws.

Sharon lost herself. "*Laws!* Tell me, Father Thiele, how would you like it if you were trying to build a church, you'd made plans, and everything has to go *just so* or else you wouldn't have enough money to keep the church? And how would *you* like it if every time you turned around you were *banged up* again?"

The priest blushed, Sharon froze. Scott gathered up his wife and kids and they drove back to the Cheslik-DeMeyer Farm in silence, Sharon mortified at what she'd said and Scott trying to figure out a way to tell her it was the funniest thing he'd ever heard in all his life. They didn't return to Our Mother of Piety again. Or any church, for that matter.

Four days later, it was Sunday again. The usual calamity of dressing four young boys and two adults and driving an hour away to church, disappeared barely noticed and never missed. Checkmarks started appearing more rapidly on the Things To Do chart. With all the free time Scott had on his hands, the barn was nearly complete by the time Steven was born.

On the afternoon of March 22, 1968, Scott was in the barn tinkering with his motorcycle, too anxious about the imminent birth to do anything else. Grandma Thayer had told him it would be any minute now.

At a quarter past three, Grandma Thayer stuck her head out of the upstairs window and said "Hi" to the oldest three boys playing in the yard between the house and the barn (Mike was in a dresser drawer-crib in the room with them). The barn door was slightly ajar, so instead of having one of the boys fetch their father, Grandma Thayer yelled out, "Hey, Scotty, it's time!" The boys cheered and Scott took a deep breath and walked to the house, patting Junior on the head as he passed him.

Steven must've sensed the stress his parents had been going through, 'cause he didn't take long to arrive. About a half-hour after the screen door slammed behind Scott, Grandma Thayer slapped Steven's behind and he let out the first musical note of his life.

✪✪✪

Four years later, Steven's mother had another baby. They wanted to have one on *purpose* for a change. Also, Steven's mother really wanted to have a baby girl and Grandma Thayer convinced her that the right foods could make it happen.

Kay was born on October 7, 1972.

My Family Tree

He kept leaving his family, he kept moving away,
She always found him eventually;
When she found him, she always found him shacking up
With the man who's not in my family tree.

I wonder now if he were living
What he would have to say to me;
But I'll never know too much about my father's father
Or the man who's not in my family tree.

Chapter Three

Cousin Mandy

Spring has a very special place in my heart for several reasons. Most importantly, it was the spring of 1992 when I decided to stop feeling sorry for myself. Since October 28, 1991, my birthday, I had been on a downward spiral of personal despair. I had turned twenty-four and was still living with my parents in old Mrs. Jackson's double-wide, the Nicki 2000, in Freedom Acres. Freedom wasn't something I felt the least bit of, much less acres of it. My attendance at the revival meetings slacked off. Slowly at first, and then after the Christmas of '91 I stopped going altogether. I told myself there were other more important things I needed to do. Like lying on my bed, staring at the ceiling and feeling sorry for myself. The big question on my mind was: What am I gonna do with my life? I had no idea. I'd read in a magazine somewhere that if you weren't doing what you really wanted to do in life by the time you turned thirty, you never would! My time was ticking away.

Nights, I dreamed of exotic and exciting places. But it was like I was looking at a picture postcard or watching a movie on TV. I never seemed to be *at* any of those exotic and exciting places. Even still, I'd open my eyes each morning, hoping and believing I was gonna wake up in the place I'd just been dreaming about. But, alas, every time I opened my eyes I saw the same four wood-paneled walls.

✪✪✪

Just on the other side of I-10 Uncle Joe's big illuminated sign towers high up over the highway:

OKEY-DOKEY MOBILE MADNESS!

A beacon for many. On Saturday, March 21, 1992, it was a beacon for me. Just about everybody in my immediate family — and in their immediate families — was piled into our trailerhome. All were aware of my "recent state" and were walking on eggshells because of it. I figured the only place I'd be able to get away from all their loving attempts would be out at Uncle Joe's trailerhome sales lot. He'd likely be busy with customers and I'd be able to just sit in his back office — the one he keeps as cold as the north pole most of the year — and brood.

Surprisingly, Uncle Joe was in his office. He'd sent his other salesman home and he was the only one at Mobile Madness. A hidden camera peered at the sales lot entrance, and its monitor hung high up on a wall in the office, but Uncle Joe didn't expect any visitors 'til the Early Spring Sale-A-Thon that was starting up Monday evening (after the First Spring Monday Potluck was over — I'll explain it later). Banners all over the sales lot announced it. He knew I didn't have any interest in this subject. From the look on my face, I guess he knew it was time for one of his stories. Mamaw Byrd was the original story-teller in the Byrd blood line, as far as I know, and she passed it down to both of her sons. But unlike his brother (my Daddy), Uncle Joe has a limited number of stories in his repertoire and I've heard them all a dozen times. But for the record: they're worthy of repetition.

As I sat across the desk from him in the office trailer, Uncle Joe thought about his stories and which one he should tell me this day. As he thought about it, one finger unconsciously ran back and forth on his shoulder seam. Maybe he was checking to see if the seam was still holding (even though he and Aunt Nicki are divorced, they're still friends and she repairs his dresses when they need it). Or maybe he just liked the way the fabric felt; this dress was a gaudy purple color and looked like it might've been made out of cashmere. I always told him my favorite dress of his was still the Lucky Green Dress.

As if he read my mind, Uncle Joe said, "Ahh! Ya want me to tell ya the story of the Lucky Green Dress?!" "No, Uncle Joe, I'm not really in the mood."

"Or maybe the story about the time Sylvia and I went on that shopping spree in Galveston that lucky week when three dress shops went out of business?" Sylvia is old Mrs. Jackson.

"No, I can't ever keep all the facts in that story straight."

Uncle Joe knew I didn't want to hear either of those stories. He always knew exactly which story would help my mood the most and he always offered it third on the list, don't ask me why.

"How's about I tell you the story of Cousin Mandy? I haven't told that one in a while!"

I didn't really think I wanted to hear any story, but I considered Uncle Joe's keen ability to get to the heart of things and said, "Oh, alright."

"When Cousin Mandy was a little girl, the age of about eleven or twelve," Uncle Joe said, "She got a bad case of the ringworms. So her Momma, my Aint Alice, mixed up a special ringworm-killin' salve, made up out of the different herbs an' plants in their garden. But before this special potion could be applied, the affected area had to be shaved. Well, the affected area on poor ol' Cousin Mandy was her *head.* Her entire scalp.

"So her Daddy, ol' Artie Bean, took her down to Frank Snow's an' had him shave her head so Aint Alice could apply the special potion. Well, this was some years back an' there weren't any young ladies with bald heads back then. So Frank Snow took ever' precaution to make Cousin Mandy feel as comfortable as possible. He took all of the barber cloths (what he normally uses to put over his customers) an' he tied 'em all together by their back straps. Then he strung 'em 'cross the front window so nobody could look in on 'em. An' he had ol' Artie Bean stand guard at the door an' send away anybody that might decide they needed a haircut right then. Then he hiked Cousin Mandy up on the red Naugahyde barber's chair an' did the job quickly an' painlessly.

"I tell you what, the look on poor ol' Cousin Mandy's face musta been a sight for sore eyes. Frank Snow gave the girl the whole jar of penny suckers for it. He usually just handed 'em out one at a time to the youngest customers, y'know. (Or sometimes when some of the older fellers'd got liquored up an' needed a breath freshener for the ride home!)

"Well, anyways, Frank Snow didn' even charge ol' Artie Bean for the haircut. An' he guarded the door while Artie Bean went out an' got his car an' pulled it right up to the front door. It musta looked like they were robbin' a bank or somethin'! Frank wrapped Cousin Mandy from head to toe in two of the barber cloths. An' he carried her like a log to the front door an' handed her off to Artie who had the back door of his car open an' waitin'. Then ol' Artie Bean jumped in the driver's seat an' tore off, slammin' the back door that he'd forgot to shut before.

"Same thing when he got her to the house. They lived in that ol' shack out on Cedar Bayou Road which is over in Goose Creek. (This was when ever'body was still livin' over in Goose Creek. An' it was before Cousin Mandy bought 'em that ol' *roadhouse* they travel all over the country in nowadays.) But anyways, ol' Artie Bean drove up there in the back yard. Real close to the back porch. An' he hopped out an' opened up all the doors leadin' into the house. Then he come back to the car, scooped up Cousin Mandy an' ran her into the house, swiftly. Like she was a stolen piece of art or somethin'.

"Cousin Mandy just laid there in her mummy costume without sayin' a word; didn' move a muscle the whole entire time. In her mind she musta been pretendin' she *was* a stolen piece of art! Soon as Aint Alice saw ol' Artie Bean, she clasped her hands to her bosom an' cried, 'Oh, Artie Bean, what are ya doin'?! That poor child!' Course, ol' Artie Bean was a drinker, y'know. An' though his intentions was always good ones, his actions were pretty often questionable. I think he's cleaned up now, though, praise the Lord.

"So anyways, Aint Alice took the wraps off a'Cousin Mandy an' swears to this day that her head was slightly aglow an' beautiful as anything the Good Lord ever made. She applied the ringworm-killin' salve to Cousin Mandy's head. An' while they timed it doin' its job, the three of 'em separated the penny suckers by colors. Ol' Artie Bean accidentally let slip out that the purple ones was his favorite. An' then he stupidly added 'When I was a boy.' But Aint Alice knew good an' well ever' time ol' Artie Bean stopped by the saloon. 'Cause his kisses tasted like beer an' bourbon an' grape candy. Ol' Artie Bean was a real cross for Aint Alice to bear back then, I tell ya what.

"Well, as ya know, the ringworm-killin' salve did its job alright. It killed all the ringworms. It also killed all a'poor ol' Cousin Mandy's hair follicles. To this very day her head is smooth as the diaper-side of a baby.

"Now, Aint Alice was quite distressed about this. Quite distressed. She tried to keep her emotions to herself. But it wasn' always easy. She had a lot on her mind an' was now bearin' two crosses in her life, *po'shang*. One good thing, though, it was the summertime, so there wasn' any school for a while. Aint Alice figured that'd give her time to try to resolve the matter.

"Cousin Mandy wore scarves on her head all summer long. Mostly on accounta they were afraid of the sun burnin' her head to a crisp. At the end of each day as she laid down to go to sleep, Aint Alice'd take the scarf off an' check for hair by softly rubbin' her hand over Cousin Mandy's scalp. But it was always as smooth as the night before. She'd rub her head 'til Mandy fell asleep.

"One night, 'bout a week 'fore school was set to start, Aint Alice broke down to cryin' when she finally faced facts that Cousin Mandy wasn' ever gonna have her beautiful hair again. Or even any ugly hair! No hair at all!

"But then Cousin Mandy did a beautiful thing. She'd always

been a real quiet girl, y'know, so whenever she spoke up, folks were pretty apt to listen. She said, 'Please don't cry Momma. I don't mind havin' no hair. Really. In fact, if I did have hair I'd cut it all off anyway. An' do you know why? 'Cause like it is now, I can feel love comin' through your hand when you rub my head.'

"Aw, that did it! The flood gates opened up an' the tears gushed out! Aint Alice's got that big ol' bosom, y'know, an' she pulled poor ol' Cousin Mandy up into her bosom an' gave her the biggest ol' Momma Hug ever. She held her there an' they laughed. An' as they laughed, Cousin Mandy realized she could breathe out better then she could breathe in. An' finally she got a little panicky an' had to scream to get Aint Alice to let her go! I tell you what!

"Well, anyways, Cousin Mandy went to school an' she didn' even wear a scarf or nothin' to cover up her bald head. Just as bold as ya please. Back then, they were still bussin' the kids from Goose Creek to schools in Highland an' Clover Crest. Cousin Mandy went to school in Highland. An' none of the other school kids except the ones from Goose Creek knew anything about what'd happened to Cousin Mandy that summer. I think it was her first year in junior high school, or something like that. So she really stuck out. An' all the kids stared at her. Sure. An' they pointed. An' they 'bz-bz-bz' talked about her behind her back.

"Well anyways, they were electin' the class president at her school an' crazy ol' Cousin Mandy marched right down to the office there an' signed up to be a candidate for the presidency. She's got a real purty face, y'know. An' as it turns out, a nice shaped head, too. An' whenever the kids stared at her an' pointed an' 'bz-bz-bz' behind her back, Cousin Mandy'd walk right up to 'em an' say, 'Do ya think it looks funny or do ya *like* the way it looks?' An' no matter what their answer was, she'd hand 'em one a'them penny suckers Frank Snow'd given her. An' she'd say, 'Don't forget to vote for the bald eagle Mandy Bean on election day!'

"Well, Cousin Mandy was elected class president by a landslide.

"An' she became very popular. She got good grades all throughout school, an' she became a lot more talkative. A lot more talkative! An' she married that boy Gilbert that she met at that Austin university. An' now they travel all around the country teachin' folks how to be as happy an' successful an' popular as they are. They make money at it, too! 'Course her message is very simple. An' it's one I believe in very strongly. An' you've heard me spout it many a time. But I might as well say it again now since Cousin Mandy's the one who came up with it, an' since it's kinda the moral of the story. It goes: *Ya can't never tell what might happen to ya if folks have reason to stare*!

"End of story."

No sooner had Uncle Joe said Mandy's words than I realized what I'd do. I borrowed his car and drove the forty-five minutes to Goose Creek (unfortunately, the Bumpity-Bump road was long ago turned into a small craft airport). There was a parking space right in front of Frank Snow's barber shop, probably close to where old Artie Bean had parked his car for the getaway back when. On the big glass front window, slightly chipping gold letters spelled out in a circle FRANK SNOW on the top half and BARBER SHOPPE on the bottom half. Sometime between Cousin Mandy's famous visit and now, "Jr.'s" had been painted in the middle of the circle with a slightly different gold paint. It wasn't done professionally like the original sign. It was a little too far to the right, and the "S" looked a little sad and droopy — probably because it's the hardest letter of the alphabet to paint backwards. There was a dingy white curtain in the window blocking out the sun; it made me think of the barber shop cloths that were once draped there.

I went to the door. There was one of those funnel gunshot holes in the glass. And behind it was a cigarette ad with OPEN printed on it dangling from a smoke-stained suction cup. I looked into the window and saw only two people in the barber shop, and they were dancing, oblivious to me. When I opened the front door, the string of bells could barely be heard over the Tejano music blaring from the dust-covered transistor radio sitting on the top of a cabinet in the far corner. Other than all of the framed pictures of Jesus in various poses on the walls, and a Jesus calendar on the mirror, the barber shop looked just like Uncle Joe had created it for me time and time again in his stories.

The couple pulled apart when they saw me and the man jumped up on a chair that was waiting there by the cabinet and turned the music down. The woman smiled, said, "Hi." She was a beautiful woman with dark skin and teeth so white, they seemed to glow. "Do you need directions somewhere?" A slight Mexican accent came through. They must've gotten more requests for directions than for haircuts here lately — on the way, I'd noticed a billboard on the highway advertising a Super Cuts hair salon in a strip mall somewhere nearby.

"No. I came for a haircut."

The man grabbed a whisk broom and swept the dust from the seat of the middle chair. Its red Naugahyde cushions were patched with dirty red duct tape. I sat tall in the chair and waited while he popped the barber's cloth behind me and swooped it over me in a grand gesture.

"What'll it be, sir," the man asked me in an accent similar to the woman's. He was very light-skinned. Lighter than me. But his thick black hair and his clothes and jewelry were the style of a Low Rider. He seemed to be performing, as if he were here merely for the fun of it. I tried playing along, not sure if he would follow me.

"Give me the Cousin Mandy Special!"

"*Whoa*, wait a minute. That sounds familiar to me. Why does that sound familiar to me?"

He looked to the woman. She shrugged her shoulders way up behind a shy smile that revealed her beautiful teeth again. I'd never seen such white teeth before and was mesmerized by them. I occasionally glanced back at her through the mirror in hopes of getting another glimpse, particularly when we all laughed.

As it turned out, this man was Frank Snow's son Junior. I told him the story of the ringworms. He'd never heard the whole story but he had heard about Cousin Mandy 'cause once a month this was where Uncle Joe still came to get his hair trimmed. "That crazy man in the dresses is your uncle, man?"

"Very nice dresses," the woman said very sincerely, shaking her head.

"Yeah. Joe Byrd's a really good tipper, man. He can come in here *nekked* for all I care!"

We all laughed and I answered his questions about Uncle Joe and Cousin Mandy while he transformed my head into a shiny dome.

When Junior finished the job, he gave me a hand-mirror and spun me around and around slowly so I could look at my head from every possible angle over and over again. I was happy that the Byrds had gotten the same good head shape gene that the Beans had gotten.

I paid Junior the five dollars for the Cousin Mandy Special and tipped him two, apologizing that I wasn't as well off as Uncle Joe. He apologized that he didn't have a whole jar of lollipops to give me; he didn't have any lollipops at all. He *did* have a dusty old box of unbreakable plastic combs with

FRANK SNOW BARBER SHOPPE

imprinted on them, and he gave me the whole box.

I drove Uncle Joe's car back to Okey-Dokey Mobile Madness. When Uncle Joe saw me — or, more specifically, when he saw my shaved head — his eyes clouded up and I thought he was gonna cry. For somebody who puts a wink and a poke to almost everything he says, Uncle Joe was oddly serious when he said, "It looks real good, son." He told me if I wanted to wait, he'd be closing up in about an hour and I could ride home with him. But I felt like walking; I didn't think I could sit still for an hour anyway. I gave him a comb and left.

Everybody I passed on the street stopped me or said something as they passed. Nice things. I gave them all combs. The mailman Carl even thought to ask if he'd see me "in service" Sunday.

"Hey, that's tomorrow!"

"That's right, Jay Byrd!"

"Sure thing, see you there, Carl!" I gave him *two* combs (one for his son).

When I got home, supper was about on the table. Rose Anne and Deana were still there, and so were Deana's daughters, Leah and Deanne. Momma squealed with delight when I walked through the door. Daddy smiled and said, "Cousin Mandy." He said it slowly, like he could've fit "Oh-my-Lord-what-happened-to-your-head?!" in the same amount of space. He was certainly pleased when I announced I was gonna be at the revival meeting the next morning. He probably knew I wanted to show off my new 'do. But Daddy never questions folks' reasons for going to revival meetings, he just likes it when they do, 'cause once they're there he can do his job.

As the day came to an end, we all sat in the living room and chatted. My two nieces were taking turns rubbing my "stubble head" — as Rose Anne called it — and giggling uncontrollably about the way it felt on their palms. As their giggles reached a near-disastrous level, Deana finally said, "Alright, that's enough. Bedtime." And as if any mother's command is good enough for all of us, we all went to bed.

Throw Away the Dove

I
No - ah loved the an - i - mals, but he
V
threw a - way the dove. Well, act like Je - sus
I
show your love. Throw a - way the dove.
Bridge:
I
In the sky, fly - in'
high. With my wings of
V
gold some - day. In the
pro - mised land,
I
with my wings of gold some - day.

Chapter Four

The Vision

On Sunday, March 22, 1992, in Kornflake, Indiana, Steven's Momma and Grandma Thayer were up early in the morning, doing everything they could to make Steven's twenty-fourth birthday party the best yet. Steven wasn't having a very good time of it himself (I'll tell you why later). But there was nothing I could do about that; in Okey-Dokey, Texas, we were still oblivious to the little farm and Kornflake — and even Indiana, at least on this day.

Our Sunday was filled with Daddy's tent revival meeting. The original tent, the one that we had pulled in the old U-Haul trailer behind us all those years, had long since been replaced. Each strong wind that came along had taken another little piece of it, and finally, Hurricane Agnes put Uncle Joe to insisting on building a new one. The new structure looks somewhat like a tent on the outside but is actually a cleverly disguised aluminum structure wrapped in canvas. It's about four times as big as the old tent, and Daddy's congregation is growing into it. I must say, it's one of Uncle Joe's most ingenious creations, very modern for Okey-Dokey, Texas.

That Sunday morning I gave myself too much time, got up much earlier than necessary, seeing as how I didn't have any hair to "do." I was a little bit anxious, sure there'd be a lot of cheek-pinching and hand-shaking (and head-rubbing) going on when folks realized it was the first time I'd been to a revival meeting in months. I tapped on the bathroom door, behind which Momma was mysteriously putting on her face, and told her I was gonna walk on to the tent revival. She started to say, "Don't get your shoes dirty," or something like that, but caught herself. What came out was, "Don't — I mean alright, honey!"

When I got to the tent revival, Uncle Joe and Daddy were talking about the new robes Uncle Joe wanted to buy the choir with some of the money he'd just made off of the sale of another new trailerpark. It was quite a sight to see Uncle Joe in his sparkling dress trying to convince Daddy in his plain brown suit that the choir would be more exciting with "The Abiding Joy Songsters" written in rhinestones across the backs of their robes and Daddy trying to keep Uncle Joe's excitement to a normal conversing level. Uncle Joe told Daddy, "As long as they're up on the risers, they'd just be wearing pretty deep blue silk robes with white fringe sashes, but when they exit at the end of the sermon, *ta-daa!*"

Daddy just chuckled and said, "Fringe?"

Although the Okey-Dokey Abiding Joy Songsters aren't as big or as professional as the Austin Angels Halleluia Heaven-Bound Gospel Choir that Daddy always talks about being at the preaching competition the night I was born, I don't believe there's a choir more enthusiastic than the Songsters. Especially not with Uncle Joe and his money on their side.

No decision was made that day about choir robes, but Daddy made Uncle Joe feel useful by asking him to choose a song from the hymnal for the congregation to sing. Daddy always likes to start off the revival meetings with a gospel song or two, and he likes to pick the songs himself. It sets the mood for his sermon and gets everybody fired up and ready. (His favorite gospel songs are the ones that haven't been sung to death.) So it was actually quite an honor for him to give the decision over to his brother, and Uncle Joe knew this and immediately went to work.

Now, I'm sure everybody's wondering, so I'll tell ya: Uncle Joe was wearing one of the late Mrs. Jackson's hand-me-downs. It was a decidedly fashionable spring outfit, pale peach with lace overlay on the top half and little pearl droplets dangling from the lace. I complimented Uncle Joe on the outfit but told him my favorite dress of his was still the Lucky Green Dress. He said that it was at the cleaners. I figured he was having it cleaned to help him with sales at the upcoming Mobile Madness Sale-A-Thon, 'cause my Uncle Joe is pretty superstitious.

Momma led the Songsters in their song of the day and then the congregation joined in for the song Uncle Joe had painstakingly selected from the hymnal: "Won't It Be Grand." (It was really a shame to see Uncle Joe's outfit covered up with a choir robe, especially since it was one of the old maroon ones with no rhinestones *or* fringe, but I can certainly understand why a preacher wouldn't want somebody like Uncle Joe behind him without a robe on, for fear of being upstaged!)

Afterwards, Edna Joy, the former mayor's former wife, was helped up to the pulpit by Daddy for the announcements of the day. The most notable announcement was that the First Spring Monday Potluck, organized by Edna herself, would be held the following morning at the old revival grounds. First Spring Monday is a holiday that has been celebrated in Okey-Dokey, Texas as long as I can remember. School is let out, and many folks take off from work. The potluck part of the holiday began in 1987.

When Daddy returned to the pulpit, he mentioned that he'd try to keep the sermon down-to-size so that everybody could get home and start cooking their specialties. Edna laughed out loud in that way she does, traveling up the scale and back down again, only this time she caught herself before she went back down. (Edna Joy has had a crush on my Daddy since 1967 when she "discovered" him.)

The sermon of the day came from the Book of Daniel. It's really a good book, very entertaining. You should read it if you haven't already. I don't wanna go over the whole sermon for ya 'cause I don't think it's necessary to get the gist of what happened to me on March 22, 1992. But I will give you a rundown. Daddy's sermon covered only the first two chapters of the Book of Daniel. Like I said he tends to go on and on, so he's learned over the years to limit his intake to match his intended output.

So, here we are in Babylon. I don't know what year it is, but it must be Something B.C., 'cause it's the Old Testament. The king of Babylon is Nebuchadnezzar (harder to spell than to say: Neb-a-ka-nez-er). The king keeps having a vision, and he's disturbed by it. There's a big statue in his own image. The head is made out of gold, and all the body parts below that are made out of weaker and weaker materials, all the way down to the toes, which are made out of dry clay. Well, a mountain comes crashing down out of Heaven and hits the clay toes and they crumble. And then the feet crumble because the toes were supporting them, and then the ankles crumble because the feet were supporting them and the calves crumble and the knees crumble and the thighs and so on and so on 'til the whole statue crumbles and ends up in a big pile of dust with the king's head sitting on top of it. And then a big strong wind blows the pile of dust, and the cloud of dust gets in the king's eyes. This vision appears over and over to the king, and he's beginning to think he's going crazy. And maybe he is — he's not one of the good guys in the Bible.

But *Daniel's* a good guy. Daniel's like one of the superheroes of the Bible. Later on in the Book of Daniel, he'll end up in the lion's den — but that's not what Daddy's sermon was about this day and I don't wanna give away the ending in case you haven't read it yet.

Anyway, one of Daniel's superhero abilities was that he was able to interpret dreams and visions. So Daniel is summoned to the king to tell him what the vision he's having means, and if he doesn't tell him the truth, the king promised he'd kill Daniel and all the other strong and handsome young men in Babylon. Talk about a meanie!

Well, at about this point in Daddy's sermon, things started happening to *me*. First, I started feeling a little warm and took off my suit coat. Then I started hearing noises, like music or something, in my head. I tried to ignore the noises and just keep on enjoying Daddy's sermon, but it was impossible to hear over the noise. And when Daddy spoke, his words got muddled with the noises in my head. "*Bawwwww, bawwwww, bawwwww....*" That's about all I could make out.

I thought maybe I oughta go outside and get a little fresh air. I turned around to look at the exit, but something got in my eye. And every time I blinked, it only made it worse. I tried rubbing my eyes and knocked my glasses off. I reached down and put them on and when I sat up, I could see clearly. Crystal clear. Except for what looked like smoke coming out of Daddy's head. I blinked hard a couple of times, but the smoke didn't go away. I looked around but nobody else seemed to be having the same problems as I seemed to be having, so I decided I still had something in my eyes and ignored it.

But I couldn't ignore the noises in my head. No matter how hard I concentrated, I couldn't understand what Daddy was saying. It was hard to keep focused on him anyway because I was sure smoke was coming out of his head! I watched the smoke rise up from his head and form into a cloud at the ceiling above him. The cloud was about five feet wide, two or three feet tall, and it was shaped like a flat-bottomed football.

Then, a dot appeared in the center of the cloud. And it grew 'til it was a large imperfect circle within the cloud. The circle started moving about, wiggling and growing and changing colors. I looked around again, convinced that everybody should be able to see what I was seeing, but none of them looked as shocked and surprised as I thought they should. When I looked back to Daddy, the dot in the cloud had formed into the image of a man's head. It was a *Vision!* A Vision of a man wearing glasses and a farmer's straw hat.

The face came to life. He looked around the tent revival congregation 'til he found *me!* And he smiled.

My first thought was "God." God was looking down from Heaven and giving me some sort of a sign. But it sure seemed odd that God would be wearing a farmer's hat, much less glasses! Wouldn't God have 20/20 vision? I decided that this was just a Vision of a man. An ordinary man. (As ordinary as a man in a cloud gets!)

But what was an ordinary man in a cloud doing floating at the ceiling of my Daddy's tent revival and smiling at me? Something was definitely going on. Now, nobody talks about seeing Visions these days like they did so often back in the days of the Bible — at least nobody that doesn't want to be put in a padded room! But I can't think of any other way to describe it. So tap me on the shoulder and take me away because the man in the cloud spoke to me. He said, "Come and go with me." He said it slowly but I didn't understand him. I wasn't really expecting to be visited by a Vision that day (much less talked to), so I guess I wasn't really paying attention. He repeated himself, "Come and go with me."

I mumbled, "Huh?"

"Come and go with me."

And I said, "What?"

And he shouted, "*Come and go with me.*"

I stood and slapped my hand to my chest and said, "Do you mean *me*?"

And he said, "Yes!"

I suddenly noticed that *everybody* in the tent was looking back at me, most of them smiling oddly. I looked up at Daddy, and he was smiling down at me and nodding his head. I looked up at the man in the cloud and pointed and passed out cold.

When I woke up, I was laid out on a back pew. The sermon was over and there was a circle of people standing over me, praying. I was a little embarrassed but very excited. Daddy was more excited than me. He pushed his way through the congregation to me and asked excitedly, "Was it the angel Aint Pearl?"

"I don't think so."

"Well, did she have white hair and brown skin?"

"It was a man."

"A man? Was he in a choir robe?"

"No, he had on a straw hat, and glasses."

Daddy's questions opened the flood gates for everybody else. "Glasses?" "Did he tell you his name?" "Is there a farmer angel,

Brother Roy?" "Who could it be?" They probably hoped it was Daniel or John the Baptist, or even Joan of Arc.

"It was just a man. Just a man in a cloud." They were disappointed, and some of them let it show.

Daddy piped in, "'Just a man in a cloud!' It was an *angel.* You had a *Vision,* son. I always knew you were gonna get a callin', ever since the angel Aint Pearl was there for your birth!"

Somebody asked, "Did the man in the cloud say anything to you?"

"Mm-hm."

"What did he say?"

"He said, 'Come and go with me.'"

Carl the mailman said, "Go where?"

That was the best question of all of 'em. "I have no idea."

Daddy said, "Don't you worry, you'll know soon enough."

✪✪✪

We ate Sunday dinner at Nana and Dad's trailerhome that day. Nana and Dad are my grandparents on my Momma's side. Nana had been planning this meal for a while. It was another loving family member's attempt to get me out of my doldrums, but now it was more of a celebration dinner. Nana made her famous Chicken 'n' Dumplin's, my favorite dish.

At the dinner table, I seized an opportunity to make an announcement. "I'm gonna be leaving Okey-Dokey tomorrow." I didn't have to say it for them to know that my intention was to follow the man in the cloud. There wasn't much of a discussion about the what and the where and the how of it all, it just seemed as natural as saying, "I'm going to college in the fall."

That evening, back at the tent revival, Daddy repeated my announcement for the benefit of the rest of the congregation. Edna Joy was taken over with inspiration and stood up and asked Brother Roy if it wouldn't be a good idea to turn the First Spring Monday Potluck that was already planned for the following morning into a going away potluck for me. Daddy said that it would indeed be a great idea.

That night my head was so full of thoughts I thought I'd explode. After months of days that I thought would never end, this day was over way too soon. I even attempted to recreate the slow-moving days by lying on my bed and staring at the ceiling, but the ceiling was alive with my thoughts.

I didn't sleep a wink that night. Out my bedroom window, up over the tops of the other trailerhomes, the sky was clear and full of stars. There was only one small cloud in the sky. It hovered alone in the northeast, the direction of Louisiana. I pondered the question Carl the mailman had asked earlier that day. And as I looked out at that single cloud, I thought about the legend of the rainbow. As you move toward it, it moves away from you. But when you finally catch up with it, you find a pot of gold. I wondered if I'd find a pot of gold at the end of my journey.

Nana's Famous Chicken 'n' Dumplin's

2 large fryers
1 stick oleo
4 stalks celery, chopped
2 medium onions, chopped
10 chicken bouillon cubes
2 cups milk
8 teaspoons flaked parsley
salt (at least 2 tablespoons)
pepper

In a large pan, place chicken, with water to about 5 inches to the top. Add oleo, celery, onion, chicken bouillon cubes, salt & pepper. Boil 3 to 4 hours. Add a little water if needed. Cut fire down so it won't boil so hard. *Debone chicken*. Set aside. Make 2 double pie crusts:

4 ½ cups flour
1 ½ cups Crisco
1 teaspoon salt
12-16 tablespoons ice water

Roll out. Work some flour in as you roll. Cut into squares. Drop in chicken broth while it is *boiling hard,* keep it boiling as you drop. Simmer with lid on for 20 minutes. Add chicken, milk and parsley flakes. Simmer 10 minutes more.

Gotta Be A Big Man

Though the mountain is tall, and the valley is low,
When I hear my call you know that's where I'm gonna go;
And though the water is so deep and I don't know how to swim,
My faithful word I'm gonna keep, and I will cling to him.

Chapter Five

Eduardo

When the Summer of 1991 rolled around, Steven was the only Cheslik-DeMeyer kid still living at home, and he wasn't happy about it. One at a time, his brothers had flown the coop to pursue exciting careers. Scott, Jr., moved to Virginia Beach, Virginia, to pursue underwater welding; Jack moved to Indianapolis in hopes of one day becoming president (or at least the mayor) — but for the time being he's still a City Councilman; Eddie joined the Peace Corps and still lives overseas; and Michael moved to Columbus, Ohio, to build and fly small airplanes.

Kay graduated from high school in 1991 and moved to Evansville, Indiana, that same summer to prepare for four years at the University of Southern Indiana studying mass communication. They all seemed to know exactly what they wanted to do with their lives and they went for it. Steven was twenty-three years old and hadn't figured out what he was gonna do with his life yet. He wondered if he ever would.

Grandma Thayer told Steven, "Start saving your money, 'cause sooner or later *something's* gonna come along and you're gonna wanna have money for it." That sounded like pretty good advice, so Steven asked his father if he could work for him. His father said he would figure out something for Steven to do.

Steven's father is a popcorn farmer. This was a surprise to me, since my sisters had me convinced that popcorn is manufactured and not grown, same as green peas. I should explain. For the first thirteen years of my life in the back seat of the Rambler station wagon, my sisters told me stories, playing a secret game with each other to see how outlandish they could make their stories and still get me to believe them. Neither one of them lost very often because I believed just about everything they told me. I still embarrass myself once in a while with one of their stories. (They told me that green peas, unlike other kinds of peas, like black-eyed peas or pigeon peas or snow peas, were made in a factory out of spinach and potatoes, created for parents who couldn't get their kids to eat their greens. They told me that Japanese were men and Chinese were women and their babies were called *Vietmanese*!)

With Pop's untimely death in 1984 from a heart attack while making love to Grandma during a blizzard, the Cheslik-DeMeyer Farm had doubled in size to a hundred acres. Pop was the region's main popcorn grower in his day, so Steven's father grew "regular" corn at first so as not to compete with Pop. But Pop left most of the Thayer farm to the Cheslik-DeMeyers, so, as a sort of memorial to Pop, Steven's father changed his entire crop to popcorn. The rest of the Thayer Farm was bought up by a big agricultural corporation after Pop died, and Grandma moved in with Steven's family — Steven's mother stood on the road and wept when they tore down the Thayer house and barn. The company grows field corn (that's what they use to feed livestock, and to grind up for cornmeal).

The problem was, Steven's father had all the hired help he needed for the popcorn fields, so he gave Steven little odd jobs to do. Besides, he didn't want to overwhelm Steven with too big a job since Steven had a tendency to take on too many things and then get bored or give up on most of them; he was always looking for exactly the "right" thing to do. Like, for instance, when the Thayers gave Steven a fiddle at the age of five. He never practiced so he never learned to play very well (and therefore, when he was asked to play, he would only do so if everybody listened from the next room). He also tried crocheting and other crafts, but became frustrated with all of the different stitching styles.

One thing Steven took to unusually well, though, was the guitar. It was a gift from his sister Kay, and that could've had something to do with all the time and effort he put into learning to play it. Y'see, Steven and his sister were best friends all throughout their childhood. It started before she was even born, actually. Seven months before, to be exact.

For his fourth birthday Steven had gotten his first pair of glasses and the promise of a baby sister. Steven took that to mean that the baby was a belated birthday present for *him*. When she was born, Steven claimed Kay as his own. He'd hold her for hours at a time and rock her to sleep, or just stand over her crib and pet her, pushing his older brothers away from her.

When she got older, Kay studied dance and Steven always went with his mother to pick her up from class; and he'd always work the record player for her when she was practicing; and he'd always be the one who started clapping first and who clapped the loudest and the longest at her recitals. No matter if it was ballet or jazz or tap or modern dance or twirling, Steven was Kay's biggest fan.

For her eighth birthday, Kay got a guitar. But about the same time, Pop bought an old saloon piano and put it on the stage in his barn. Kay preferred the piano over the guitar, so the guitar rarely left its case and eventually everybody forgot about it. Two years later, Steven asked Kay whatever happened to her old guitar. She said, "I don't know," but then she dug it up and gave it to Steven for his fourteenth birthday.

Steven loved the guitar because, among other things, it gave him an excuse to spend more time with Kay. He spent hours teaching himself to play, mostly by listening to songs on his mother's favorite radio station. And he got pretty good. Soon he was playing along with Kay on the piano.

For Steven's parents' twentieth wedding anniversary, the Thayers threw a barn dance. Steven and Kay learned "You Are My Sunshine," "Will The Circle Be Unbroken," and "Mom & Dad's Waltz" and performed them for the crowd of people there. At every barn dance after that, there was always a request for the Cheslik-DeMeyer kids to play their songs.

✪✪✪

So, Steven's father found a big job for Steven to do. The fences between the Cheslik-DeMeyer Farm and the old Thayer Farm needed mending. It was a good job for Steven because it was on the outskirts of the farm and therefore pretty secluded. His mother said, "You can even take your guitar out there and play it on your breaks. It's nice and quiet out there."

Everybody knew how much Steven loved the guitar, and they all knew he hadn't played once in the two months since Kay had left.

The following morning, Steven dragged the new oil-treated fenceposts and crossbeams to the edge of the property with the old tractor. It was the middle of August and the sun was already a menace by nine-thirty a.m. Steven's mother called him in for lunch, then afterwards, he took off on foot with a bucket of nails, a saw and a hammer, his lunch and water bucket, and the guitar. The walk took a little more than thirty minutes.

When he got there, he was drenched with sweat. He sat against the fence and drank some water. As he sat there, he thought about Kay, and looked over at his guitar. He picked it up and sang one chorus of "You Are My Sunshine," adding his own comments:

> You are my sunshine — "Go *away*!"
> My only sunshine — "Who *needs* you?"
> You make me happy — "*I'm* not happy!"
> When skies are gray — "I *wish* skies were gray, then
> maybe it wouldn't be so *hot*!"

He squinted up into the sun and laughed, then laid the guitar down and told himself he'd better get to work. He stood up — too fast! His ears started ringing and his head started spinning. Quickly, he squatted down. A gust of wind blew dirt right into his eyes. He fell to his knees and rubbed his eyes and knocked his glasses off. He got on all fours and felt around the ground, but he couldn't find them. That was the straw that broke the camel's back. Steven admitted defeat and fell onto his stomach, on the verge of tears.

He laid there silently for a few moments, resting his forehead on his forearm. Then he heard a noise. Like somebody shaking a cornstalk. Steven looked up, but nobody was there. He wasn't spooked or anything, he just thought it was odd that he heard a noise but nobody was there.

"Hello?"

Nobody answered. He squinted into the cornstalks and thought he saw fumes — like gas fumes — coming up out of the ground. The fumes made the cornstalks look like they were doing a hula dance.

Steven looked at the fumes, into the fumes — through the fumes — down the row between the cornstalks in front of him. Even though he didn't have his glasses, he could see a black dot in the midst of the fumes. It was dancing in the fumes close to the ground. As it danced, the black dot got bigger and bigger. And then beneath the black dot, a light brown dot appeared. The brown dot was the color of milk chocolate. Steven thought of that because he really likes chocolate. And that made him happy.

The black dot and the milk chocolate dot came together to form a bigger dot, and the bigger dot moved around until it formed an imperfect circle. It was the shape of a head. It was a milk chocolate head dancing about in the fumes of the popcorn field — with hair made out of licorice sticks!

[*Steven wants me to put a disclaimer here and tell you that this isn't* exactly *the story the way he told it to me. But I wanna disclaim Steven's disclaimer and say, "Yes it is,* too*!"*]

Steven pulled himself up on his knees. The chocolate head rose up from out of the ground, like it was growing, and a torso followed after it, the whole thing milk chocolate.

Steven thought to himself, "Is this real?"

Maybe it was some kind of cornfield mirage. He couldn't move toward or away from it, he just sat there on his knees watching as an entire milk chocolate man with nothing on but a pair of blue jeans grew up from out of the ground in front of him.

And then the man started walking toward Steven! Steven frantically searched the ground for his glasses, but he couldn't find them. When he looked up again, the chocolate man was standing over him.

He held out a milk chocolatey hand toward Steven and said softly, "Are you okay? You seem sad."

Steven fainted.

✪✪✪

When Steven came to, it took him a second to figure out where he was. He was looking up into the emerald green eyes of the chocolate man. His head was resting against the man's naked chest and his hair was being stroked by one of the man's hands. Steven felt like he was in a horror movie. "Chocolate Man From The Popcorn Field" or something like that. The blood started rushing to his head and he figured he'd better speak before he fainted again.

"My glasses...." That was all that came out. The man handed them to Steven.

Steven put them on and sat up. He could see clearly that this man wasn't made of chocolate at all. He was flesh and blood, perfectly sun-baked flesh and pulsating blood. (Oh, alright, he didn't have a stethoscope, but he found out soon enough!)

"Who are you?"

The man told him his name was Eduardo, that he had come from Puerto de Amor, Mexico.

Steven asked Eduardo what he was doing in Kornflake, Indiana, and Eduardo said, "I'm here to meet you, no?" (It was an unusual answer but Steven didn't question it. A beautiful man appears out of nowhere and says he's there for you, do you ask him why? I don't think so.)

Steven smiled and opened his arms and Eduardo fell into them laughing gently. The sun didn't seem to bother them the rest of the day. In fact, neither of them noticed that the sun had ducked behind a cloud and was riding it into the horizon. Steven's heart was riding a cloud, too; he fell for Eduardo, and Eduardo told Steven he was falling for him.

As they laid there in one another's arms, a cool breeze blew through the cornstalks. Eduardo said it sounded like maracas in the distance. "It sounds like they are singing, 'I love you. I love you.' Listen."

Steven listened but he could only hear the dull glub-glub thumping of Eduardo's heart. Everything that Eduardo said sounded like music to Steven.

Suddenly, the sun was gone; night was upon them. Steven stirred from his comfortable place on the ground and gathered up his tools and his guitar.

"Would you like to come have supper with me and my family?"

Eduardo didn't answer. Steven turned around and the beautiful man was gone. Steven called out for Eduardo, but there was no response. He had disappeared.

A stiff breeze blew past Steven and the cornstalks bristled in the wind. He could hear them singing, "I love you. I love you."

Steven was late for supper. His mother and father and Grandma Thayer were just starting without him when he walked through the kitchen door. He apologized and washed up quickly to join them. Over dinner, he told them all about Eduardo. His father figured Eduardo worked on the old Thayer Farm but Steven said, "He told me he works on a coffee bean farm in Mexico. Puerto de Amor."

Steven's mother said, "Do you have enough water out there?"

They didn't seem to understand.

Grandma Thayer understood. She said "The Gates of Love. That's what Puerto de Amor translates into." Grandma Thayer thought it was *real* special that Steven had made a friend in the cornfield. She said she would crochet Eduardo a sombrero.

Since Pop's death, Grandma had taken to making the oddest things: thirty-foot mufflers, ten-foot square afghans, monster-size mittens and footsies. She even made twenty-nine "corn caps" and gave them to Steven's father for Christmas one year; she said she'd make the rest as soon as she could. She'd planned to make enough for every ear of corn in the field 'til Steven's mother took her out to the field to show her that the cornstalks didn't need any winter caps because they'd all gone away for the winter. (They attributed this and other bizarre Grandma Thayer antics to the marijuana plants she grew and protected like a hawk. She said she just liked the way they looked. But when Steven's father found them — quite by accident — and started pulling them up, she appeared out of nowhere and attacked him with her knitting bag.)

✪✪✪

The following day, the sun was every bit as hot, but it didn't seem to affect Steven nearly as much. At lunch time, after he finished eating a leftover meatloaf sandwich, he took out his guitar. He had an idea for a song about his sister Kay. He sang a few lines, then sang them a little bit different, but he stopped short, dissatisfied with the way it was coming out.

Out of nowhere, Eduardo's voice said, "Who is *she*?" He was standing behind Steven, leaning over the same post Steven was sitting against.

Eduardo jumped over the fence and sat down next to Steven. Steven told him about his sister. Eduardo hung on every word. At one point, his eyes teary, he said, "You have so much passion, it strokes my heart and makes me feel love for you."

Steven didn't return to work that day. Time just slipped away in Eduardo's emerald eyes. As dusk set in, Steven told Eduardo he shouldn't be late for supper and invited him again to join them.

Eduardo stood up and paced nervously and said, "I don't think that would be such a great idea." He wouldn't tell Steven why, and he disappeared again while Steven wasn't looking.

Every day for the rest of the summer, Eduardo would appear to Steven in the popcorn field. Steven never saw him come or go. Every day, Steven asked Eduardo to go with him for supper and every day Eduardo declined. Steven's parents kidded him about the "Phantom Man in the Cornfield" but Grandma Thayer always listened with interest whenever Steven talked about him.

When fall came, there was less work for Steven to do, but he still made his way into the cornfield at least once a day and Eduardo always seemed to find him wherever he was. As the hot sun turned cooler, Eduardo told Steven that he was going back to Puerto de Amor for the winter, but that he'd return in the spring and they could be together then. Steven begged him to stay, but Eduardo said he had to see his family. He asked Steven to come with him. After thinking about it, Steven said he would, but that Eduardo would have to meet his family first.

Eduardo got angry. "Why do we have to meet anyone? Why can't we just be together the two of us in our world? Why don't you just run away? I know a place in Puerto de Amor where you can hide and then we can be together and love each other, and nobody can make us stop."

Steven told Eduardo that his family wouldn't stop them from loving each other. "They don't care who or what you are, they just want me to be happy. And you make me happy, so they'll love you, too."

Eduardo screamed, "No!" and disappeared into the cornfield. Steven chased after him, but he didn't see him again.

That night at supper, Steven told his parents the whole story. They decided they should comb through the cornfields the next day and find Eduardo. Late in the afternoon, after chores, Steven's father and mother got in the cab of the beat-up old tricolored Chevy/Ford truck that used to belong to the Thayers, and Steven and Grandma Thayer got in the back. Steven stood and looked out over the cab and called out to Eduardo. Grandma Thayer sat on a cushion of hay with the newly completed red and yellow crocheted sombrero in her lap. She wanted to offer it to Eduardo as a token of friendship.

They drove around their hundred acres for nearly three hours, 'til the setting sun played tricks on their eyes with shadows. As they drove back to the barn, Grandma Thayer had the sombrero on her head and she softly sang "Cielito Lindo":

Ay ay ay ay,
Canta y no llores;
Porque cantando se alegra
Cielito lindo los corazones.

Steven looked down at her, his face wet with tears; Grandma Thayer smiled up at Steven and said, "Sing, don't cry...beautiful sky." The sight of her with the droopy brim of the hand-crocheted sombrero falling around her face made him laugh, and his laughter combined with sobs as he hugged her tightly. She hugged him back and said, "That's better."

✪✪✪

Christmastime is usually a very joyous season on the Cheslik-DeMeyer Farm. No matter where they are, all of Steven's brothers and Kay come home for Christmas to uphold their family traditions, like going out to a Chinese restaurant in Terre Haute on Christmas Eve. You might think this is a particularly odd Christmas tradition, but it makes perfect sense when you understand it. Y'see, back when Pop was alive, Grandma Thayer always made oyster stew on Christmas Eve 'cause Pop loved it. But after two years without Pop, as everybody choked down the milky broth, Grandma Thayer looked up from her first spoonful and said, "Hell, he's gone, can't we go out for Chinese food or something?"

Grandma Thayer's cookie platter is another tradition that continues to this day, only now, it's Steven's mother's cookie platter.

Grandma Thayer is always too busy crafting an odd assortment of gifts to do any baking.

The Christmas of '91 was a little more subdued than the years before or since. Steven didn't speak much at all and everybody talked in whispers about the mysterious Mexican Eduardo. Steven spent most of the holiday season up in his room, lying on his bed and staring at the ceiling. He couldn't even be coaxed into singing carols around the Christmas tree, usually one of his favorite holiday traditions.

Kay had met somebody at college and came home and announced, "I think he's the *one*!" She planned to go to Tennessee with him the next summer to meet his family and then would bring him to Kornflake for Christmas 1992.

Steven thought about how Eduardo said he'd return in the spring. But would he still be returning after what'd happened? What *had* happened? Steven had to believe that Eduardo was coming back, or else he'd never make it through the winter.

✪✪✪

On February 2, 1992, the groundhog saw his shadow bright and clear. Steven had never paid much attention to what the groundhog saw before, but this year it gave him a really bad case of Spring Fever. What was worse, it was Leap Year, so there was an extra day before spring.

On March 21, the first day of spring, Steven packed a picnic basket and headed out early in the morning to the fencepost where Eduardo had first come to him. He laid out one of Grandma Thayer's patchwork quilts and set out two plates and two cups and then leaned back on the fencepost and played through the song about Kay that he was still working on.

He came to a stopping point in the song and just sat still and listened. A breeze blew across the field and Steven laughed to himself and said, "I love you."

"Do you?"

Steven's heart jumped up into his throat. He looked up and Eduardo was standing there above him, leaning over the fencepost as he had before. He got up as fast as he could, grabbed Eduardo and held him for a long time, afraid to let go. When he stepped back, he realized Eduardo was very dressed up. His jeans were new and pressed, he was wearing a crisp white shirt and he had on black leather shoes. His hair was longer and pulled back into a ponytail and it reflected the sun brightly. He looked down at the picnic spread and said, "All this, for me?"

"All this and more, Eduardo."

Eduardo didn't say much all afternoon, and neither did Steven; they stayed in each others' arms until the day was close to an end. Finally, Steven said, "I wanna be with you, Eduardo. I wanna go with you. Wherever you want me to go, I'll go there. I love you." Steven looked up and a tear rolled down Eduardo's cheek, but he was smiling. Steven asked him what was wrong but Eduardo just pulled him in and held him tight.

As Steven packed up the picnic basket, he said, "I'll say goodbye to my family tonight. Tomorrow at noon, I'll be here. We can go then. Wherever."

Eduardo nodded and kissed Steven. Steven bent down to pick up his guitar and when he stood up, Eduardo was gone.

Steven didn't say a word to his family that night; he hoped he would be able to convince Eduardo to go and meet them. The next day at noon, Steven was there in the field, but Eduardo wasn't. Steven's excitement turned into anxiousness, and then a sinking feeling came over him that grew as the sun made its way farther west. He thought, "Maybe he'll come tomorrow." But he knew he was kidding himself.

Kay was coming that evening for his birthday so he thought he oughta get home. He picked up his duffel bag and then he picked up his guitar. Beneath it on the ground was a bright white square of paper. He stood staring down at it for a long time. Finally, he bent over and picked it up. It was folded in half. He unfolded it. It was a letter from Eduardo:

> My deer Steven.
>
> My hart is braking and yours will be to becaws I will brake it. It is no what I want to do it is what I will do becaws Im an afrade. I am hapy that you hav your famaly. They must be good and full of lov like I dont ever no. Promis me will not reed this to them or to anyone els. Im an afrade for anyone els to no how I feel.
>
> I want you to no how I feel, that Im afrade. I want you to no that Im am back in Mexico for good. My famaly is hapy for me that I hav a wive and she will hav my baby soon. This is how it is supos to be.
>
> Pleas do no com heer to Mexico for me. Pleas do no think about me. I will mis you. Eduardo.
>
> PS: you wer the only man I ever let myself love.

As Steven's tears fell on the letter, the words caught in them and trickled off the bottom of the page. A crack of thunder pounded in the sky and the sky opened up and rain came down hard and fast. Steven stood looking down at the letter as the rain washed the words completely off of the page. He started laughing.

When he got home, Steven could smell a chocolate cake baking. Chocolate cake with *cooked* chocolate icing, that's what he always asked for and that's what he always got for his birthday. His mother was the first one to see him when he walked through the kitchen door. He was soaking wet and still laughing.

"What's gotten into you?" Steven just shrugged. She looked

down at the duffel bag. "Are you going somewhere?"

"I don't know. Maybe. Someday."

He went up to his bedroom and laid on the bed. He just stared up at the ceiling and his mind was blank. A couple of minutes later, Grandma Thayer tapped on his open bedroom door. Steven barely raised his head and said, "Hi." He invited her in but didn't move from his position.

In her hand, Grandma Thayer was carrying a small crocheted thing, like a small sack, all red with a little black heart-shape in the middle. She sat on the bed next to Steven and set the sack in her lap and played with it as she spoke.

"You know, before I met Pop, there was another boy. I was fourteen years old. It was nineteen-hundred and thirty. Can you believe it? Well this boy, his name was Robert, he told me he loved me and that he would never leave me. Oh, I fell for him, really hard! He was so handsome with his missing tooth and his curly black hair. Well, Robert suddenly decided that Mary Sullivan was a much better girl for him than me. She was *fif*teen. But the worst part about it was he wouldn't *tell* me. I knew he was sweet on her, but he just wouldn't come out with it and tell me like a man. He wanted to bow out of it gracefully. Well, he did bow out, but let me tell you, there wasn't thing *one* graceful about it!

"The thing I remember the most about the whole episode was how my chest hurt. It was like somebody had put a block of ice where my heart used to be. It was actually *cold* in there! Well, you don't wanna hear an old girl's sad story. The reason I'm telling you all this silliness is because I know what you're going through, Steven. I can feel it. And I'm *sorry*."

Hot tears ran into Steven's ears and he just laid there with his arms spread open.

"I made you this heart-warmer."

Slowly, Steven sat up.

"I hope that if you're feeling that coldness in your heart like I was feeling, you'll take it out and put it in here for a little while." She had her hand inside of it now and held it up as if to demonstrate. "Guaranteed to make your heart feel better!"

Steven hugged Grandma Thayer and sobbed for a long time. She held him and rubbed his head until he pulled away from her.

"Another thing. Maybe you oughta take off for a while. You know...you aren't finding what you're looking for here in Kornflake; maybe you oughta look a little farther. Go out into the deeper waters!" She smiled, kissed Steven on the forehead, tossed the heart-warmer on the bed, then stood up and sashayed to the door. At the door, she turned around and said, "Don't you dare tell your Mom and Dad this, 'cause I'll deny it 'til my dying day, but there's a little something in there that'll make your traveling a little easier." She blew a kiss to him and walked down the hallway singing "Happy Birthday To You."

Steven laughed to himself. He figured Grandma Thayer had probably put some marijuana in the crocheted bag. He reached into the heart-warmer and took out an envelope. Inside it were twenty-four twenty dollar bills.

Does It Feel Like Home?

I used to dream she was in danger
On a cliff or at the river's edge;
And in my dream, I would save her
From whatever lay ahead.
Now there's a distance between us,
And we're both so far from home;
But it will be like Mama told us,
We will reap what we have sown.

Chapter Six

The First Spring Monday Potluck

Edna Joy has a fetish for organizing things. This fetish is particularly active when she's under a lot of pressure or is stressed out about something. The preaching contest my Daddy won back in 1968 was organized because Edna's immediate family was upset that her husband Frank Joy had decided to go into politics; and the stress of organizing the preaching contest prompted her to reorganize her entire house. The first annual First Spring Monday Potluck was organized in 1987 when Edna returned from a holiday cruise *without* her husband, the former mayor. He was elected the Coconut King onboard, off the coast of Florida, and apparently took up with the Grass Skirt Queen and sent Edna home alone. It's a long and sordid story that changes every time Edna tells it, so I'd rather not get into it. (But if ya *really* wanna hear a story, ask Edna Joy!)

First Spring Monday has been a holiday without the Potlucks as long as anybody can remember, but in 1987 Edna Joy was seeking the comfort of friends and food and invented the Potlucks to get both. I guess because this stress was a particularly monumental stress in Edna's life, the First Spring Monday Potlucks weren't just a gathering of friends with some covered dishes. Edna wrote letters to every household in Okey-Dokey, Goose Creek, and Highland, and she made the Potlucks a major event in the tri-community area. She gave each family a choice of three different courses to bring, according to what they felt best-equipped to handle: an appetizer, a side dish, or a dessert. Edna thought that this would create a variety of foods at the Potlucks, but it tended to produce more desserts than anything. Not that anybody complained!

The lot where my Daddy's new tent revival now stands permanently was manicured to golf course-type grass surrounded by tall pine trees in the spring of 1982. Edna thought the revival grounds were the most beautiful and inspiring place to have the Potlucks and, fortunately for her, Daddy agreed.

Edna rented banquet tables from Houston, and borrowed red checkered table cloths from a linen supply company in Highland and beverage-dispensing coolers from the Goose Creek Consolidated Independent School District construction department. Uncle Joe provided paper cups and plates (with "Okey-Dokey Mobile Madness" printed on them) and made batches of ice tea and five different flavors of Kool-Aid. The First Spring Monday Potlucks were an organization-fetishist's dream.

1992 was a particularly special First Spring Monday Potluck. For one thing, it was the tenth annual. For another thing, I had had my Vision the day before and by now even folks who never came to Daddy's revival meetings had heard about it. Edna Joy figured that these factors would make the 1992 First Spring Monday Potluck the most attended Potluck ever, and she was right. She ordered extra banquet tables and was on the revival grounds with her clipboard by eight in the morning, March 23, pointing delivery men this way and that 'til the tables were all in just the right places. Four of the tables were covered with butcher paper and set apart from the rest. The children who helped bring out the extra wooden folding chairs that were stored in the old U-Haul (which is now kept behind the revival tent) were given strict and repeated instructions *not* to put chairs around those tables, and as soon as Nana arrived with a big pot of leftover Chicken 'n' Dumplin's and was instructed to put it on the butcher-papered tables, the children understood why. Soon, the butcher paper would be barely visible under covered serving dishes of all shapes, sizes, and colors, with serving spoons resting neatly beside them.

1992 was certainly no different as far as types of dishes that were brought to the Potluck. My Momma always cooks up a few appetizers and side dishes to offset the large number of dessert items at the Potlucks, but her efforts were still way outnumbered by Heaven & Heck (a devil's food/angel food combo cake), Aunt Konk's Pineapple Upside-down Cake, Ruth's Texas Dirt Cake (made in a clay flowerpot with Gummi Worms and a plastic flower sticking out of the top), French Apple Cheesecake, Coca-Cola Cake and Tunnel-O-Fudge Cake; apple pie, pecan pie, sweet potato pie, peanut butter pie, rhubarb pie, and German-Chocolate Pie; Coke Salad and a whole rainbow of Jell-O mold desserts; cookies, brownies, muffins, and turnovers; et cetera, et cetera, et cetera. Twenty miles north of Highland, the northernmost town in the tri-community area, is one of Texas's largest sugar farms; its influence is obvious in the number of visits children in the area make to the dentist each year — my oldest sister Rose Anne went four times one year.

✪✪✪

I always tell Steven that my first taste of fame came on March 23, 1992. Early that afternoon as the buzz from the second helping of desserts was wearing off, everybody at the Potluck seemed to wanna hear me tell the story of my Vision. I must've told that story a hundred times. They were all undeniably impressed by the story, but the cloud — the cloud that was the climax of the story — seemed to confuse them. I'd finish up the story each time with the same words: "I've promised myself that I'll follow the man in the cloud wherever he leads me!" I'd proudly point up above the pine trees to my fluffy little cloud waiting patiently for the Potluck to end so we could hit the road, and I'd say, "That's it right there!"

Everybody would look up into the sky with great anticipation on their faces, but then somebody would always say, "Where?" or "That's *it*?" Or, worse yet, they'd just look back at me blankly, their looks of anticipation replaced by doubt.

Every time I told the story, I was fueled by the crowd's anticipation, and then crushed by their confusion. Noticing my distress, Daddy finally came over and said, "It ain't *their* Vision, Jay Byrd, it's *yours*."

From that point on when folks asked me to tell the story, I just said that it was way too incredibly exciting and unbelievably terrific to put into words, and that would send them running off to hear a version of the story from one of the groups that had formed on different parts of the revival grounds.

✪✪✪

Around three-thirty, the crowd was beginning to thin out. The curiosity-seekers had all gone home to sleep off their sugar highs and the only folks left on the revival grounds were close friends and family members. The butcher paper was splattered with spoonfuls of food that didn't make it all the way to their intended paper plates, and the pots and bowls and platters that were still on the tables were scraped nearly clean. I got up from my seat between Daddy and Momma and went for another glass of Kool-Aid, but all that was left in the coolers was sludge, five different colors of it.

When I returned to the three banquet tables in the center of all the others where everybody who was still there had migrated, Edna Joy had taken my seat and was whispering in Daddy's ear. I made my way to a chair by Nana at the far end of the same table. As I looked around, I noticed all my aunts and uncles and cousins — and all of the folks I just *called* Aunt or Uncle or Cousin — staring at me with odd smiles on their faces. I smiled back and said, *"What!"*

Daddy lifted a Corning Ware bowl and a metal serving spoon he had taken from one of the food tables (since all of the cups and plates were paper) and hit them together over his head. *Clang, clang, clang, clang, clang!*

Everybody was startled by the clanging and then laughed. Edna stood up. On the table in front of her was a stack of papers of varying sizes — each of them hole-punched and joined together by a chain — and an envelope. On the hundreds of scraps of paper were the names, addresses and phone numbers of family members and close friends of just about everybody in the tri-community area who lived outside of the tri-community area, folks who said they'd put me up for a night and feed me if I happened to end up near them on my journey. They were as close by as Houston and Galveston and as far away as the Dominican Republic (Mr. and Mrs. Lester's son is an Episcopalian missionary there). Except for that one, all of them were in the United States, and most of them were in the southern half of the country. Edna Joy carried the names and numbers by their chain to my end of the table and gave them to me and said, "No matter where the man in the cloud leads ya, there'll always be somebody close by who's willin' ta put a roof over your head or a meal in your belly!"

I wasn't really sure what she meant at first but I thanked her anyway as she put the chain over my head like a medal.

Edna returned to her place next to Daddy and picked up the fat envelope and brought it back to me; it was an offering she had taken up at the Potluck and it turned out to be nearly a thousand dollars. She held it out and I took it, but she didn't let go. As we stood there, both of us with a hand on the envelope, everybody's eyes on us, Edna said, "I was the first child born in Southeast Texas in the year nineteen and twenty. I first met Frank Joy in nineteen and thirty. He was seventeen and I was too young for marryin' yet! Father was a sugar farmer and a drinker. I don't know if ya knew that. I don't really tell it much. Durin' the Great Depression *we* lived on sugar and *he* lived on homemade rum. In nineteen and forty, I was seventeen and Frank Joy was twenty and he came a'callin' again. This time around, we married. But we didn' have any children. Couldn'. Everbody figured it was me but I found out different in nineteen and fifty. There was the matter of a little affair with a gentleman who shall remain nameless."

There was a noticeable shudder around me and Daddy started to break in, but Edna continued. "Those were some terrible days; it was before I knew the Lord, mind ya. By nineteen and sixty, ever tooth in my head was fake. I never ate sugary snacks after my weddin' day, but it was too late, the damage was already done. In nineteen and seventy, I met your Daddy, Brother Roy (right over there!), on the day you were born. Then in nineteen and eighty, y'all had the sense to settle down here for good. And now you're leavin' us! Well, I'll be...where do the years go?"

As I stood there wondering where the years *did* go, she let go of the envelope and everybody stood up and applauded.

I made my way through everybody, exchanging final goodbyes. My sisters gave me two hundred postcard stamps so that I could always keep in touch; Nana and Dad gave me a small canvas sack, heavy with ten rolls of quarters. Nana said, "Those are for callin' your old grandmaw — an' washin' your clothes!"

Dad said, "An' if anybody gives ya any trouble out there, just swing it over your head like David to Goliath!" He illustrated with the sack.

Nana slapped his arm playfully and said, "Oh, Dad!"

Everybody else gave me words of encouragement for my journey:

"The Good Lord'll keep a watch over you!"

"Your Daddy gave you his good genes!" (At first, I thought they meant "jeans" like blue jeans, but then I decided that couldn't have been what they said since I'd packed my own backpack).

One last goodbye and I turned to leave, but then Uncle Joe pulled into the tent revival parking lot, laying on his horn. That's when it dawned on me that he'd been missing from the Potluck for the last hour or two. Truth be known, old Mrs. Jackson had passed away on First Spring Monday back in 1980 (before the Potlucks began), and so Uncle Joe wasn't too terribly sociable at the Potlucks, he just kinda sat around watching everybody else, and reminiscing, I guess.

But on this day, Uncle Joe was unusually full of energy. He jumped out of his truck with three bulky white boxes in his arms and called me over.

Everybody gathered around me in a circle and Uncle Joe handed the boxes to me one at a time. In the first box was a cowboy hat with a fake white sunflower on it.

"The flower'll keep the sun shinin' down on ya an' the hat'll keep it from burnin' ya to a crisp!"

Everybody said, "Mmm!" — meaning, I guess, that that was a good thought.

In the second box was a pair of python snake cowboy boots; everybody let out an "Oooh!" I'd had my eyes on them at Don's Western World for months, but I didn't remember telling anybody how much I liked them.

He said, "Ya gotta have some sturdy walkin' shoes!" He was right. I looked down at my old Pay-Less sneakers and realized I hadn't given much thought to my feet. Then I looked at Uncle Joe's feet and realized he was wearing a brand new pair just like mine! I kicked off my sneakers and pulled on the boots. They fit like gloves.

The third box was sealed up a lot tighter than the first two, with tape on all four sides. When I finally got it open, whatever was in it was wrapped in several layers of different colored tissue paper; pink and blue and green and purple. And just behind the purple tissue paper was a sparkly green dress. It was Uncle Joe's Lucky Green Dress.

Everybody gasped, including me. I said, "Are you kidding?"

Uncle Joe said, "Put it on!" He obviously wasn't kidding.

Everybody cheered. I'd never actually worn a dress before (and I wasn't sure I was ready to), but the cheering overtook me — and I didn't want to disappoint Uncle Joe — so I stepped into the revival tent and put it all on (dress, boots and hat). I had no idea what I looked like, but when I stepped out and walked down the stone path, everybody exploded into applause and happy screams. Cameras flashed and I couldn't close my mouth, I was smiling so big. I walked over to Uncle Joe and hugged him.

When I pulled away from Uncle Joe I was surprised that his face was wet with tears. He said, "The future's as big as the sky, Jay Byrd. Go get em!"

Again, everybody cheered and I looked up into the sky and noticed that the cloud had moved slightly northward. That was my sign. I hiked my backpack up on my back and headed out of the parking lot and down Cedar Terrace Road toward I-10. I didn't look back 'cause suddenly I was scared. I thought if I looked back, something in their faces might keep me from being able to leave.

Close to the edge of town I passed Carl the mailman. He shook my hand long and hard and said, "Neither rain nor snow nor sleet nor dead of night shall keep our fearless couriers from their appointed rounds, huh, Jay Byrd?"

I laughed and said, "Uh-huh," but I didn't have any idea what he was talking about.

"Will we be seeing you in service again next Sunday, Jay Byrd?"

"I don't think so, Carl. I don't think so."

"Well, we're all very proud of you, Jay Byrd. Especially your Daddy!"

"I know, Carl. Thank you!"

Then he said, "Is that a *dress* you got on?" I nodded and waved and we continued going our separate directions. When I got to the huge sign at the edge of town, the one that says:

YOU ARE NOW LEAVING
OKEY-DOKEY
ALRIGHTY?!

I ducked behind it and changed out of Uncle Joe's Lucky Green Dress into my regular clothes. I just *couldn't*....

The Cottonwood Tree

Part Two

The Journey

Fancy Pants

Your toothy smile don't make our skin all goosey.
Your sinewy physique don't make us hot.
Your belly button's cute as a potater.
But, I tell ya, I'd rather have a tater tot.

You're smooth and you move just like an old serpent.
But remember Satan also was a snake.
And Satan hasn't got a pot to pee in.
Or a tree limb in The Garden left to shake.

Chapter Seven

Ruther Jean's Closet

I've always called my Uncle Joe's ex-wife Aunt Nicki's second cousin Nonie Bruscato "Aunt Nonie," even though she's obviously not very related to me. I always wished she was though. She's younger than anybody I've ever called aunt, and she's definitely more "cool" than any aunt I've ever known — even Aunt Nicki. The first thing that always struck everybody about Aunt Nonie was her head. It's like one of those Fix-Me-Up doll heads my sisters both had, only Aunt Nonie's head was fixed up to perfection. Platinum blonde hair, candy-apple red lips, big movie star sunglasses — worn even on cloudy days — and humongous shiny earrings that sent out blinding death rays when the sun hit 'em. And powdery-white, *perfect* skin. That's the way I remember her, though I haven't seen her in years. She always smelled like candy, too; she wore cinnamon oil as perfume. (To this day, cinnamon is my number one favorite hard candy flavor, and I blame that on Aunt Nonie!)

Aunt Nonie and Aunt Nicki were best friends when I was growing up. Whenever my family was taking a break in Goose Creek from the tent revival circuit (before everybody up and moved to Okey-Dokey) Aunt Nonie always made a point of dropping by and taking me and my sisters for a ride in her souped-up candy-apple red convertible GTO to the house where the Mexican lady sold tamales out of her kitchen window, using the driveway as a drive-thru and the backyard as a turn-around. They were the best tamales in the world, authentic and delicious, and the driveway was sometimes so busy that there would be a traffic jam in the backyard around the big old pecan tree, and folks would cuss at each other and Aunt Nonie would beg us not to tell our parents or else they might not let us ride in her car again, or they might not let us hang around her anymore if they knew what kind of a scary neighborhood she was taking us to. My sisters and I never uttered a word about anything we did with Aunt Nonie, not even to each other; we were members of a very secret club: Aunt Nonie's Secret Keepers.

By the time Uncle Joe and Aunt Nicki split up, Aunt Nonie had moved away from Goose Creek. I was real mad at her for moving, and I tried to make myself *not* forgive her (thinking that that might make her come back), but when I saw her the next Christmas, I ran to her and hugged her long and hard, hoping to squeeze out all the guilt I'd caused myself from the bad thoughts I'd had about her.

Over the years, I was able to let Aunt Nonie out of my heart and mind a little bit, but never completely. Once in a while she'd arrive in my dreams riding a cinnamon stick, and she would take me and my sisters to a "Willy Wonka/Wizard of Oz" Mexico for magical candied tamales. She never came back while I was awake, though. It made sense that she moved; Goose Creek, Texas, was no kind of town for somebody as bold and beautiful and cool and perfect as Nonie Bruscato. She had to make her way out into the big world and I came to understand that.

She moved to Beaumont, Texas.

Occasionally, kinfolks brought Aunt Nonie up in conversation. "Nonie got married," then "Nonie got divorced." Neither statement was much of a surprise to me. I pictured her husband, handsome and muscular and neat, but not quite up to snuff. It was natural that Aunt Nonie would marry and divorce him. And even though divorce wasn't looked on too kindly by some folks in the community, Aunt Nonie's reputation wasn't tarnished in my mind at all — in fact, I think it made her even cooler. That's why I was so excited that the first piece of paper I saw on my names-and-numbers necklace that Edna Joy gave me had "Nonie Bruscato" on it. I felt myself blush when I read it; it was like I'd gotten an autographed picture from a movie star.

Beaumont became the first goal of my journey. I walked to the Greyhound station in Highland and had to wait for what seemed like forever to catch the next bus to Aunt Nonie. On the bus, I practiced in my head what I'd say to her when I got there. It was close to midnight when I got off the bus in Beaumont. I saw a pay phone on the far side of the parking lot and called from there.

Her answering machine picked up after the second ring. "Hey. Noan here. Well, I *ain't* here! Leave a message and I'll call ya back....An' Delbert, if that's you, I left your hat at Ruther Jean's," and she gave out Ruther Jean's phone number. The beep sounded and I must've stood there for thirty seconds watching the "TION" in the neon bus station sign across the parking lot short out. Finally, I hung up. Then I called right back.

"Aunt Nonie, it's your long-lost nephew Jay Byrd. I missed ya. I'm sorry I missed ya. I came to town — I'm in *Beaumont*! — but I missed ya — ya aren't here. Sorry I missed ya." Something like that. I know I babbled a lot and said, "Sorry I missed ya" a lot, 'til her answering machine got tired of hearing me say it and cut me off.

I hung up and stood there with my hand on the receiver, thinking. Thinking hard. But no brilliant ideas came to me. An unlit sign beneath the bus station sign said:

RESTAURANT!

I decided to get a bite to eat. I walked across the empty gray parking lot and into the metal bus station building. On a bench in the main waiting area, a rotund older man and woman (of the same exact proportions) slept, leaning against each other.

They were very dirty and had a rickety pushcart in front of them full of what looked like neatly organized bags of garbage. Beyond them on one wall was a closed ticket window with a sign:

RING FOR TICKETS

Behind them was the restaurant, or what used to be and would possibly someday again be the restaurant. A greasy sign told the story:

OPEN 24 HOURS TODAY

"The Restrant is Close"

I looked again at the sleeping couple. This looked like the end of the line for them. I decided this wasn't where I wanted to end up.

As I walked across the parking lot, I looked up into the clear black sky. Right over my head was my cloud. The man I'd seen so clearly in the cloud when it was in my Daddy's tent revival was now just a shadow — but I recognized the shadow as the shape of the man's head. I said, "Alright, cloud...."

The phone rang. I smiled to myself as I hurried my steps to the phone. I didn't run; I didn't wanna look desperate! Besides, the phone wasn't that far away; it only rang two and a half times before I got to it and picked it up. I said hello to a dial tone. Weird.

I hung up and waited a moment for the caller to call again, but then I wondered who I was thinking might be calling. I wasn't even sure I'd know what to say to somebody who'd call a pay phone in the middle of an empty parking lot outside of a bus station in the middle of the night. But I didn't find out 'cause the phone didn't ring again.

When I went to turn around in the phone booth, my backpack pushed the door shut and kinda wedged me into a corner. The harder I tried to get out the more stuck I seemed to get. I got a little panicky and called Aunt Nonie again, but halfway through her outgoing message I realized that if I left a panic-stricken message for her, she wouldn't get it 'til she returned the following Sunday and by then I'd either be dead or gone. I slammed the phone down. "I *hate* Beaumont!" I screamed as loud as I could, "Aaaagh!" Then I pictured what I looked like from above (very clearly — perhaps it was a cloud's-eye view) and I laughed. I laughed for a little while, but my laughter came to a sudden halt when I realized what an ignoramus I'd been. I *did* have somebody to call. I called Aunt Nonie's number one more time. "...An' Delbert, if that's you, I left your hat at Ruther Jean's...." I wrote the number with my finger on the steamed up glass of the phone booth.

I was a little bit worried that I might wake this Ruther Jean person up, but I wasn't so worried about it that I considered staying in the phone booth all night long to wait for a better time. The phone rang less than a whole ring before Ruther Jean said, "Yello!" She sounded so awake, I figured she was either wide awake or so dead asleep she didn't know what she was saying. What I didn't know at the time, and what I still haven't gotten around to telling my Momma and Daddy (but I did tell Steven and I'll tell you right now) is that Ruther Jean is one of them exotic dancers; y'know, she dances and takes her clothes off while she's doing it. For money! Well anyway, what I'm trying to say by that is that Ruther Jean *was* awake; lucky me, it was her night off.

I told her my hard-luck story and as soon as I mentioned the part about being stuck in a phone booth, she said, "Don't move a muscle, Russell, I will be there in a jiffy!" I tried to tell her that my name wasn't Russell, but all I heard was a dial tone. I hung up and tried to wait patiently. I could lift my feet off the ground a couple of inches and rest my forearms on top of the telephone and that way be a little bit more comfortable. I stayed in that position for who-knows-how-long; my mind was blank.

Suddenly, I heard tires squealing and saw a gold Dodge Duster barreling through the parking lot toward me, its muffler sputtering like a race car in need of a tune-up. I had seen cop shows on TV, I knew what came next: the car would run over the phone booth, and it, me and a couple of just-arriving Greyhound buses would all blow up sky high in slow motion. Fortunately, I was wrong. It was Ruther Jean in the Dodge Duster. She jumped out of the car, left the motor running, ran to the phone booth, and grunted as she pried the door open a little. She saw a loose strap on my backpack hanging out, grabbed it, and shimmied me backwards. The glass accordion phone booth door inched open slowly for a second, then popped off its track and fell to the pavement, splintering into a spider web design. Instead of tossing me aside and letting me fall to the ground, Ruther Jean counterbalanced me and we went spinning in circles until I was able to catch myself. In the spinning, the loose strap had tightened around a couple of her fingernails. She screamed, "Hold it! Hold it!" as I tried to turn around and thank her; I was jiggling one of her nails loose. She cried out a funny fake-cry that I didn't recognize as fake at first. She said, "You pulled my *fangernail* off!" My stomach tensed. I turned to face her and she was squeezing one finger with her other fist. I saw splashes of red all over her hands. The nails that were still attached were painted blood red, and I was sure the end of one of her fingers must be squirting blood like a shook-up bottle of Coke.

When I finally got her to stop squeezing her finger and let me take a look — *carefully!* — I realized that all that had come off was a fake fingernail, a blood-red polished fake fingernail, like the other nine that were still attached. I screamed, "It's fake!"

She screamed back, *"Hey!"* And we laughed.

Ruther Jean took a step back to look me over, so I looked her over at the same time. She was dressed in a red rhinestone-studded bright orange jumpsuit. Her hair was platinum blonde — just like Aunt Nonie's! — and her lips were heavily colored, but hers were blood red and not candy-apple red (the difference may have only been a matter of me being older, I'm not sure). And then there were those fingernails! This was something I'd never seen before, not on Aunt Nonie or anybody. Other than that, though — and the fact that Aunt Nonie was tall and thin and Ruther Jean was not as tall — these two women seemed to have been poured out of the same pitcher of "Cool."

Ruther Jean pulled her dislodged fingernail out from under my backpack strap and told me to toss the pack in the back seat. When we got in the car, she was laughing. The only word she could get out through her laughter was "Sorry—." I stared at her, waiting for her to finish. The flickering bus station sign caught my eye, then I looked up into the sky at my cloud, a little more north than before. When she got control of herself she said, "I am *sorry*! My Daddy was tall and thin and ball-headed like you. I swear, when I came driving up here across the parking lot, I had a flashback on the old man and I almost ran you down, fella!" She went on to tell me that of *course* she wouldn't have run over me — "I hardly know you!" Then she said, "Please don't think of me as an escaped lunatic." (To be honest, I wasn't thinking of her as an "escaped" anything, but I hadn't made up my mind yet about her being a lunatic or not! I pulled on my flowerdy cowboy hat to keep her from thinking about her Daddy, just to be safe.)

On the way to her apartment, Ruther Jean asked me if James Dean Jay Byrd was my stage name and I told her that it was my real name and that I didn't have a stage name 'cause I'd never been on a stage. She said, "Not yet, anyway, huh?!" Then she told me *her* stage name. She motioned to her chest and said, "Ruther Beaucoup. *That* is the French way of saying Ruther a'*plenty*!" I blushed and she laughed at me and put her hand on my leg, "You sure are shy for a jaybird!" I blushed some more.

Before I knew it, we were pulling into the parking lot of "The Spire" apartment complex. Unlike Ruther Beaucoup, The Spire didn't even come close to exemplifying its name. It should've been called "The Block," 'cause that's what it was, a solid block of apartments, as square as it could be, six stories high and six apartments wide. Ruther Jean lives in apartment 6F. I knew which apartment was hers as soon as we pulled into the parking lot. Or, at least, I figured I knew. It was on the top floor, the farthest apartment to the right. A string of lights with small plastic jack-o'-lanterns on it hung from the overhang above her porch; the front door was adorned with a lanky scarecrow with moveable limbs reaching out as far as it could in every direction; and in the front window, backlit by the orange glow from a hidden light shining on the beige curtains, a limp-wristed plastic skeleton did his best to wave a haunting hello to the world as one hip twitched uncontrollably, powered by a small motor that made a whirring, ghost-like noise whenever the apartment was quiet.

Yes, it was March, but Ruther Jean's a self-confessed Halloween fanatic. She told me so as she was turning the key in her front door. This was when I noticed that her apartment was "6F," but the door actually read "6FRIGHT" because of the alternating orange and black letters she had stuck to the door. The Halloween theme went all the way through her apartment, through the living room, the kitchen, her bedroom, and the bathroom — the deepest spot in the apartment, where the tiles were black and the toilet paper was peach and therefore orange enough.

The only room that didn't contain round orange plastic buckets of penny candy or ghost-shaped platters or strings of orange lights was the hallway closet, halfway between the living room/kitchen and the bedroom/bathroom. It was about five square feet in size, so it made a pretty big closet, but a really small room. Maybe it was a utility closet or a baby's room at one point. Who knows?

Ruther Jean pushed her shoulder hard against the door to get it to open. It slid slowly over the deep-pile, multicolored, earth-tone shag carpet. She said, "Sorry it's *so* full of crapola." I didn't realize she was offering it as my sleeping quarters 'til I saw the single foam mattress on the floor against the back wall under a couple of stacks of boxes.

But it was some time before I saw that. What first caught my eye was the reflection of the hall light in about a thousand rhinestones. Ruther Jean had installed a grid-work of poles about a foot from the ceiling. From the poles hung dresses. Beautiful dresses. Sparkling, silky, feathery, bright, sexy, slinky, perfumed dresses. My first thought (I'm ashamed to admit) was that Ruther Jean was the madam of a whorehouse! My next thought was that these were Halloween costumes. As it turned out, both of my thoughts were a little bit right and a whole lot wrong.

Ruther Jean told me that she's the star attraction at the Tiger's Den, a go-go club in downtown Beaumont. I'd never heard of a go-go club before. The term meant as much to me as if she'd called it a "stop-stop club." She filled me in on all the graphic details and even told me she'd show me one of her routines later if I liked. I thought it'd probably be better to catch "Ruther Beaucoup" at the Tiger's Den, since that's where she usually appeared. She laughed and touched me on the cheek and said, "You are a funny little bird, Jay Byrd!" She got me to move the boxes that were on the mattress to the hall while she went to get sheets and a pillow for me.

I stepped into the closet. At first I was a little afraid to touch the dresses, but the only way I could've completely avoided touching any of them was if I crawled on my belly. I figured Ruther Jean would've told me if she'd expected me to do that, so I took a step into the closet and pushed my way into the forest of fancy dresses. Silk and lace and fishnet material hung all around me like Spanish moss; brightly colored feather-trimmed sleeves and collars caught on the stubble of my "ball head" and tickled my face. Every size and color and shape of rhinestone that exists in the world I believe was represented in Ruther Jean's closet. The dresses were heavy with rhinestones. Some were lightly sprinkled with rhinestones, some had designs drawn on them with rhinestones, and one was even made *entirely* of rhinestones — I couldn't find a piece of exposed fabric on it. I forgot my manners and took the solid-rhinestone dress down to get a closer look. It must've weighed twenty pounds. It seemed like every rhinestone was a different color. It sparkled like something from Heaven. I couldn't take my eyes off of it.

"That's my favorite dress for lookin', but my least favorite dress for wearin'. You know what I mean?" She gave me folded sheets and a pillow and took the dress from me and hung it back on the pole, grunting as she hung it up. I was pretty embarrassed. "It's *sooo* dat-burned heavy! If I wear it for too long before I take it off, it leaves these unsightly rhinestone dents in my shoulders. I am serious! Serious as a heart-attack!" She stopped, sniffed the air, then said, "Jay Byrd, you sure are cute, but you *smell* like the part of the pig ya don't eat. I think you oughta take a shower before ya fondle too many more of my dresses!"

When I got to the bathroom, my shaving kit was on the counter top. I was afraid to open it at first; I knew I hadn't brought it in from the car and I didn't see Ruther Jean bring it in, so I thought maybe she had one that looked just like mine. I felt kinda weird about having taken her dress down without asking; I didn't wanna invade her privacy again. I stood there looking down at it when I heard her calling from another part of the apartment, "I put your toiletries in there — I hope that was good."

"Yes, ma'am."

"Jay Byrd, I *swear*, if you ever call me 'ma'am' again, I...I don't know *what* I'll do!"

I smiled and turned on the water and shaved. While I

shaved, the toilet paper-wrapped cotton ball ghosts hanging from the ceiling tiles made me think that maybe Ruther Jean was hiding some kind of real-life voodoo behind all the Hallmark Halloweenery. But in the shower, I decided that if she *was* a witch, she was the good kind and I didn't really need to worry about it.

I didn't wanna put the same smelly clothes on, so I wrapped the towel around my waist and walked quickly back to the hall closet, my room for the night. I kinda knew that my backpack would be there (since my shaving kit was in the bathroom) and I was right. I dug into it for some fresh undies and socks and came across my Uncle Joe's Lucky Green Dress. I shook it out and hung it up on a puffy satin hanger among Ruther Jean's dresses. It was wrinkled and shabby-looking next to all of her glorious outfits.

On the inside of the closet door was a full-length mirror. A couple of feet down the mirror a hanger bar went across the door. Hanging from that bar was the most beautiful blue-sequined turtleneck backless floor-length dress I'd ever seen. (Actually, it was the *only* blue-sequined turtleneck backless floor-length dress I'd ever seen!) The way it hung on the door, if I bent my knees just a little bit, my reflection in the mirror made me look like I had the dress *on*! I took the dress off of the hanger rack and held it up to my body to see what I looked like in it when I moved around. The sequins were about a quarter-inch round each and they were attached from their tops so that they swung back and forth. Each row overlapped the row below it so it had a kind of fish-scale appearance. They were made of thick, heavy plastic so they made a lot of noise as they knocked against each other. The material beneath the sequins was so thin it could hardly keep still; it seemed to dance, even without an exotic dancer in it. It didn't quite reach the floor on me, but it still made me look and feel sorta glamorous.

I wondered if this was how it had happened for Uncle Joe.

Was there some experience in his life where he was locked in a closet with a bunch of beautiful and sparkly dresses? And was I in the midst of the very same sort of discovery about myself? I mean, why else would I be standing in front of a mirror in my birthday suit holding Ruther Jean's blue-sequined turtle-neck backless almost-floor-length dress up against my body doing model poses?

Well, I didn't really have a chance to think it through because Ruther Jean burst into the closet — and I do mean burst, full-shoulder into the door *burst* — with a ghost-shaped plate of Oatmeal M&M Cookies in her hand. I didn't have time to put the dress away or throw it down or even react. There we were, face-to-face, a plate of cookies and a dress the only two things between my nakedness and her. All I could do was say, "Hello."

She stood there looking at me for a while, then tucked her free hand under her cookie plate arm, chuckled and said, "So, tell me, Jay Byrd...are you, uh, out of the Closet yet?" I figured that honesty was the best policy and the only way to possibly save face in this situation. I hugged the dress to myself and said sincerely, "Oh, Ruther Jean...I could just *live* in this closet!"

She laughed so hard her hand went weak and she dropped the plate of cookies and they went rolling in every direction. I didn't know exactly what she was laughing about, but I started laughing, too. We laughed so hard, we cried, and I came close to losing my blue-sequined covering a couple of times. I finally begged Ruther Jean to leave me alone so I could put on some clothes. She didn't mind leaving me because she said she was about to pee in her jumpsuit!

✪✪✪

In Ruther Jean's kitchen and living room were at least a dozen ceramic and tin and plastic cookie jars, some of them your basic pumpkin, black cat and witch shapes, others were modeled after more famous spooky characters (the Munsters, the Hunchback of Notre Dame, Casper the Friendly Ghost, Frankenstein, things like that). Every last jar was full to the brim with Ruther Jean's Oatmeal M&M Cookies. They were good cookies, too. They were really good. It's a good thing they were so good, 'cause we finished off quite a few cookie jars that night. This seemed to be Ruther Jean's only source of nutrition: Oatmeal M&M Cookies and sweet, sweet ice tea (tea so sweet, it almost overpowered the sweetness of the cookies). We talked and ate cookies and drank ice tea all night long.

Ruther Jean told me about running away from home a lot when she was a kid; she was supposed to be one of the heirs to the Coca-Cola fortune, but "things just didn't work out," as she put it. I figured that's why we were drinking ice tea and not Coke. She told me about the first man she loved, a man named McBee who could do things with his glass eye that she thought I was too young to hear about. She told me about the first woman she loved, a woman with the stage name of Clairol who modeled herself after Janice Joplin and chain-smoked cigarillos. Clairol was the one who got Ruther Jean into exotic dancing in the first place. Ruther Jean said that she hasn't loved anybody since them, because everybody she's met since them seems to be named *John*!

When I told her that I was almost twenty-five and hadn't had a first love yet, she laughed and called me a late bloomer and said it like she was making fun of me. But then she turned around and said, "That's alright, Jay Byrd, I was a late bloomer, too. I smoked for two years but then I got asthma and had to quit, and when I quit smoking, *that* was when my bazooms blossomed to where they are now! And *nothing* happened to me when I was flat-chested, I kid you not!"

She told me lots of things that made me laugh and lots of things that made me blush and once in a while she'd even stop talking and ask me to tell her something about *me.* When the morning light out-glowed the front curtain, Ruther Jean said, "Let's hit the sack, Jack!"

While I was putting sheets on the mattress in the hall closet, Ruther Jean appeared with a quilt. Before she said anything, she noticed Uncle Joe's wrinkled green dress hanging there with hers. "Hey! That ain't mine. Are you holding out on me, Jay Byrd?!"

"It's my Uncle Joe's Lucky Green Dress."

"Oh, yeah, Nicki's ex. So, what are *you* doing with it, then?"

"He gave it to me when I left Okey-Dokey, as a good luck charm, y'know, for my journey. I think he kinda expects me to wear it — but, hey! Do *you* want it?"

She held a hand to her mouth for a long time, thinking very seriously, then she said, "Do you realize how dangerous that could be for me, Jay Byrd, wearing *your* Lucky Green Dress?"

"It's my Uncle Joe's, really."

"No! No, don't say that. Joe gave you that dress. *You!* Not anybody else. Your uncle gave you his Lucky Green Dress, and you're just gonna toss it away? I thought we were *friends*, Jay Byrd. I mean, I could fall off the stage and break my neck wearing that dress and be paralyzed and it would be all your fault. And what about *you*? If you have no concern for *my* safety, what about your own safety?! What will happen to you, Jay Byrd? I hate to *think* about what will happen to you. Terrible things. *Horrible* things. Very un-lucky things."

She was on an Oatmeal M&M Cookie-induced rampage. I had to stop her. "Alright, alright, I'll keep the dress."

But that wasn't enough anymore. She wanted me to put it on. *Immediately!*

"Ruther Jean, it's already light outside. *Sane* people are asleep at the crack of dawn."

"Are you calling me insane, Jay Byrd? Insult to injury! I

invite you into my house, give you a foam mattress to sleep on, Oatmeal M&M Cookies for your belly, and *this* is how you treat me? *Put the Lucky Green Dress on.*"

Her blue-sequined turtleneck backless floor-length dress caught my eye. I picked it up and held it out to her. "Alrighty. I'll put on the Lucky Green Dress for you if you'll put on this dress!"

She tried to refuse, said, "But I have to wear it onstage first — I have to break it in."

"Well, if you won't put on *your* dress, then I ain't gonna put on *my* dress!"

"Fine, then!" She took the dress, marched to her bedroom and slammed the door, giggling.

I could hear her struggling to put the dress on behind her bedroom door. "Oh, my boobies are too fat!" I laughed so hard, I could hardly keep my balance long enough to put a leg into the green dress. The outfit wouldn't have been complete without the python boots and cowboy hat Uncle Joe gave me with it, so I put those on, too. I pulled open the closet door and at the same time, Ruther *Beaucoup* opened her bedroom door. She screamed like a siren, starting low and rising to an eardrum-piercing tone. She strutted to the living room and I followed after her, trying to learn how to walk from her example.

She exotic-danced across the room and back, and sang like a trombone, "Da-dum, da-dum, dum-dummmm, da-dum da-da-dum-dumm, da-da-da-dum, da-dum, da-dum-dum-dum-dum" — something like that, and then I exotic-danced across the room and back for her, mimicking her song. We did this for a while, laughing all the way, and then she started *unzipping* her dress.

I could feel my whole head turning red. "Hold it! Hold it! Wait a minute!"

"What's the matter, Jay Byrd, don't you want to see *Ruther Beaucoup*?!" Her voice was different, kinda weird and playful.

She squealed with delight and I didn't know what to say.

Finally, I said, "Maybe later — at the Tiger's Den."

"*All* the world's a stage, Jay Byrd; Billy Shakespeare said so."

"Yeah, well, it looks just great *on*."

She squealed again.

I changed the subject. "Let's figure out a way to test my Uncle Joe's dress, to see once and for all if it really will bring me any luck."

Ruther Jean shook her head, suddenly very serious. "A test. Very good." The phone rang. "How about if I answer the phone!" I wondered who in the world would be calling at this time of the night — or morning — but Ruther Jean didn't seem to mind. She picked it up before it rang a second time. "Yello! —Well, hello, Sweetie! No, it's a *perfect* time, honey! Yes, he is, as a matter a'fact! Hold the line, Clementine!" She held the phone out to me and whispered with conviction, "*Lucky Green Dress*!"

I took the receiver cautiously and put it to my ear. It was Aunt Nonie! She was in Oklahoma and had called in to get her messages and heard mine. She was glad I'd thought of calling Ruther Jean. We talked about Ruther Jean for a while and then I told her that Uncle Joe had given me his Lucky Green Dress and all about the man in the cloud and my journey and my life and she said, "Well, Kiddo, I sure hope that man in the cloud brings ya back my way again when I'm *around*!"

We said our goodbyes and everything seemed complete for me in Beaumont, Texas. I guess I hadn't really gone there to look up my dear old Aunt Nonie after all; fate had taken me there to meet Ruther Jean and to see her amazing closet.

✪✪✪

The next day I woke up close to four in the afternoon. The first thing I did was to look out the front door. My cloud had traveled quite a bit in the night and I knew I'd better put a hop in my step if I wanted to keep up with him. Ruther Jean had washed, dried and ironed my dirty clothes and hand-washed the Lucky Green Dress and rolled it up in a special dress bag. (Does she *ever* sleep?) When she told me what she'd done, she made me *promise* that I'd wear the Lucky Green Dress *every* day — even if I just put it on and took it right back off again. She said, "You hafta have *faith* in the Lucky Green Dress, Jay Byrd." That reminded me of my Daddy and the Vision and the man in the cloud, so I promised. She offered me cookies for breakfast, of course, but I told her I'd get a bite on the way out of town, so she packed a Tupperware container of cookies for me and put it in an outside pocket of my backpack. She also slipped a copy of the recipe for the cookies in the Tupperware, rightly sure that I'd need a fix once in a while.

Ruther Jean was disappointed that I wouldn't be staying the night to see her show at the Tiger's Den; she was planning on premiering her blue-sequined turtleneck backless floor-length dress. To be honest, I was kinda disappointed, too, but the show didn't start 'til ten and I hoped to be close to the Louisiana border by then. She said she understood and gave me a very sexy autographed picture of herself in a tiger-striped nightie and said it would hold me over!

Ruther Jean's Oatmeal M&M Cookies

Preheat oven to 350 degrees. Whisk together:

1 ¾ cups flour
¾ teaspoon baking soda
¾ teaspoon baking powder
½ teaspoon cinnamon
½ teaspoon nutmeg
½ teaspoon salt

Beat together until well blended:

2 sticks margarine
¾ cup brown sugar
¾ cup sugar
¼ cup molasses
2 eggs
2 ½ teaspoons vanilla

Stir the two mixtures together until smooth. Stir in:

3 ½ cups rolled oats (not quick oats)
1 cup M&Ms

Drop by heaping measuring tablespoonfuls onto greased cookie sheets about 3 inches apart. Grease hands and press each down to about ½" rounds. Decorate with additional M&Ms — press 3 or 4 into the top of each cookie. Bake until lightly browned all over, about 6-9 minutes. Let stand 2 minutes before transferring to rack to cool completely.

Leavin' Town

There's no sorrow in my eyes now,
There's no trouble in my brow;
I'm taking nothing to remind me,
Not a single thing I will allow.

It's too late to turn around now,
The life I left behind is dead;
All my wondering lies behind me,
And the open road lies ahead.

Chapter Eight

Steven's Five-Pointed Star

To look at Steven, you'd probably see a soft-spoken and thoughtful man with above-average good looks, intelligence and charm. I'm looking at him right now and that's what I see. But to spend a week with him under a highway overpass swapping stories during a terrible thunderstorm is to really know Kornflake, Indiana's Steven Cheslik-DeMeyer. That's how I got to know him. And everything you've learned about him so far in this book came directly out of his mouth, into my ear, through my brain, down my right arm and onto this piece of paper. Oh, and there were several stops at my heart, too!

Since you're probably never gonna get the chance to sit under a highway overpass with Steven for a week during a terrible thunderstorm, I've made it my job to expose as much of him as I see fit (and as much as he'll allow). I'll tell you all about the terrible thunderstorm in due time; right now, you've gotta hear about Steven's incredible journey — actually, all five of them! That's why this chapter is called "Steven's Five-Pointed Star"; if you traced all of his journeys on a map, they would roughly form a star.

First, I oughta back up and get you all caught up. We'll go all the way back to Sunday, March 22, 1992, Steven's birthday. It was a beautiful day of realizations and beginnings for me in Okey-Dokey, Texas, and it was a day of realizations for Steven, too. But it wasn't a beautiful day at all, it was dark and ended with a rainstorm. As you'll remember from Chapter Five, Steven met, fell in love with and then lost a beautiful and mysterious Mexican man named Eduardo. In fact, as

Chapter Five was ending, Steven had come in from waiting most of the day in the popcorn field, his duffle bag packed and him ready to run away with Eduardo to Puerto de Amor or wherever their love took them. But Eduardo never appeared. (I, for one, am quite glad Eduardo didn't appear — otherwise, this half of the book would've been a lot shorter and a lot less exciting.)

The rain washed the letter out of Steven's hands and the tears off of his face and when he got home for his birthday party, he didn't think anybody would be able to understand what'd happened. But Grandma Thayer knew something was up and she followed Steven up to his bedroom after the birthday supper was eaten and the birthday candles were blown out and the presents were opened. She hadn't given him a present downstairs because her gift to him was private and very special; it was the heart-warmer that she crocheted by herself. Now, do you remember? And remember, it had twenty-four twenty dollar bills in it (one for each of Steven's years on Earth).

After Grandma Thayer left Steven's bedroom, Kay came in to tell Steven goodbye — she had to get back to Evansville, Indiana, for a test at school the next day. Steven told Kay that he might run away from home for a while. She was scared for him and asked, "Where will you go?"

"I don't know, I just have to get away from Kornflake for a while; I can hear him calling me in the rain — he just won't stop."

Kay begged Steven not to run away without telling their mother and father and he promised he wouldn't. She wanted to stay longer — she could tell he needed her to — but she had waited as long as she could and the storm was letting up and her friend was there from Terre Haute, Indiana, to go back to school with her so she had to leave. Kay hugged Steven and said, "You can always come to school with me." He kissed her and thanked her and laughed nervously and she was gone.

He listened while a car he never even saw drove away from the farmhouse through the rain as he stared at the ceiling thinking of his options. He said to himself, "Oh, what am I gonna do with my life?" About that time, he noticed his duffel bag by the hallway door. The canvas exterior was dark with wetness. He pulled himself up off of his bed and went to the duffel bag and unzipped it and felt around its insides. Amazingly, the clothes inside were dry.

A large shadow appeared on the duffel bag and Steven looked up to see Grandma Thayer standing over him in her nightgown and hand-crocheted housecoat. In her hand was a book, but Steven couldn't see its cover. She said, "Looky what I found. I think it belongs to Pop, although I don't have the foggiest notion why I think that." She tossed it on top of the clothes in the duffel bag.

Steven didn't speak, so she turned to leave but turned back right away. "Remember what I said earlier, about you needing to take off for a while?" Steven nodded. "I don't know, maybe that book will give you some big ideas."

After she was gone, Steven picked up the book. It was called *Tom Brown's Field Guide To Wilderness Survival.* He chuckled and flipped through the pages and stopped once in a while to look at drawings of edible wild trees and plants and shelters that could be built out of sticks and other wilderness "debris." He was confused as to why Grandma Thayer had given him the book, but he was fascinated by the book at the same time. He ended up falling asleep with the book open in front of him on the bed.

That night, he dreamed he was a fish swimming underwater, then a hawk flying high over a forest, and then part of a family of bears sleeping in a cave. It was like a fairy tale because they were all wearing clothes. The bear cub in a pretty dress had a little stick and was tickling Steven the Bear's foot with it. Steven woke himself up laughing and decided the little bear in the dress was his sister telling him to go camping. It was surely some sort of a sign.

Steven left Kornflake, Indiana, the next morning, taking with him the survival book and the duffel bag full of clothes and snacks, eliminating the need to really "survive." He walked north along Highway 231 and then Highway 421, his back to the oncoming traffic, his left thumb pointing toward the sky. Nobody even slowed down when they passed him. He walked for five days and slept in cheap motels until he reached the Indiana Dunes State Park on Lake Michigan. Once there, he rented a personal-sized campsite in a pup tent village and barely left his little tent for two days and three nights. Steven pondered his life as best as he could in such primitive surroundings. He read the survival book from cover to cover and realized that he wasn't really living all that primitively. But he couldn't bring himself to eat grass and roots when he had drumsticks and corn-on-the-cob and chocolate cake wrapped up and waiting in little containers in his duffel bag.

Early on the morning of his third day in the park, Steven heard the song of a trumpet bouncing through the trees. As soon as he heard it, he realized he'd forgotten to bring his guitar with him and he felt disappointed and anxious. The trumpet playing wasn't coming from any of the pup tents nearby; it was a far-off sound, beautiful and kinda mournful. It matched the way Steven was feeling to a tee. The trumpeter played throughout the morning. He played a variety of styles: jazzy songs, classical songs, folk songs, country songs. Most of them seemed only vaguely familiar to Steven, none were familiar enough for him to be able to sing along. But then he heard a song he knew all too well. When the trumpeter got to the chorus, Steven found himself singing along.

Ay ay ay ay,
Canta y no llores;
Porque cantando se alegra
Cielito lindo los corazones.

It was the song Grandma Thayer sang in the back of the pickup truck that day they all went searching the popcorn fields for Eduardo.

Steven began trembling, even though it was a warm spring morning and he was sitting by a little built-in gas campfire. It was his heart that was cold, just like Grandma Thayer had said. He wished he *could* take his heart out and wrap it in the heart-warmer she had crocheted for him, just for a minute.

The trumpeter played many songs, but he kept coming back to "Cielito Lindo." With eyes full of tears, Steven turned the campfire switch to OFF and put on his heavy boots, determined to find the trumpeter and make him stop playing that song. There were no breaks between any of the songs and Steven never noticed when the trumpeter changed to another song, only when he changed back to "Cielito Lindo." He cut through brush that he normally would've walked around, trying to make a direct path to the trumpeter. As he pushed through spiky vines that caught on his clothes and tried to hold him back, Steven got the crazy idea that it was *Eduardo* playing the trumpet, calling Steven to him. He knew it was a crazy idea, but he couldn't shake it.

Soon, Steven came upon a clearing surrounding a large man-made pond. A pair of swans floated on the water side-by-side, enjoying the music of the trumpeter who sat against a tree on the far bank. As soon as he saw the trumpeter, Steven could tell that he wasn't Eduardo; he didn't look anything like him — he was old and had reddish-gray hair — but Steven was still drawn to him. He walked around the pond toward the trumpeter who was now playing "Cielito Lindo" again. But then, halfway around the pond, Steven *saw* Eduardo. He was sitting on a park bench on the far side of the path, facing away from the pond. Steven's heart dropped into his stomach. What would he say? Would Eduardo run away? What did he *feel*? *Cielito lindo.* Beautiful sky.

Steven looked up to the sky; it was truly beautiful and clear, unlike his mind. When he looked down again, Eduardo had vanished. His heart jumped up into his throat. He stood there looking at the empty bench for a long time. When the trumpeter stopped playing, Steven came out of his trance. He looked over at the trumpeter, fifteen or so yards away; he was putting the trumpet in its case. Steven walked to him.

The trumpeter smiled up at Steven. "Did you see her?"

"What?"

"The pretty young lady with the long brown hair, heh? She was sitting on the bench there. I thought for sure you were watching her, heh?"

"Oh, *her*. I'm sorry. Yes. I did."

"Heart-broken young lady, heh? She got me to play that song 'Cielito Lindo.' Know it? And then she went and sat on that bench over there and cried and cried. Beautiful song, heh? Ever' time I finished it, she'd dry her eyes and come over here and beg me to play it again. And then she'd go back over there and cry. Over and over, all morning long! It's funny how a song can do that to a person, heh?"

"Yes, it's funny...."

"Well, that's it for me. My lips are bleeding, heh?" He stood up, groaning about his old legs and disappeared into the woods without saying another word.

Steven sat where the trumpeter had been sitting; the ground was warm and the weeping willow growing there supported his back perfectly. The view of the pond was completely unique from this perspective. Flowering water lilies were suddenly visible. A turtle was sunbathing on a log in the middle of the water. The swans swam close to the bank and he could hear low, gurgly swan sounds coming from their throats. They were in love.

✪✪✪

Four and a half days later, Steven was back home. His experience in the park had left him confused, exhilarated, a little undernourished, and scruffier than he'd ever been. He shaved and took a long, hot shower while his mother made a huge supper. For the next three days, he moped around the house, feeling like he'd really failed at the most important journey of his life. He didn't realize that this was only the first of several important journeys he would take.

Grandma Thayer went to Steven's room on Sunday evening after supper and found him reading *Tom Brown's Field Guide to Wilderness Survival.* She said, "Eat any good trees lately?" Steven was soon opening up and telling Grandma Thayer that he was afraid he had no purpose in life. She said "That's sheep dip, Steven. Let me tell you something about farming. You don't just make one trip to the field with the seeds and call yourself a farmer. You have to plow the earth and fertilize it and plant the seeds and water the ground and talk to the plants and give them sun and pluck the corn and shuck the ears and sell the kernels. And *then* you're a farmer! Why, all those fields out there wouldn't be there if Pop had just gone out there once in his life. Do you know what I'm saying?" Steven said he did, but she clarified anyway. "You have to keep going out to the field 'til there's corn to bring in!"

The next day, Steven strapped his guitar to his back, tucked the survival book, a spiral notebook and pencil under his arm and headed out of Kornflake without even a change of clothes, this time by way of the west side of town. He told everybody he was going to California!

✪✪✪

Well, he didn't quite make it to California (I'm happy to say). He didn't even get all the way to St. Louis, Missouri.

Just this side of St. Louis is a tiny little town in Illinois called Saint Louise. It's such a tiny little town that nobody even lives there. But there is a church there, a beautiful old Baptist church made of wood and painted white, with stained-glass windows and a steeple that towers up into the Midwestern sky and scrapes the bottom of Heaven, so they say. It's called the Saint Louise Baptist Church. People come from all around to visit that church, but not so much because the preacher there is so good — although I'm sure the preacher is fine (not nearly as good as my Daddy, of course, but that's beside the point!) — but because a lot of famous folks have been known to worship there. Jazz musicians and famous fans of jazz musicians. Half of the congregation is made up of just regular black folks, another part are famous folks, and the rest are folks trying to get a glimpse of the famous folks. Apparently, the famous folks stay up all night long Saturday night in St. Louis, Missouri, at the jazz clubs, and then get to feeling guilty come around nine a.m. Sunday morning, so they head over to the Saint Louise Baptist Church, twenty minutes east of St. Louis. They say the gospel music that bellows out of that church on Sunday mornings is so sweet, folks in nearby communities eat their pancakes dry!

Now, as you know, Steven never went to church when he was growing up and he didn't even know anybody who was Baptist, so he didn't know what to expect when he came upon the Saint Louise Baptist Church. He heard organ music, beautiful organ music, before he even got to Saint Louise, Illinois. (It wasn't the church's Sunday morning gospel music because it wasn't Sunday morning; it was late in the afternoon, Tuesday, April 14.) Steven followed a winding dirt road up a tall hill in the direction of the organ music. And then suddenly the church appeared. It seemed to rise up to meet him, steeple first, as he topped a wildberry-covered hill. He squatted there for a long time, eating berries and listening to the music. Then the sky began to darken with rain clouds. It looked like a storm was coming — although not the terrible thunderstorm that I mentioned earlier. (I'll tell you about that in due time.) Steven made his way down the west side of the hill into the valley where the Saint Louise Baptist Church stood, surrounded by nothing but meadows.

Steven came upon the little church from the backside. There were no windows on the back wall, so he walked around toward the front, passing the beautifully ornate stained-glass windows on the side wall. When he turned the corner to the front side of the church, the music poured out louder because the front doors were wide open. Steven eased up the front steps and into the small foyer of the church. Just beyond the foyer was another set of doors, propped open to reveal the rich wooden interior of the church. At the front of the church on one side of the pulpit was a shiny black grand piano. Steven moved to the opposite side of the foyer and from there could see the organ. Sitting at the organ was a nun in her habit. (That's what they call their uniforms: "habits"; I told Steven it sounds more like a "rule" than a habit to me; he thought I was being funny.)

As the nun played, her eyes remained shut and her mahogany face glistened with the tears that were streaming down it. At first, Steven thought he should leave, but he couldn't pull himself away, so he quietly and carefully snuck in and sat down in the back pew and looked at the Bible scenes in the stained-glass windows while the nun played, avoiding looking at her. The stained-glass pictures seemed to be alive because of the movement of the storm clouds in the sky outside.

Suddenly, the music stopped. Steven looked toward the organ and froze. The nun had lifted her hands up from the organ keys in position and her eyes were wide open and she was staring directly at Steven. They stared at each other for a long time, then the nun quickly and quietly stood up and rushed past Steven out the front door. Steven sat there baffled, still looking at the organ. A moment or two later, the nun put a hand softly on Steven's shoulder. Steven jumped and screamed and the nun gasped and jumped back, apologizing. Steven apologized for screaming and the nun apologized for scaring Steven and he said, "No, that's okay."

And she said, "No, it was *I* who should be apologizing."

Steven said, "I'm sorry."

The nun said, "No, *I'm* sorry," and they apologized back and forth like that for Lord-knows-how-long, and then suddenly their conversation fell off a cliff into silence.

After a while of that, Steven asked her a funny question. He said, "Are you a nun?"

She answered, "Yes, I am. My name is Sister Mary Patrick." She sat next to him and they talked for a long time (even though Steven's not very talkative and the nun wasn't very talkative either).

The thing that drives me crazy about this little journey of Steven's — and, believe me, it's gonna drive you crazy, too — is that Steven never asked the nun why she was crying and playing the organ in a Baptist church in the middle of nowhere. I had no choice but to come to some bizarre conclusions:

1) She was born a Baptist, but was abducted by Catholic recruiters and forced into a life of nunhood; or

2) She's a Baptist trapped in the body of a Catholic nun.

Those are the only two examples that Steven would allow me to tell you — there are plenty more; he just wants everybody to understand that she was a very nice nun-lady with a real talent for playing the organ. As it turned out, she was a composer. She played a couple of her jazzy tunes on the organ, and then Steven played some of his songs on his guitar and Sister Mary Patrick jazzed them up by playing along on the organ. They spent the rest of the afternoon making music together while the rainstorm blew through Saint Louise, Illinois. I imagine that was some beautiful music blowing in the wind.

Sister Mary Patrick gave Steven directions for getting around "sin city" St. Louis, Missouri, and onward to "sin city" Los Angeles, California, but he got lost and ended up back-tracking through Illinois and was a third of the way back to Kornflake, Indiana, before he realized it. He tried to convince himself that this was another sign of some sort, but he was mad at himself, and deep inside, he felt like he'd failed again. Sure, he could've turned around and headed back toward the West Coast again, but I for one sure am glad he didn't. Instead, he just set up camp in another state park, the South Shore State Park on Lake Carlyle in Illinois.

His first day on Lake Carlyle, Steven sat for hours on a cliff overlooking the lake and did nothing but let the thoughts run through his head. He closed his eyes for just a moment (or so he thought), and when he opened them again, several hours must've passed by because a squirrel was about fifteen inches from his face and a sparrow had made a nice little perch out of his boot toe. Steven jumped up and gasped and the squirrel and the bird both disappeared in a flurry. But the bird left Steven a warm little gooky present on his boot!

That evening, Steven built a perfect shelter for himself using the survival book as a guide. He thought maybe he was discovering that his purpose in life was to be a forest ranger or some such thing like that. Over the next couple of days, he experimented more and more with living off the land; he steamed cattails and boiled wild carrots (the roots of the Queen Anne's Lace flowers) and grasses in a bowl that he made by burning an area on an old log and rubbing it smooth and deep with rough rocks. He cooked sassafras and wildberry tea and made acorn burgers. It was a real survivalist's experience! Tom Brown would've been very proud; he probably even would've given Steven an award or a ribbon or something. But after nearly three days of living like a wild forest creature, all Steven really wished was that somebody would give him was a chicken-fried steak and a Dr Pepper! He decided to go back home again.

When Steven got back to Kornflake, he was welcomed with open arms, a big meal and a hot shower, of course. He entertained his family with stories of his adventures, but confessed that he didn't feel like he was getting anywhere with his life outside of Kornflake any better than he was getting anywhere on the Cheslik-DeMeyer Popcorn Farm. His mother was perhaps a little overly-understanding; she didn't wanna pressure Steven into doing something he didn't wanna do, even if that was exactly what he *needed* somebody to do.

His father just said, "You can have a job here anytime you want it." So Steven took a job on the farm. He thought maybe, just maybe, he hadn't given the option of being a farmer enough of a chance.

On Thursday, April 30, five days after Steven started working for his father in the popcorn field, Grandma Thayer went into Steven's room again. He had just showered and was lying on his bed, exhausted, waiting for supper. She'd been sent to tell him supper was ready, but first she said, "What are you doing here, Steven?" She almost sounded angry.

"I'm waiting for supper," he answered, a little wary.

"Well, supper's ready." He started to get up, but Grandma Thayer pushed him back onto the bed. "What are you doing *here*? You think you're a farmer now? Horse-feathers! Let me tell you something about farming, Steven. You don't just make one trip to the field with the seeds and call yourself a farmer. You have to plow the earth and fertilize it and plant the seeds and water the ground and talk to the plants and give them sun and pluck the corn and shuck the ears and sell the kernels. And *then* you're a farmer." Well, maybe she didn't say the same exact words like that, but it was pretty close. She definitely ended it with, "You have to keep going out to the field 'til there's corn to bring in!"

Steven knew that she knew that deep down *he* knew that this wasn't where he wanted to be. (He wasn't sure if she knew she'd given him the exact same pep talk the last time he came home, but it didn't matter because it seemed to be exactly what he needed to hear again.)

At supper, Steven sat quietly while his mother talked about the upcoming Indiana State Fair in Indianapolis that she was getting crafts ready for. (She thought maybe Steven would be interested in going.) Grandma Thayer said she was gonna crochet some hot pants to sell. "That *Cosmo* magazine said they're back in style again."

Steven's mother told Grandma Thayer that she was looking at a very old issue of *Cosmopolitan* and that she didn't remember crocheted hot pants *ever* being in style, but Grandma Thayer got up from the table immediately and went to her room, presumably to start working on the hot pants right away, even though supper wasn't nearly done.

Steven seized the silent moment that followed to ask his father if he could quit working on the farm. His father was more concerned than upset. He asked Steven what was wrong. Steven told his parents that he just couldn't work on the farm, that it was just too hard on his heart. (He didn't mention Eduardo but he didn't have to, his mother and father knew exactly what he meant.) Steven's father said that his friend Duke Longfeather down at the hardware store had a cousin named Charlie Broswell down near Fort Branch, Indiana, who was always looking for farmhands. He was pretty sure Steven could get a job there, if he wanted to try a different farm. Steven's mother said that it was close to Evansville where his sister Kay was going to school and that he would be able to visit her on long weekends. Steven thought maybe a different farm — especially one close to his sister — might be a good idea, so that Saturday his father and mother and Grandma Thayer (crocheting away) drove him down to the Broswell Farm and he was hired on the spot.

✪✪✪

Working on the Broswell Farm helped Steven decide once and for all that he wasn't cut out for farming. Maybe it was the back-breaking work, but more likely it was the fact that most of the other Broswell farmhands were young and dark-skinned and beautiful, like Eduardo. None of them looked anything like Eduardo, but they reminded Steven of Eduardo enough to make him feel queasy. Four days after he arrived, Steven slipped off of the Broswell Farm in the middle of the night like a fugitive. The next morning, when he woke up in a nearby state park, he regretted what he'd done, but he couldn't make himself go back.

He went to Evansville to visit Kay. He slept on the floor of her dorm room that night, but her roommate was a religious fanatic and insisted that boys weren't allowed to sleep in girls' dorm rooms overnight — even if it *was* a distraught brother. So, Steven spent the next night back at the state park.

One of Kay's girlfriends loaned Kay her car so she could take Steven back home, against his wishes. (Kay has a way of making Steven do whatever she wants him to do.) Kay's boyfriend, "Mr. Right," was home in Tennessee visiting a sick relative that week so Steven wasn't able to meet him, and he was glad about that. He'd already had his fill of squirrel couples and swan couples and bug couples that spring — a happy human couple was bound to push him over the edge.

The car Kay borrowed was actually a Volkswagen bus, white with hand-painted smiley faces all over it (the girlfriend was a graphic arts student). The front passenger seat was broken and had been removed from the bus so Steven sat on the pillow on the front floorboard and serenaded his sister almost all the way home. He sang her all of the songs he had written, including the one he wrote about her, "Does It Feel Like Home?" Kay was crying so hard by the time Steven finished singing it that she nearly drove off the side of the road! They laughed about it, but Steven sat on the long seat in the back of the bus for the rest of the ride.

Steven told Kay that he didn't really wanna go back home because everything there reminded him of Eduardo. But, then again, everything everywhere reminded him of Eduardo. He told her how he'd hitchhiked to the state park on Lake Michigan, about the trumpeter there, about the crying nun at the Saint Louise Baptist Church, about surviving in the wild at Lake Carlyle, and about the advice that Grandma Thayer kept giving him (which he didn't understand)— *and why was he letting her take him home again since every time he went there, it was more obvious what a failure he was and how he had no purpose in life at all?*

Kay took a deep breath, smiled and said, "Have you ever thought about being a songwriter? I love your songs!"

Hmm. Why hadn't he thought of that before?

"But, how does somebody go about *being* a songwriter? How does anybody make money doing something like that?"

"Maybe you should go to a big city like Los Angeles or Chicago or New York, or even Nashville. There's gotta be lots of other songwriters there."

Of *course!* Steven said, "Maybe I should just enroll in school because *you* sure are smart!"

Kay said, "Oh, I don't know how smart I am, I don't think I could figure out how to turn trees and grass into lunch!"

"It's easy, you just read this book — and hold your nose!"

✪✪✪

That night, over a supper of chicken-fried steak, mashed potatoes, green beans, and cornbread, Steven announced that he was gonna go to Nashville to become a songwriter. His mother and sister were thrilled because they love country music and they loved the way Steven glowed when he talked about it. His father was happy, too, even though he likes classical music more than country. Grandma Thayer seemed to be in another world at the time, in a dilemma about how to crochet pockets into hot pants.

That night as he was falling asleep, Grandma Thayer walked through the darkness of Steven's bedroom and sat on the bed next to him and startled him awake when she nearly sat on his head and said, "I want to tell you something, Steven. You don't just make one trip to the field with the seeds and call yourself a farmer...." That's right, she went through the whole story again, ending with, "You have to keep going out to the field 'til there's corn to bring in!"

Steven told her that he was on his way to Nashville to be a songwriter.

Grandma Thayer sat there silently in the darkness for a long while as Steven dozed in and out, and then finally she leaned toward him and kissed him squarely on his left eyelid, waking him again. "I like songs! Especially *corny* songs!" She stood up and walked slowly toward the light of the hallway coming in through the open bedroom door, singing, "By the light of the slippery moon, da-da-da-daa, da-dada-dada-day...."

✪✪✪

On Saturday, May 9, Steven left Kornflake, Indiana, for the fourth time, this time heading southeast, roughly in the direction of Nashville, Tennessee. He took his duffel bag with him again because he planned not to rough it as much this time. He wanted to be able to change clothes and shave and look presentable when he arrived in Nashville to sell the stack of songs he was gonna write on the way.

At one point in his journey, he walked through a field of wildflowers and lost the road. Five days later, he happened upon the My Old Kentucky Home State Park outside of Nazareth, Kentucky. Now, it's interesting to point out here that around the same time, *I* passed through Nazareth, Kentucky, too, on the Blue Grass Parkway in an eighteen-wheeler driven by a nineteen-year-old Skoal-dipping guy named Tucker. We even laughed at the sign pointed toward the My Old Kentucky Home State Park. It makes my heart speed up to think about how close Steven and I came to crossing paths then; I bet if he hadn't gone off the road, and if Tucker and I hadn't gone to the rest stop just before we got to the My Old Kentucky Home State Park turn-off, we might've run right into each other! But, of course, I wouldn't have noticed him because my eyes were steady on the clear blue sky and the one little cloud that was leading me evermore northeastward. Fate wasn't quite ready for us to meet yet.

There weren't any pup tents for rent in the My Old Kentucky Home State Park, so Steven was forced to live off of the land as best as he could remember (he hadn't taken the survival book with him this time). Fortunately, it was a warm night, so he didn't have to make a hut or anything like that to sleep in. He made some bluegrass soup and honeysuckle tea and got a bad stomach ache — no surprise to me — and he couldn't sleep. As he laid there gazing up at the broad Kentucky sky, alive with shooting stars, the song of a harmonica suddenly wailed into the night. He thought maybe it was his mind and his upset stomach playing tricks on him, so he sat up to listen closer. Off in the distance he saw a glow that was unmistakably the glow of a campfire. He stood up and walked toward the glow. He knew he was going in the right direction because the harmonica wailed louder and louder and the glowing campfire got brighter and brighter the closer he got.

In a clearing, Steven saw a real-life cowboy sitting by the campfire. Steven hid behind a tree to investigate. The cowboy's boots were next to him and they were so worn out they hunched over like two little old men. His hat and leather vest were tan and stained with sweat and his clothes were all black. He looked like he'd stepped out of an old Western movie. The campfire was surrounded with nearly-matching five-inch thick rocks with a handmade spit over the fire. On the cross-stick was a duck, roasted deep golden. The wind kicked up and swept through the clearing and the fire beneath the bird swelled up and touched the meat, and the wind carried the smell of the cooking meat to Steven's nose and he stepped out from behind the tree without thinking about what he was doing, intent on the smell of the bird. The cowboy looked up and waved Steven to the campfire without saying a word. Steven sat across from the cowboy and picked a piece of meat off of the duck every time the cowboy did, 'til it was all gone.

After supper, the cowboy picked his teeth for a while, then started playing a sad song on the harmonica. He stopped suddenly and looked up at Steven and said, "Ya play that thang er jess carry it aroun' wit ya?" Steven took his guitar out of its worn case and strummed along while the cowboy played.

Later, the cowboy rubbed his tired feet while he told Steven a truly sad story.

Calypso

Verse:
I I V
I once had a horse named Ca -
I IV
lyp - so. and man, oh man, could she
I V
fly; Got her from a gyp - sy
I IV I V
side - show. in the mid - dle of the
I IV
night. I was told that she had some
I IV
ma - gic, but the price was way too
V IV
good. At this point my sto - ry turns
I IV V
tra - gic, but I swear I did
I
ev - 'ry - thing I could. Ca -

We traveled down yonder to Texas,
We traveled up to Tennessee;
Calypso was my best friend, you betcha,
An' she would do anything for me.
We came 'cross a clan of old hobos,
It turns out they're as mean as they look;
One said, "I'm so hungry, I could eat a horse."
Then the barrel flames blazed up to cook.

I do all my travelin' on foot now,
I'm so sad I can't even cry;
I don't want another horse, not even a cow,
I'll just punish my travelin' feet 'til I die.
And when I die, then I'll be happy,
But I cannot be happy 'til then,
'Til I'm joined up in Heaven with Calyppie,
And can ride her to Texas again.

Steven fell asleep while the cowboy was playing his sad harmonica. The next morning, the fire had been cleared, the big rocks were gone and the dirt and leaves had been spread around so it looked like there had never been a fire there at all. There was no sign of the cowboy. At first, it didn't strike Steven as odd, but after he told me about it, we realized it was *very* odd.

Steven went to the entrance of the state park and easily found the highway. Once there, he stuck out his thumb and caught a ride almost immediately with a little old man named Joe Miks in a baby blue Dodge Dart with Indiana plates. Steven told Joe that he was going to Nashville and Joe said it was right on his way. He drove forty-five miles an hour in the fast-lane with cars honking and drivers speeding by and shouting at him all the way. Joe didn't seem to notice them, and Steven didn't notice that they were going in the wrong direction 'til Joe pulled into a small town gas station and said, "Here we are, Nashville, Indiana."

Steven started laughing; he laughed so hard that Joe started getting scared. Steven got ahold of himself and told Joe what'd happened. Joe was so upset, he said he'd drive Steven back as far as Kentucky. But Steven knew that that would be way too hard on the old man. They were closer to Kornflake than Kentucky, so Steven got Joe to drop him off near his parents' farm, since Joe was heading on to Terre Haute. Steven stayed home only one night, just long enough to eat a meal, pick up *Tom Brown's Guide To Wilderness Survival* and to hear Grandma Thayer's encouraging words one more time: "...You have to keep going out to the field 'til there's corn to bring in!" He'd already traveled unsuccessfully in the directions of Chicago, Los Angeles and Nashville; the only place left on the list of places that his sister said he oughta try to go to was New York City. Why not?

Chapter Nine

The Queen Of The Rodeo Contest

I kept my promise to Ruther Jean of wearing the Lucky Green Dress every day. Usually, I took it with me when I went to take a shower wherever I was staying for the night and slipped into it for a quick moment after I was dry. There was never a magical *pprring!* sound or anything like that when I put it on, but I had faith that there was some luck in the lace or rhinestones; Ruther Jean gave me that faith. If I ever had any trouble hitching a ride on the road, I'd poke my hand down into the special Lucky Green Dress dress bag and rub my hitch-hiking thumb on the fabric, and I swear not five minutes would pass before I'd have a ride. I got rides with some pretty interesting folks during my journey.

For example, there was Annie in the rusted out old sea-foam colored '62 Chevy Biscayne with her three children: Garth, seven, Reba, four, and Dwight, three. Reba kept popping her red curls and bright little face over the seat at me in the back. It made me laugh every time, but it made Annie very nervous; she'd yank the girl out of my view and scream, "Reba, I swear to *god*!" The car would rock from side to side for a few seconds because the shocks weren't very good.

But Reba wasn't swayed by the scoldings, she'd just say very innocently, "Yes, Mommy?" Annie would continue telling me a story I wasn't really interested in (about the time she *almost* met her oldest kid's namesake, Garth Brooks), and a minute or two later Reba would inch up again and the whole process would start over.

Garth sat in the back seat with me, on the far side of the car behind his mother, shooting *everything* with a (thankfully) empty pop gun. And Dwight slept the whole time I was in the car 'til Annie pulled over and dropped me off outside of Creepy Crawley, Louisiana, to head south to Sweet Bay to look for her "old man." When I opened my door and thanked Annie and said goodbye to Reba (who said "Boo-bye!") and Garth (who shot me), Dwight suddenly screamed out *"Hunnnnngry!"* I was glad I was getting out of the car.

As they drove away, Reba climbed over the back seat and waved out the back window at me and then she suddenly disappeared and the car rocked from side to side and almost off the road and I could almost hear Annie saying, "Reba, I swear to *god*!"

I rode on motorcycles, in station wagons, sports cars, and eighteen-wheelers. Once, I even got to ride in a Winnebago! For those of you who've never been in a Winnebago, believe you me, they're *really* neato! It was like a trailerhome with a steering wheel! I wish my Momma and Daddy had known about Winnebagos when I was growing up.

Sometimes, I didn't try to catch a ride at all; sometimes, I just walked.

Each and every night, I found a place to sleep with one of the folks on my names-and-numbers necklace. (Edna Joy had organized them geographically so it was easy to find a person to call no matter where I was.) I stayed in Lake Charles, Louisiana, with Dad's second cousins, then in Creepy Crawley, Slaughterhouse, and Greenberry, Louisiana.

From Greenberry, I caught a ride on the morning of Saturday, April 4 and got all the way to Jackson, Mississippi. I took a vacation from my non-stop traveling for a day with some more friends of Aunt Nicki's named Pat and Pete and they took me to a place called Club Hey! Hey! where a bluegrass singer and fiddle player I'd never heard of before named Alison Krauss was playing. I screamed so hard for a second encore, I just about lost my voice!

Late the next day, I caught a ride to Duck Hill, Mississippi, then I walked a whole lot between short rides to Coffeeville, Denmark, Hickory Chip, and Tigerlily — all of them in Mississippi.

I stayed the night in each of those towns with folks I didn't know or have anything in common with; they were all very hospitable folks who tried to entertain me with stories about whatever family members or close friends they had back in Okey-Dokey, Goose Creek, or Highland, Texas. Most of the time, I had no idea who they were talking about, but it was nice talking about home anyway.

Then I hit Tennessee: Pocahontas, Peach Bluff, the Chickasaw Reservation (my Daddy's Momma, Mamaw, was one-quarter Chickasaw and, I guess, from those parts), White Lightning (the one-time national capital of moonshine!) and then Henry-Henry, Tennessee. *Whew!*

The most exciting stop on my journey — up to that point, anyway — was the four days I spent in Paris, Tennessee. I arrived in the late morning of Thursday, April 16. It was a scorcher and I was starving.

Now, once in a while, particularly when I was alone and walking, I'd talk to my cloud, to the man in the cloud who was leading me on my journey — even though I hadn't actually *seen* the man in the cloud since that day at the revival meeting; but Daddy told me to remain faithful no matter what, so I did. I'd just chitchat, y'know, saying things like, "How's the weather up there?" and silly stuff like that. I'd also sing, mostly gospel songs, since those were what I knew best.

Sometimes, I'd just stare up at the cloud and marvel at the way it maintained its shape. I've always been a cloud-watcher and I know for a fact that most clouds change their shape a lot; y'know, one minute they look like an elephant, and the next, they've turned into a witch on a broomstick, complete with puffs of exhaust. But not my cloud. It maintained its flat-bottomed football shape and density until its job was done. And, amazingly, it never came in contact with any other clouds in the sky. True, the sky was almost always cloudless up to this point in my journey, but on the odd occasion when a patch of clouds did appear, they were always way over there and my cloud was always right here, right ahead of me, leading me on my unbelievable journey.

On Thursday, April 16, I was walking along, admiring my wonderful cloud when I walked smack-dab right into the city limits sign of Paris, Tennessee (population 9,332). It knocked me on my behind and I thought I saw stars floating around the big green sign, but actually somebody had glued big plastic flowers all around the edge of the sign. They had probably been bright colors at one time, but were all faded now to grayish-white — kinda star-like. I sat there looking up at the flowers for a while, almost sure I could smell their sweetness. When I stood up, I realized that the "sweetness" I was smelling was actually the smell of freshly digested hay. I'd landed right in the middle of a pile of horse-apples! I pulled up a bunch of dandelion stalks from the side of the road and wiped myself off as best I could. All about the road and the sides of the road were more horse-apples. I took a deep breath and tiptoed carefully up the street 'til a blinding beam of sunlight hit me in the eyes, stopping me in my tracks. When I moved out of the glare of the sunbeam, the street came alive. Right above me was a traffic light that marked the beginning of Main Street, U.S.A., or so it seemed. It was a freshly washed red brick street, with colorful flags, banners and other signs of festivity all about. All of the buildings were painted a variety of happy colors (I never knew there were so many happy colors at the paint store), and it seemed I was just in time for the Paris, Tennessee, rodeo — or, at the very least, the Queen of the Rodeo Contest. A banner strung over the street announced it:

Farmer Jack Braxton Sez:
"IT'S RODEO-TIME, Y'ALL!"
Paris, Tennessee
Home of the Queen of the Rodeo Contest!!!

In smaller print across the bottom of the banner was a phone number and the announcement of cash prizes: $500 for First Place, $250 for Second, and $100 for Third. I didn't pay any more attention to the sign than it took me to read it. Even still, it wasn't hard to tell that the Queen of the Rodeo Contest was what Paris, Tennessee, was famous for. Every effort was made to get the word out about the event. Banners on sides of buildings, posters in store windows, flyers on telephone poles, car windows, and mailboxes. There was even an old man barely strong enough-looking to wear a sandwich board out in front of a restaurant called Tiffany's advertising the contest, along with the Tiffany's menu. (As it turns out, he was Mr. Tiffany.) The flyers Mr. Tiffany had were different than all the other Queen of the Rodeo Contest flyers and posters (which were all the same); his were photocopied with a coupon for Tiffany's Restaurant, offering ten percent off of the Queen of the Rodeo Breakfast Special there.

I took one of the flyers from the old man and went in. At the register was a stack of *The Paris Banner Graphic*, the local paper. I dropped a quarter in the empty coffee can next to the stack that said "Newspapers — 20¢." I chose the booth farthest from all the other customers and put the newspaper on the seat and sat on it, concerned about the mess on my pants.

The waiter was a very tall, full-voiced black man. He made his way to me casually with a glass of water and a menu. His name tag was covered up with a paper sticker that had hand-printed on it "TENDER." He was in high spirits when he approached the table; he said, "Howdy, cowboy — shooo-*weee*! Smells like you brought the fairgrounds in here with you!"

I'd never heard an accent like his before but I soon came to the conclusion that it was the accent of the region, since everybody talked like that (although none of their accents were as thick as his). He disappeared then reappeared on the far side of the restaurant and walked back to me, spraying a steady trail of Lysol above his head. Everybody in the restaurant craned their necks to look at me and I blushed.

I apologized to the waiter and asked him to explain the Queen of the Rodeo Breakfast Special to me. "That's three buttermilk pancakes topped off with one scrambled egg an' a patta butter shaped like the Queen's crown — it's very purty. An' all that's surrounded with two links a'sausage, two strips a'bacon; an' it comes with a side a'cheese fries. Coffee an' juice 'er extry."

It sounded like a lot more than I wanted. "Oh, no, thanks, I'll just have the blueberry pancakes and coffee with one egg on the side, over-easy." He didn't write my order down; he was most intent on getting me to order the special. I said, "Do ya get a *commission* on those things or what?"

He got kinda tense and huffed and *tsk*ed. "Well, since you made me go through the trouble of explainin' the whole thing, I figgered the least ya could do is take it." He waited for me to change my order holding the order pad and pencil up so that his face was hidden behind them.

"No, the blueberry pancakes and coffee with one egg on the side will be fine. Over-easy."

"You want juice 'er not?"

I was pretty sure the juice in this restaurant was made from frozen, and I didn't really want that because made-from-frozen juice always burns my tongue, but I didn't wanna ask him if it was made-from-frozen because I didn't wanna make him think I was giving him a hard time. (He seemed kinda moody.) "Okay, yes, that'll be fine — good." When the orange juice came, I mixed it in little portions with my water so I could get it down without burning my tongue and without being detected by the waiter.

At the register next to the newspapers was a small display with a few different Tennessee postcards on it. One of them was a picture of a fresh cow patty that had

Paris, Tennessee — Wish You Were Here

written on it. I bought all of those and wrote notes to everybody I could think of while I waited for, and then ate, my breakfast.

By the time my breakfast and third cup of coffee were finished, Tender was being friendly with me again. I was the only customer still there besides an older woman in the far back corner who kept applying red lipstick to her cheeks like rouge. (As it turns out, she was Mrs. Tiffany!) Tender sat down across from me as he poured my fourth cup of coffee and let out a "shoo-*wee*," which this time I think meant he was tired. The flyer for the Queen of the Rodeo Contest was lying on the table between us. Tender pushed it toward me and I smiled, picked it up and glanced over the information, even though I knew just about as much as I thought I needed to know about the contest by this time. I didn't wanna offend or upset him in any way, so I let the words mingle in my head a little longer than usual before I spoke.

"This seems like a really big deal around here."

Tender said, "Oh, it *is*! Ain't that what yer here for?" He assumed that since I was in Paris, Tennessee the day before the Queen of the Rodeo Contest, and since I was wearing cowboy boots and a hat with a flower on it, that I was there to enter the contest. (He hadn't even heard about the Lucky Green Dress yet!)

Well, come to find out, the Queen of the Rodeo Contest isn't like any other contest in the world. Tender explained it all to me. Everybody who enters the Queen of the Rodeo Contest pays one dollar for the privilege. For their dollar, they get a contestant number, printed boldly on a square piece of paper, and a safety pin. The numbers are available a month prior to the contest and can be gotten at the rodeo arena box office, the Piggly Wiggly manager's booth or at Lolly's Beauty Parlor on the corner of Wright and Matlock Streets. In 1991, there were over nine hundred contestants; they were expecting more than a thousand for the 1992 contest.

Most of the contestants wear outrageous outfits — kinda like they do in the Mardi Gras festival down in New Orleans, Louisiana — but some of them just wear whatever they happen to have on, focusing more of their energies on their talent. Tender told me that the ones who don't dress up *never* get to the finalist round, and that they're "just a big waste of time." They all pin their contestant numbers to their collars, if they have collars, or tape them to their necks, and mill about the rodeo arena. A soft-spoken female announcer in a glass cage at the top of the bleachers starts calling out the numbers of the contestants who have been eliminated. This is all done starting at one p.m., without any of the public present, "so nobody'll be unnecessarily embarrassed."

The Queen of the Rodeo Judges walk around the center of the rodeo arena in yellow sports jackets loaned to them by the local Century 21 real estate office, the rectangular logo patches on their breast pockets having been covered over with temporary "Queen of the Rodeo Judge" patches. They call in their personal eliminations to the announcer in the glass cage by way of walkie-talkies.

This round of the contest lasts about an hour, 'til there are only ten contestants left in the rodeo arena. And while this is going on, every kind of souvenir imaginable is being sold from booths crowding the parking areas on three sides of the rodeo arena. T-shirts with "QUEEN OF THE RODEO" or "I Ain't the Queen" on them, coffee cups, beer mugs, teddy bears, spoon rests, coasters, ashtrays, all of them with some message that lets folks know that the purchaser was there that year. One whole section of booths is dedicated to hand-crafted items: crocheted things, things made out of foam egg cartons, beer can hats, fancy photo album covers; those sorts of things, and more.

Once the Queen of the Rodeo contestant pool is whittled down to ten, fog horns scream and dinner bells clang for one solid minute. Everybody all over town stops what they're doing and cheers. There's a break 'til five p.m. Then, at the stroke of five, the big wooden doors to the rodeo arena are pushed open and the audience piles into the bleachers. It costs only fifty cents to just be an audience member.

At six o'clock, the Queen of the Rodeo Horses enter the cleared arena floor to wild applause. (These horses are as famous in these parts as the Budweiser Clydesdales are all over the country.) There are ten Queen of the Rodeo Horses. The horse in front is gigantic and pink — brilliant pink. On his back is a silver-colored saddle that has "The Queen" embossed on either side in black. His hooves sparkle when he prances, and on top of his massive head — attached by twisty-ties to his mane — is the coveted Queen of the Rodeo crown (a contest-winner itself, created by one of Paris, Tennessee's, high school kids and made out of papier-mâché, foil, gold paint and glitter, and plastic gems). Behind the front horse are two more horses. These horses are the brightest blue you can imagine, and their hooves sparkle brightly, and they're saddled up as well — although their saddles are regular brown leather and don't really match (an overlooked detail that drove Tender to near insanity when he told me about it). In the third row are three more horses, these are green in color; they have sparkly hooves but no saddles. And in the fourth row are four horses, all of them bright purple with sparkling hooves and no saddles. The ten Queen of the Rodeo Horses walk in a triangular formation one full time around the perimeter of the rodeo arena and then exit again the way they entered. This is the sign that the finalist round of the contest has begun.

Of course, you're likely to be wondering where in the world you could find pink and blue and green and purple horses with such sparkly hooves. Well, ya can't — except in Paris, Tennessee, and then only on the day of the Queen of the Rodeo Contest. Y'see, Jack Braxton's Horse Farm is right outside of Paris in Braxton, Tennessee. He raises huge snow-white Arabian horses and they are used in the Queen of the Rodeo Contest — gussied up by the town's cosmetologists and veterinarian's assistants with dye-jobs and multicolored rhinestones glued to their hooves — in exchange for an abundance of advertisements all around town and in the rodeo arena. The dye is temporary but the rhinestones have to be shucked off by hand with a big metal file when the contest is over. The horses are brought into town on the Thursday morning before the contest day (which explains all of the horse-apples).

✪✪✪

For the finalist round of the Queen of the Rodeo Contest, the ten finalists enter the arena one at a time and make their way to the small stage in the center. The audience cheers the entire half a minute or so it takes them to get there. Once there, the finalists display their talent. Again, I'll repeat, the Queen of the Rodeo Contest isn't like any other contest in the world. What the judges (and the audience) are most interested in is originality and peculiarity.

About this time, the next-shift waitress, a grumpy, frumpy woman named Brenda, showed up at Tiffany's Restaurant. Tender took me to his garage apartment overlooking the rodeo arena to show me a video and photo albums of the 1991 Queen of the Rodeo Contest. Of course, you're probably wondering why Tender had a video and photo albums of the 1991 Queen of the Rodeo Contest. Well, it's very simple, actually: Tender was crowned the 1991 Queen of the Rodeo. This would be the first year in five that he wouldn't be able to enter the contest (the previous year's Queen is not allowed to run in the current year). Tender had been desperately searching for someone to groom as the Queen and little did I know at the time that *I* was the chosen one!

I got myself into it, really. As I flipped through the photo albums, looking at all the outfits that people wore to enter the contest, I blurted out that I oughta put on my Uncle Joe's Lucky Green Dress and enter the contest. I didn't even realize I'd said it out loud, but the next thing I knew, I was modeling the Lucky Green Dress for Tender.

He propped the 1991 Queen of the Rodeo crown on my head and sounded like he was gonna cry when he said, "It could happen...." He *had* to get me entered in that contest. My reluctance was only a minor obstacle for him to get over. After all of his begging and gushing compliments didn't do it, Tender said he'd wash my dirty pants for me if I'd enter the Queen of the Rodeo Contest.

I said, "Tender, the only way you could get me to enter that contest was if you washed every stitch of clothes in my backpack!"

He wasn't in the mood to bargain with me; he had a tub full of water and a washboard out and was busy with my laundry before I knew what was happening. He washed my clothes, hung them out the back window to dry, then ironed them to crisp perfection (even my socks and underwear!) with an old-fashioned iron he heated up in his oven.

As he worked, I watched the video of the 1991 Queen of the Rodeo Contest. The first contestant was a teenage girl named D'wana Tucker. The sound wasn't very good on his television, so I couldn't tell what she was singing, I could only tell that she was singing *off*-key. The other contestants included a female caballero, a tap-dancing aluminum-foiled alien, a rope trickster, a farmer who sang a duet with his small pig, a sexy woman in a bathing suit made of banana peels, a circus clown, a midget riding a huge white dog painted (not dyed) pink to look like the lead Queen of the Rodeo Horse, an albino fiddle player and the Grim Reaper.

The only act I could understand at all was Tender's, because when his part of the video came up, he stood behind me and performed along with the video. He was wearing a ten-gallon cowboy hat, a huge Western shirt, chaps and extra long cowboy boots. He carried a tape deck with him and sat it on one side of the stage. He took the microphone out of its stand and swayed back and forth rhythmically while his head bobbed up and down double-time.

Boom-chicka-boom-chicka-boom-chicka-boom,
Boom-chicka-boom-chicka-boom-chicka-boom.
Now listen up, an' y'all shall see
The delicious moves of Tender Mercy!
Boom-chicka-boom-chicka-boom-chicka-boom,
Boom-chicka-boom-chicka-boom-chicka-boom....

He continued his "boom-chicka-booms," and quickly sat the microphone on the stage next to the tape deck and pushed Play. A funky beat roared out over the loudspeaker and he did a dance that was part gymnastics and part tribal dance. As he danced, he stripped out of his cowboy outfit to reveal a huge Afro wig and a jungle man outfit. A few moments later, he stripped off the wig and jungle outfit and under that he was painted up to look like a snake. He did snake-like moves on the floor of the stage and stuck out a tongue that looked like it must've been ten inches long!

The audience loved it! By the time the song was over, they were all clapping along in rhythm and chanting, "Ten-der! Ten-der! Ten-der!"

He fast-forwarded the video to the awards ceremony which follows a short break at the end of the talent part of the contest. The caballero woman won third place, the banana peels bathing suit won second, and, you guessed it, Tender was crowned the 1991 Queen of the Rodeo. He snapped his fingers and said, "Mm-hm, Queen for a day!"

Right after the crowning ceremony, Tender turned off the VCR and put a record on his old-timey wind-up record player. He held his hand up in the air the entire time the song was playing (which I took to mean I shouldn't say a word, so I didn't). It was a scratchy record and the singer was singing in a foreign language so I didn't really know what was going on. After it was over, Tender put the big needle to the side of the player and flashed a big smile at me.

"What was that?"

"That's your talent, Baby!" He strutted around in a circle on the floor.

"But what *was* it?!"

"Don't you know Edith Piaf?" he asked in a funny accent. "Darlin', with your purty green dress on, you look just like her!" He told me that Edith Piaf is the most important French singer ever.

"I don't know how to speak French!"

"Oh, Sugar, that's the beauuuuty of the French language. Ya

don't gotta speak it t'sang it!" He said some weird words that sounded foreign and then asked me, "What'd I just say?"

"I don't know."

He threw his head back and laughed. "Me either, Baby — I didn't say nothin' a'tall! It's what I call Tender's Fakey-fakey French Tongue." I nodded. "Jay Byrd, Darlin', the Queen of the Rodeo Judges just *love* foreign acts — *ever'body* loves foreign acts — even if they ain't really foreign!"

"No, Tender, I just can't."

"You will do it."

"No, Tender, please."

"*You will do it.*"

"No."

"Don't make me use my Black Magic on yore beehind, Jay Byrd, 'cause you will surely regret it."

I kept protesting, but I ended up losing the battle. He said, "I already washed *all* your clothes by *hand*, Jay Byrd, I can't unwash 'em. So *sang*!"

I couldn't exactly argue with him, so I did my best to learn the song. It was called "La Goualante du Pauvre Jean," but the only way I could put my mouth around the words, it came out sounding like "The Goulash to Papa John." It was garbled and foreign-sounding enough for Tender. He clapped his hands and said, "Brilliantine! Brilliantine!"

✪✪✪

Bright and early the next morning, I got my contestant number at the rodeo arena box office. The line at the rodeo arena box office was pretty long and slow-moving; I figured out why when I got to the front. The woman in the booth was Mrs. Tiffany, bright red cheeks and all. She couldn't seem to keep her bifocals on her face. She was very nice, though and she smiled real big when she gave me my number and said, "Hey, number one thousand — it's your lucky day!" That's the exact same thing Tender said when I got back to his apartment.

The rest of the day is sort of a blur to me. I think that's because Tender wouldn't let me eat anything. He was afraid I wouldn't be able to get into the dress, even though it fits me perfectly. At first, I was really nervous about wearing the Lucky Green Dress out in public — even though Tender was right there by my side the whole time; but after a while, I got so weak, I completely forgot about my nervousness.

Many of the same contestants were there, the farmer and his cute little pig, the midget (but not his Queen of the Rodeo Horse-dog — Tender said the paint-job the previous year killed it). In the hour that we were milling about the rodeo arena as the eliminations were being announced, I remember looking up at my cloud, directly above us, wishing it would block out the sun. I also remember the scream of the fog horn, and I vaguely remember Tender feeding me saltines and Coke during the break, slapping me lightly on the face and saying, "Come on, Jay Byrd, you can do it."

The next thing I remember, they were calling out over the loudspeaker, "Contestant Number One Thousand for the last time."

Tender was frantically chasing me around the stall they had set aside as the waiting area for the contestants — next to the Queen of the Rodeo Horses' stalls — screaming the words to the song at me and demanding I repeat them, but when he heard my number called, he said "Just do your best, child — that's all I can ask," and he shoved me out into the rodeo arena, shaking his head in shame.

I don't remember the walk across the dirt to the stage in the middle of the arena. Tender said I took it very slowly. He said everybody could see my knees knocking as I stood in front of the microphone. He cued somebody in the glass cage and the French song blared out of the loudspeaker, but I didn't sing. The audience went wild — they could tell it was gonna be a foreign act. Tender begged them to rewind the tape and restart, but again I didn't sing along; I just stood there, dizzy and numb. The music went off and one of the judges stepped up on the bottom step and asked if I was alright. I don't know if I answered. The crowd was very worked up about the prospect of a foreign act, and I remember them clapping and chanting in unison — though I couldn't understand what they were chanting — but it had a nice rhythm to it and it made me think of the video of Tender on this very same stage. I started tapping my toe and bobbing my head up and down. I tried to snap my fingers in rhythm, but my hands were soaked with sweat. I wiped my hands down the front of the Lucky Green Dress, and I swear I heard a magical *ppring!* sound. And then, from out of nowhere, a song came to me. It wasn't the French song Tender had taught me; it was in English, but I'm sure I'd never heard it before. It kinda matched the chanting of the crowd. I started singing the words to the song as they came to my mouth, not sure what I was gonna sing next, but it made sense when it came out and the crowd loved it! It was unbelievably incredible.

(I Am The) Queen of the Rodeo

I am the Queen of the Rodeo,
I ride the horses in the show,
My smile is permanent;
I am the Queen of the Rodeo,
My hat's just right, my boots just so,
I am the one who's confident.

'Cause when I'm singin',
Joy bells are ringin'
In the heavens and the Lord is smilin' down;
I sing a ditty, I am so pretty,
That's the reason why they dressed me in a crown.

'Cause I am the Queen of the Rodeo,
I ride the horses in the show,
I love the way they prance;
I am the Queen of the Rodeo,
My hat's just right, my boots just so,
And now I think I'm gonna dance...

And I danced. And the audience danced along with me. And they cheered for me. And then I passed out cold.

Tender poured a bucket of ice water on me right in the middle of the stage. I jerked to, not sure if what'd just happened was real.

Tender was excited. He helped me to my feet and led me out of the arena as the audience clapped in unison chanting, "Queen of the Rodeo! Queen of the Rodeo! Queen of the Rodeo!"

Tender said, "We did it! We did it!" (It took me a while to figure out that "we did it" meant that I had been chosen as the 1992 Queen of the Rodeo.)

For the last event of the Queen of the Rodeo Contest, the rodeo arena floor is cleared of everybody except the Queen of the Rodeo (and the runners-up) and the Queen of the Rodeo Horses. They put me on the humongous pink horse at the front of the triangular formation (the two runners-up were behind me on the blue horses, but I don't even remember who they were), and we paraded around the rodeo arena a couple of times. I had to sit sidesaddle or my Lucky Green Dress would've split right up the middle!

As we paraded around the rodeo arena, Tender ran around with me in the front row of the bleachers, stepping on folks and knocking drinks over, screaming, "Yay, Jay Byrd! Yay, Jay Byrd!" Nobody seemed to mind; they all joined in with Tender screaming for me, and they tossed roses at me. I sang the song over and over again, and everybody in the bleachers sang along. Even though I was kind of in an overheated, undernourished fog the whole time, it was a truly amazing experience.

For the rest of the weekend, I was treated like Paris, Tennessee, royalty. I had dinner with the mayor of Paris and her husband (at the Mayor's Ranch), I got my picture taken with locals and tourists of all kinds at the Queen of the Rodeo Festival (which continued through Sunday). I felt so comfortable in the Lucky Green Dress that I didn't take it off all weekend. In fact, I decided I'd just keep on wearing it, even after I left Paris, Tennessee — it was bound to help me find my destiny. But then, not twenty minutes outside of town, I caught a ride with a trucker named "Stinker" who thought *he* was gonna get lucky with me and my Lucky Green Dress. I told him I was car-sick and I guess I pretended pretty good, because I got him to pull over in a little town called Murray, Kentucky, and I ran and ran and ran. When I came across a little patch of woods surrounding a watering hole in the middle of a field, I changed out of the dress, and that was that — for a while.

Heavenly Hoedown

Once I was lost, but you found me,
Once I was blind but now I see;
And I see love shinin' like a lighthouse,
And it shines on me.

(For two voices, repeat first and second verses, with second voice singing chorus simultaneously.)

Chapter Ten

The Terrible Thunderstorm

I was raised to say "ma'am" and "sir" and "please" and "thank you," so whenever I stayed with any of the folks who were on my names-and-numbers necklace, I'd write a checkmark on their piece of paper after I'd had the opportunity to write and send them a Thank You postcard.

There were lots and lots of folks who I would never meet, but I never threw any of their names and numbers out — I didn't wanna tempt fate and suddenly find myself in some strange state without anybody to call. I took off the names and numbers of the folks I *figured* I wouldn't meet and put them in a small pocket in my backpack, the one with the postcards and the stamps in it. For instance, when the man in the cloud led me into Louisiana, I took off the names and numbers of the folks who were west of Texas; then when I passed through Mississippi, I took off everybody who was in Alabama, Georgia, and Florida; Tennessee, the Carolinas, Arkansas, Oklahoma, Kansas — those got removed when I entered Missouri; and then Kentucky and West Virginia when I found myself in Ohio. And that brings us to Saturday, May 23.

Friendship, Ohio, was the last address I had that far north. I was a little worried about what tomorrow had in store for me, particularly if the man in the cloud continued his northward journey, but, like my Daddy always says: "Don't worry about tomorrow 'til there's a tomorrow to worry about." I think that's another way of saying "Live for today."

The folks whose address I had in Friendship, Ohio — Ellie Davis and Ollie Biddle — were kinfolks, of a sort. Ellie is the widow of my Nana's second cousin Floyd Davis (which makes her my great-great grandparents' brother or sister's kid's son's widow, or something like that). She told me just to call her "Aunt Ellie" and so I did. From the way he said, "The name's Ollie Biddle," and the fact that he and Aunt Ellie aren't married, I felt like I should call Ollie Biddle "Ollie Biddle." Sometimes it came out very naturally — other times I struggled with *what* to call him.

I arrived at their address late in the morning of Saturday, May 23. I soon found out that was midday for them. Ollie Biddle was sitting in a rocking chair on the front porch and Aunt Ellie was standing behind him with her hands resting gently on his shoulders, looking out at the sky. After ten minutes of telling them who I was, they finally decided I was "Agnes' boy" — (Agnes is my Nana), and they opened their home to me.

Their apartment was half of a house; a rusty screen in the middle of the porch and a wall on the inside of the house made the division. I never saw and they never mentioned a neighbor. The inside of their house was long and narrow and reminded me of a trailerhome. I felt comfortable right away. After a couple hours of being there, I stopped noticing the smell of camphor and baby powder and cooked vegetables — or, at least I *told* myself to stop making mental notes of it.

Aunt Ellie said, "We were just about to eat lunch. *Please* join us." It wasn't yet eleven a.m., but I couldn't resist her kindness, and I was a little hungry — I was always at least a little hungry during my journey. We had small portions of creamed chicken, strained peas and carrots, and white bread. I washed the dishes amid Aunt Ellie's hand-to-bosom complaints. Ollie Biddle sat at the kitchen table watching us and laughing.

When I was done, I followed Ollie out to the porch. Aunt Ellie said she'd be out soon (she didn't mention it, but she *needed* to rearrange the dishes that I'd misplaced on the drying rack and dry the counter top again).

Ollie rocked in his chair and looked out at the quiet sky with a contented smile on his face. I walked out into the yard and spotted my cloud, directly above the house, and I felt content, too. When I heard a screen door creak to a close, I looked to see Aunt Ellie sitting down on the steps and patting the spot next to her. I sat.

For the next two-and-a-half hours, we told our life stories to each other. Well, you know *my* story, so I don't have to tell you what I said, but their story is very interesting.

Aunt Ellie had spent seven years in the Friendship Christian Rest Home (she and Ollie Biddle called it "Hell's Infirmary") after her husband died and her two children moved to Saudi Arabia — both of them! Ollie Biddle was in the rest home the last five years that Aunt Ellie was there. They started playing dirty tricks on the "mean old nurses" together (the worst thing they ever did was attempt to suffocate the napping head nurse with a dirty diaper). They were punished for their pranks by being kept apart. They both pretended not to care — which got their sentences reduced each time — but it was truly the worst punishment anyone could give them because they were falling deeper and deeper in love with each other every time they pulled another prank.

In their last year at the rest home, after the dirty diaper incident, they promised they would stop their pranks if they were allowed to sleep together. Due to the religious ownership of the rest home, this was out of the question, so six months later, Aunt Ellie and Ollie ran away and rented the duplex they now live in. They hadn't yet lived there a full year; in fact, the representatives from the board of the rest home had just a month earlier stopped their regular weekly visits trying to counsel them back to the rest home.

I told Aunt Ellie and Ollie Biddle that it was hard to imagine them pulling pranks, they seemed so calm (and, I didn't say so, but, their life seemed so routine). Ollie said, "Well, when ya got what ya need in life, they ain't no *reason* t'play the fool no more, is it?" As he was telling me this Aunt Ellie got up and shuffled into the house and as she passed Ollie, he slapped her on the butt and I saw a little bit of the prankster side of him in his eyes.

Aunt Ellie didn't make a comment or even flinch in the slightest; it was two o'clock, time for the "Lawrence Welk" rerun. She watched it with the sound off, explaining to me later, "Can't hear't anyhow!"

Ollie Biddle and I stayed out on the porch for a while. He *shooshed!* me and we sat in silence while he took out his teeth, sat them on the porch railing and secretively took a pouch of Red Man tobacco out of his back pocket and pushed a chaw into his mouth 'til his cheek skin was stretched to capacity. He sucked on the tobacco leaves for a moment to get it positioned properly, then said, "Lawrence Welk!" and spit out over the porch railing. A couple of silent moments later, Ollie asked me if I knew the Carter Family.

I figured he was talking about some distant kinfolks or something. "No, sir."

He said, "Uh-huh, I figured as much. You probably listen to that old Elvis Presley." I started to deny it, but he got up and disappeared around the side of the house. A couple of minutes later, he was back, and he was carrying with him a little instrument case. He climbed the stairs carefully and when I reached up to give him a hand he yanked his dangling hand away from me. He sat back in the rocking chair, spit and said, "Ya know what this is? I betcha don't!"

I had no idea. "Is it a machine gun?" I joked.

He laughed and opened the case and said, "If it was, I'd a'shot you by now! It's what you call a bari-uke. Or a baritone ukulele." He strummed a little chord on the four-string instrument and said, "This is the easiest instrument in the world t' learn. I'll show you how." He then went about playing with such speed and precision I could barely see his fingers moving. After a few seconds of that, he looked up at me and giggled (the prankster again). Then he sang an old Carter Family song called "Keep On The Sunny Side." I knew the song somehow (even though I'd never heard of the Carter Family), so I sang along. Ollie Biddle smiled real big and said, "Yeah! *That's* it!"

After he sang that song, he sang another, and another, and in between songs, he told me stories about the Carter Family. He said they were the first folks to sing country music, and he told me that they were big stars in their day — "Bigger'n Elvis or anybody. And better, too."

I knew most of the gospel songs that the Carter Family did because they were songs we sang in my Daddy's tent revival: "Shall We Gather At The River," "Amazing Grace," "In The Sweet By And By." The other songs I just listened to him sing and play solo. His voice was smooth and soft and I found myself leaning toward him to catch every word.

Sometimes between songs, Aunt Ellie'd holler out requests. Sometimes Ollie Biddle played her requests; other times he ignored her. It's funny that Aunt Ellie couldn't hear the television, but she could hear Ollie Biddle singing very clearly. When he sang her requests, she sang along in her sweet, straining old voice. Sure, she probably knew all the songs by heart anyway, but even so, it made me think about how special music is. Being raised up in the tent revival and having a steady dose of music every Saturday evening and every Sunday evening (and sometimes every night of the week when Daddy did one of his long-term tent revivals), I guess I kinda took music for granted. But as I sat there enjoying the songs Ollie sang, something happened to me. I have a hard time trying to explain it, but it suddenly dawned on me that music is a really important thing. I *need* to have music in my life. And — as was often the case in my journey, if I had a thought that seemed significant in some way — I looked up into the sky and winked at the man in the cloud — almost unconsciously. So I looked up into the sky, and there was my cloud, peeking out into the front yard a little bit.

No sooner did I wink at the man in the cloud than Ollie Biddle said my name. It embarrassed me. When I looked at him he was holding the bari-uke toward me. He said, "Take it."

So I did. I held it and strummed on it and laughed at myself (it sounded pretty bad). I held it back toward him.

He held up a hand, paused a minute, spat a *sppwat!* stream over the porch railing and then turned back to me wiping his mouth with his shirt sleeve and said, "Keep it. It's yours."

I said, "I can't take this!"

"Too late, ya'rdy *did*! Ha-ha!" He broke out into a fit of laughter and I took the instrument back to my lap and looked at it. It was as if he'd read my mind about needing to have music in my life.

"Learn three chords and you'll be able to play any song in the world."

I couldn't say a word, so I just sat there admiring the dark wood grain, on the verge of tears — I don't think they were tears so much from the fact that I'd been moved by what had happened; I think they were tears from utter embarrassment. Fortunately, Aunt Ellie appeared at the front screen door and called us for supper and pulled me out of my mute state. "Oh, what time is it?" I asked.

It was four o'clock. As soon as Aunt Ellie ducked back into the darkness of the house, Ollie stood up, stuck a stained index finger into his cheek and in one motion rolled the chunk of tobacco out of his jaw and onto the ground. I looked down where it had landed, right on top of a large pile of previously extracted chaws.

✪✪✪

Supper was the same as lunch, with the welcomed addition of lumpy chocolate pudding. I cautiously told Aunt Ellie that Ollie Biddle had given me his bari-uke, certain she was gonna have a fit and run out of the house crying, but she hardly paused from scooping strained peas and carrots onto her plate and said, "Oh, ain't it nice! He's got about a hundred of 'em just like that one out in the shed!"

"Down to thirty-seven now!" he said proudly.

As it turns out, before he retired, Ollie Biddle owned a music store in Nashville, Tennessee. He said he just came to Friendship because Lady Destiny wanted to introduce him to Ellie. When he said Aunt Ellie's name, he patted her leg under the table and both of their faces lit up.

For the remainder of supper, Aunt Ellie and Ollie Biddle asked me questions about my life. As soon as I mentioned the fact that the man in the cloud was right out in their front yard, they both instantaneously got up from the table and went to the porch to look at it. However, their eyesight wasn't too good — they kept mistaking the transformer on top of a telephone pole for the man in the cloud. Ollie Biddle said, "Oh, yes, there he is. Fat little fellow, huh?"

After supper, we sat in the living room and watched "Live at Five" with the sound way up. All throughout the program, Ollie Biddle kept saying, "Hanh?" and Aunt Ellie just ignored him. I tried to tell him what was said three times in a row: "There's a storm in Kentucky heading this way." But each time I said it, he leaned up in his La-Z-Boy toward me and said, "What? *What?*"

I looked over at Aunt Ellie in despair and she shook her head at me and I laid back on the plastic-sealed couch and listened to the newscaster and Ollie Biddle have it out 'til a strange silence came during a commercial. I looked over and they were both sound asleep. It was barely six o'clock.

I turned the television off and sat there watching them for a while. Their snores came out like a see-saw, first Aunt Ellie: *"Snnaaawww!"* Then Ollie: *"Snnewww!"* Each round, they got a little bit louder, and then one of them would swallow their tongue, choke on it, awaken in a fit, slap at the other — whose snoring would cease — and then they'd both doze off again and it'd start all over.

I went out on the porch and sat in the rocking chair and strummed on the ukulele. I found a couple of strums that sounded like they might've been actual chords, but then I lost them. The sky turned from blue to yellow to orange to red to purple to indigo. I figured the man in the cloud was asleep because the cloud was motionless there amidst it all. Before the sky turned black, I was asleep, too.

A couple hours later, I woke up and went into the house. The couch had been made up with sheets and quilts and pillows and Aunt Ellie and Ollie Biddle were gone. The distant see-saw snoring told me that they'd made their way to bed. I laid down on the couch and fell asleep and had a dream:

> *I was walking through a meadow in the Lucky Green Dress, but my feet were a few inches off of the ground. Every once in a while, different individuals or groups of people would pop up and cheer and chant my name — "Jay Byrd! Jay Byrd! Jay Byrd!" — just like they had done in Paris, Tennessee, at the Queen of the Rodeo Contest. And then I looked up into the sky, and just as I did, the man in the cloud reached down from his cloud and held his hand out to me and said, "Come on!" I took his hand and he pulled me up into the cloud. The higher into the air I flew, the brighter everything got, and by the time I was actually up inside the cloud, it was so bright I couldn't see a thing. The man in the cloud was behind me and I was dying to see what he looked like, but when I turned around, there was a bright flash of light, and I woke up.*

The clock on the wall clicked loudly. It was one of those cat clocks, with the eyes looking to the opposite sides of the room every second, and its tail ticked as it wagged. It was four-fifteen a.m. I couldn't get back to sleep. I hadn't had much to eat since I'd been there, so I quietly looked through Aunt Ellie's cabinets for some crackers or something, but all that was in the cabinets was antique silver and china and crystal — nothing edible. The icebox was full of containers of left-over (or maybe pre-cooked) creamed chicken, "junior-size" jars of baby food, lots of little brown prescription bottles, and a metal bowl with a little bit of chocolate pudding left in it. The freezer was stocked with more creamed chicken and jars and jars of really old-looking make-up.

I slowly slid open the silverware drawer and took out a large spoon, then I sat at the table with the bowl of chocolate pudding and finished it off. It was ice cold and delicious; I ran the length of my index finger along the inside of the bowl and got every last bit of pudding. When I was done, I looked at my distorted face in the bottom of the bowl and my dream came back to me.

As I quietly washed the bowl, I started thinking about the Lucky Green Dress. I hadn't put it on in two days. That made me think of Ruther Jean and the promise I'd made to her — to wear the Lucky Green Dress *every* day. Maybe the dream was telling me that I'd missed something by not wearing the Lucky Green Dress those two days. In my defense, I gotta say that I had a pretty good reason for not putting on the Lucky Green Dress the previous Friday.

I mentioned before that sometimes on my journey, I didn't have much to say to the folks that I stayed with on my journey, and Friday night was certainly one of those times. Mostly because these folks didn't speak any English — well, one of the thirteen children apparently did, but he wasn't there. Their family name was Barrientes. They let me in when I showed them the piece of paper from my names-and-numbers necklace with their name and address on it and the short note from their Texas kin written to them in Spanish on the back. I don't read or speak any Spanish, and it was obvious that between them they only knew one sentence of English: "Victor home soon." Once in a while, one of them would attempt saying something to me, but after a few uncomfortable moments, they would finish it off by saying, "Victor home soon."

I would smile blankly, and they would smile back.

I ate dinner with them, I spent the night with them (in a bed with five others), I said "Gracias!" a lot, and I smiled at them a lot. The one thing I wasn't able to do, though, was take a shower. There wasn't a shower curtain on the shower *and* there wasn't a door on the bathroom. It just didn't seem like the right place and time to be putting on a dress, no matter how lucky it was, so I didn't. But maybe that was my test. I started thinking about all of the Biblical characters who had been tested, and I started picturing myself walking all the way back to Okey-Dokey, Texas, to tell everybody that I was a big failure.

As I stood there thinking about all of this, I suddenly thought that maybe the man in the cloud was gone. I ran to the front yard, my hands dripping soapy water all the way. I searched the sky, and, sure enough, the cloud was nowhere to be seen. I couldn't breathe and my heart felt like it was running a race. I sat on the front porch steps and put my head between my knees and took a coupla deep breaths. A drop of sweat fell from my face to the sidewalk — or maybe it was a tear. I was lost; if I didn't have the man in the cloud leading me on, I had nowhere else to go except back to Okey-Dokey, Texas.

I closed my eyes tight and said a little prayer. "Lord, please help me find my way. Please help me find the man in the cloud. I promise I'll wear the Lucky Green Dress every day 'til I get to the end of my journey. Thank you and amen."

I opened my eyes and lo and behold, there was the man in the cloud, easing out from behind a church steeple on the horizon. He was getting away from me! I had to go!

I walked back through the house briskly, carrying my backpack with me to the bathroom, which was in Aunt Ellie and Ollie Biddle's bedroom. I tiptoed through their room, careful not to wake them up. I didn't look back toward their twin beds on the far side of the room 'til I was turning to pull the bathroom door closed. The beds were *empty*! Aunt Ellie and Ollie Biddle were gone!

There was a note on the bathroom mirror:

> On a morning walk! Go back to bed! We love you very much! E.+O.

I shaved my head and took a quick bath (they didn't have a shower) and put on the outfit Uncle Joe had given me when I left Okey-Dokey, Texas, to follow my vision: the hat, the boots, and, yes, the Lucky Green Dress! I went out to the front porch. The ukulele was lying beside Ollie Biddle's rocking chair. I thought about leaving it there, but then I said to myself, "No, that was probably meant to be, too." I locked it in its case, hiked my backpack onto my back, and smiled up to the morning sky. Whoa! The man in the cloud was getting farther away! But then I realized I couldn't just leave without saying goodbye to Aunt Ellie and Ollie Biddle. But I couldn't *wait*! I paced through the house anxiously a couple of times, then stood on the front of the porch and hollered out, "Aunt Ellie!"

A dog started barking. Otherwise, silence. I couldn't wait any longer — I couldn't miss another opportunity. I couldn't lose the man in the cloud.

I quickly wrote a thank you note on a postcard and propped it against a candy dish full of ribbon candy on the coffee table. I hiked my backpack up on my shoulders, picked up the ukulele by its handle, and walked out the front door and into the world in my Lucky Green Dress a changed man.

✪✪✪

It was probably about eight a.m. I was walking north on the very hilly State Highway 23, headed toward the intersection of Highway 23 and Route 22. Church bells were echoing through the hills and I remembered that it was Sunday.

A small white school bus appeared on top of one of the hills in the distance. And then it disappeared. Then it reappeared, one hill closer, and the church bells rang out louder for a moment. And then it disappeared again, and the church bells were a little softer. The bus appeared and disappeared several times before it reached me, and each time it topped a hill, the church bells rang out a little louder than before. When it got close enough, I could see that there was a loudspeaker mounted on top of the bus and prerecorded church bells were blaring out into the countryside through it.

As the bus approached me, I waved and smiled at the glaring windshield. The bus slowed to a stop as it reached me. The bells stopped abruptly. On the side of the bus was written:

CALVARY FULL-GOSPEL CHURCH
"Where the Lord Resides"
Circleville, Ohio

The bus driver was a round-faced black man with gray-specked hair. He opened the little driver's window and pushed his face to the opening — it fit perfectly. He smiled from ear to ear. "Why, howdy, neighbor!"

I greeted him back.

"That sure is a Sund'y-go-to-meetin' dress if ever I saw one! Would ya like to go to Calvary?"

"I'm goin' the other way!"

"No, my friend, you're goin' the *right* way! It's right up there on Calvary Road, on the right — ya can't miss it. I'm just on my way to pick up the congregation! Morning service starts at nine a.m. on the *dot*!"

I said, "Maybe."

He sat up, nodded, gave me an "Okay" sign with his right hand, tooted the horn, turned on the bells, and headed on down the highway.

I started singing "When The Roll Is Called Up Yonder I'll Be There" because that's what the bus's church bells were playing, and I danced about as I walked up the deserted highway. When I topped the next hill, there was the little church two hills away and off to the right on a little dirt road. It was a cute little white aluminum building with stained-glass windows and a little white cross at its roof-peak.

The farmland around the Calvary Full-Gospel Church was hilly and a whole variety of green colors. I stood there looking out at the beautiful early morning landscape for a moment. But then I heard a weird noise behind me in the sky.

I looked over my shoulder casually and jumped back when I saw a solid line of storm clouds stretching as far as I could see in both directions east and west. They were so dark, they seemed angry, and they were moving all about within themselves, and they were moving toward me. And they were moving toward my man in the cloud — fast and furious.

I screamed out, "*Run!*" I don't know if I was screaming to my cloud or to myself, but it started me running. I stopped on top of the next hill to catch my breath, and I looked back. The storm clouds were approaching faster than ever. I ran as fast as I could and just as I topped the hill that the church sat on, the sky around me started to turn dark. I could smell rain in the air. I turned onto the dirt road and ran with every bit of energy left in me, and just as I got to the church a quarter-size drop of rain splatted me in the face. I tried the front double doors of the church but they were locked. I ran around the church; the back door was locked, too. I ran to one of the windows — but they weren't real windows; they were just painted on the outside wall of the building!

I ran toward the highway, toward the dark clouds that were overtaking me now, thinking that maybe the bus driver was on his way. The highway was still deserted. I looked back at the church and then up to my cloud. He was being swallowed up by the storm clouds! *"No!!!"*

A streak of lightning shot out of the middle of the storm clouds and touched the cross on the church's roof; the cross fell to one side. The powerful *kaboom!* immediately following the lightning knocked me to the ground. Then came the rain. It fell slowly at first (though the drops were huge) and grew steadily harder by the second. I couldn't get up with the backpack on my back so I tossed it off and stood up; the rain tried its hardest to beat me back down.

As soon as I was standing, another flash of lightning and crash of thunder hit somewhere nearby and my brain shook in my head. The church disappeared before my eyes behind a solid wall of rain. Two more times came the lightning and thunder, one right after the other, *Flash! Kaboom! Flash! Ka-kaboom!* All of the hair on my body stood on end. I figured it was just a matter of time before one of those lightning streaks came down with my name on it. But I certainly wasn't gonna just stand there and wait for it. That's not the way I was raised.

I ran! I ran as fast as I could, leaving my backpack and the ukulele behind. Just beyond the church, I came to a wooden fence. I climbed over it and stepped into a freshly planted field of some sort. The ground became softer and softer as I ran across it, but I kept running because the lightning and thunder weren't letting up. I ran toward the light part of the sky, but there was less and less light in the sky.

My feet were getting heavier and heavier; my boots were caking up with mud. I started thinking that I'd really screwed up by not wearing the Lucky Green Dress those two days (okay, I am just a little bit superstitious). I had missed out on my opportunity; the man in the cloud was gone, everything was gone. I couldn't see anything — just a solid, dark wall of rain swallowing up occasional flashes of lightning and *kabooms* of thunder. I turned around to see where I'd come from, but it looked the same as what was ahead of me. I turned back around — I thought — but I had completely lost my bearings. Had I turned far enough? I turned some more. Then it seemed like maybe I'd turned too far. The rain was coming down so hard now I couldn't see a thing! I did a few circles, I guess, 'cause when I took a step, I fell to my knees. My boots were completely entangled in vines. I pulled at them, but the vines were very strong. I started to panic. Not only was I not gonna find my destiny, I was becoming more and more doubtful that I'd even survive to the end of the day. I screamed out, "Somebody *help!*"

Suddenly, there was a humongous and blinding flash of lightning and a sonic kaboom. I fell to the ground, covering my face. When I decided I wasn't dead, I uncovered my face, and there in front of me was an outstretched arm, reaching for me. At first I thought it was a mirage — or maybe I *was* dead. But then I heard a voice that sounded vaguely familiar, but I couldn't make it out because of the rain and the thunder.

I said "What?" Again I heard a muddled voice. "*What?*"

The voice spoke once more, and this time I heard it loud and clear. He said, "Come and go with me." It was the man in the cloud! "Come *on!*"

Well, I grabbed that hand, yes I did, and the man in the cloud pulled me up, but the earth pulled back. I was stuck in the mud and the vines. He pulled once, twice, three times, and the third time, I slurped my way out of the ground. I laughed as the man in the cloud led me through the storm, and I could hear him laughing, too. I had no idea where he was taking me, but I honestly didn't care!

The terrible thunderstorm lasted for three days and three nights, and in that time the man in the cloud and I got to know each other pretty well. Except that he didn't know he was "the man in the cloud"; he was just Steven Cheslik-DeMeyer from Kornflake, Indiana. *You* know. Well, when he rescued me from the pumpkin field, he'd led me to the underside of a highway overpass where the highway went over a creek. He saw the storm coming ahead of time and ducked under the highway and started setting up camp by the time it hit. During the worst part of the storm, a mysterious sparkling in the pumpkin field caught his eye (it was my Lucky Green Dress!). The sparkling seemed to be calling out to him — well, that was me screaming out for help! Regardless, that's why Steven ran out into the field and that's how he ended up saving my life.

Once we were safely under the highway, we put on some dry clothes (Steven's clothes, which were short on me, but I didn't care), and Steven showed off some of his survivalist expertise by building a campfire with a spit over it, and by grilling up some crawdaddies he'd caught in the creek. I helped out as much as I could and while we worked, I told him my whole life story, from the Okey-Dokey Preaching Contest back in 1967 up to the present moment. I told him about my Daddy and Momma and my sisters and the angel Aunt Pearl. I told him about growing up traveling with the tent revival, and all about my Uncle Joe and his dresses (particularly the Lucky Green Dress), and all about Okey-Dokey, Texas, my hometown, and about the incredible Vision in my Daddy's tent revival that led me cross-country to Circleville, Ohio, where I finally found my destiny, the man in the cloud, which was *him*.

Steven said he felt honored to be the subject of a Vision — especially since he'd never gone to church. He told me why he'd never gone to church and all about his mother and father and how they met and fell in love and got married and moved to Kornflake, Indiana, and started having babies and couldn't stop because the Catholic Church wouldn't let them. He told me all about the Cheslik-DeMeyer Popcorn Farm and Grandma Thayer and his sister Kay and all of his brothers. He said his brothers and sister had all left home when they realized what they were supposed to do with their lives, and since he hadn't figured out what he was supposed to do with *his* life yet, he'd taken to roaming the countryside trying to figure it out.

I said, "Well, *now* ya know what you're supposed to do with your life: you're supposed to spend it with me!"

Steven laughed a little uncomfortably. "I guess so."

During the second day of the storm, my ukulele floated under the overpass on the creek. A little water had gotten in the case, but the uke wasn't damaged at all. Steven asked me if I knew how to play it, and I told him all about Ollie Biddle and the Carter Family songs. After I finished telling him all that, he asked me again if I knew how to play it and I said, "Well, no!"

Steven said, "All you have to do is learn three chords, and then you'll be able to play anything."

"That's the same thing Ollie Biddle said!"

"Ollie Biddle was right." Steven taught me the G chord, the C chord, and the D chord. He said, "Those were the only three chords Elvis Presley knew how to play."

Steven played "Does It Feel Like Home?" for me and I got all teary-eyed, then I taught him all of the other verses to "Amazing Grace" that he'd never heard before. We played songs all day and all night as the rain kept falling and the thunder and lightning kept on. He played the songs he'd written and the songs he'd learned listening to his mother's and Grandma

Thayer's favorite radio station. I taught him the songs I grew up singing in my Daddy's revival meetings. And we talked a lot, too, and we laughed a whole lot.

Late in the night one night, we finally ran out of songs to sing, and we just sat staring into each others' eyes across a crackling campfire.

The next day, we wrote our very first song together. It's as silly as it can be, but we were feeling pretty silly and giddy at the time, so that's all I can say to explain where it came from. It's called "Doggone Happy."

Doggone Happy

Daddy raised me right,
Momma raised me well;
They taught me wrong from right
And Heaven from Hell.
My head is in the right place
And my heart is, too;
I'm so doggone happy
I'm gonna share it with you.

We didn't have a pen to write the song down (Steven's had gotten ruined when he came out into the storm to save me and mine was in my backpack, somewhere). Steven handed me a long, narrow stick and had me write the words in the dirt underneath the highway while he sang and played. We sang the song over and over 'til we'd memorized it. And then, as soon as we were sure we knew all the words, we erased them and started writing another song right away. We did this every day and night and only slept in little spurts — 'til one or the other of us would jump up suddenly with a song idea, and we'd write it together. Some of the songs we actually did remember, others of 'em are lost forever.

The rain stopped early the morning of the fourth day (Wednesday, May 27), but we couldn't seem to bring ourselves to leave our cozy little home under the highway. The creek kept us stocked up with fresh water and food, and there were enough dried-up old logs and sticks and leaves around to keep a fire burning whenever we needed one. The bed Steven made us (out of weeds and brush) was really a lot more comfortable than it sounds like it would've been. And whenever we got chilly, we always had each other to keep us warm! Most of the time, though, we didn't wait 'til we got chilly to hold onto each other — there wasn't a night when we weren't completely tangled up in each others' arms (if ya know what I mean)!

Everything was perfect — that is 'til Saturday, May 30 rolled around. I'd never been in love before, but that was unmistakably what I was feeling for Steven, and it seemed like he felt the same way about me. We were sitting around the campfire that night as we'd become quite accustomed to doing, and I said, "I wish we could sing our songs together for people."

Steven said, "I'm sure we will someday."

That made me feel wonderfully confident. "Y'know what, Steven Cheslik-DeMeyer from Kornflake, Indiana," I said, "I love you!" I kinda giggled when I said it and I tossed my head back and waited for him to say, "And do *you* know what, James Dean Jay Byrd from Okey-Dokey, Texas, I love you, *too*!"

But he didn't say that. He didn't say anything at all.

After a while, my neck started getting stiff, so I pulled my head back up and I looked over at him. He was crying. I went over to him and put an arm around his shoulder. "What's the matter?"

It took him a long time to gather up the words in his mind to be able to say them to me, and even then, they came out slowly and painfully. He said, "I wanna be with you, Jay, I really do. But I have a problem." And then he told me all about Eduardo.

Well, he cried, and I cried. I tried to comfort him, but I wasn't very good at it because there wasn't anybody there comforting *me*. I mean, Steven was the Man in the Cloud — he was my *Destiny*. I was sure of that. And I wanted Steven to be sure of it, too. I didn't know anything about Eduardo, really, but I knew the way he made Steven feel was no good for anybody. And I knew that *I* was the one Steven was supposed to be with. Eduardo was history; Steven and I were the *future*.

Steven said he had to be alone to think and went up on the highway to watch the cars go by. I was terrified that a car was gonna come by and pick him up and he would disappear. I was afraid it was because I wasn't wearing the Lucky Green Dress, so I put it on. I fought back the urge to go after him.

That night, for the first time, we didn't sleep with our arms around each other. In fact, we didn't sleep much at all. We just laid there with our backs to each other. As the sun was coming up, I dozed off just long enough for Steven to disappear. I woke up from a bad dream with a start. He was gone and his guitar was gone, too.

I climbed up to the highway, but he wasn't there. I looked both ways and could feel him traveling in the back seat of a car, going away from me. I started to get choked up; I looked into the sky for an answer, but the sky was clear and completely cloudless — there wasn't a single cloud in the sky. The sun was riding high in the sky and it was a beautiful day. I wished it wasn't so beautiful. I turned around to climb back down beneath the overpass to figure out what I was gonna do with myself, and when I did, I noticed a person running, *galloping* toward me, from the middle of the pumpkin field. It was Steven!

I ran down the side of the overpass and toward him. He had his guitar in one hand and something else clenched tightly in the other hand. He leaped over the wooden fence without slowing down and ran to me with the biggest, most beautiful smile on his face and threw his arms around me and spun me around — we almost fell into a mud puddle!

I said "*What?*"

He took a moment to calm down then told me to sit down with him. We sat around the burned out campfire. He laid his guitar on the ground but held his clenched fist carefully in front of him the whole time.

"Grandma Thayer always told me, 'You have to keep going out to the field 'til there's corn to bring in.' I never really understood what she meant by that until this morning when I was out walking around. I think I found the spot where you were stuck when I found you last Sunday. I wasn't looking for it; I was just walking around, you know, trying to sort everything out, but I just happened to look down, and I was standing right in front of a circle of pumpkin vines that had been pulled up by their roots. And when I looked, there was a flash of light on the ground in the middle of the vines. I bent over to see what it was, and it was this — " Steven held out his hand and slowly unrolled his fist and right in the middle of his muddy palm was a green rhinestone. He said, "'You have to keep going out to the field 'til there's corn to bring in.' The Lucky Green Dress brought me out into the pumpkin field to find you! *This* is the corn! *You* are the corn!"

I laughed, confused, and said, "*I'm* the corn?"

"Eduardo told me he loved me. That made me feel good — *he* made me feel good. When I didn't know what to do with my life, he suddenly appeared out of nowhere and made me feel good about doing nothing at all. But then, when it came time to do something, when it came time to do something besides lying in the field doing nothing, he disappeared.

"This morning, when I found this rhinestone out in the pumpkin field, I started thinking about everything you and I have done together in one short week — we've done a *lot* this week! And I realized two very important things. One...." he squeezed the rhinestone tightly and shook his fist at me, "I realized I wasn't running away from Eduardo. I was running toward you."

He smiled at me and I could barely breathe, my heart racing again. "And what's the other thing?"

He laughed and said, "I love you — I really do! I love you, I love you, I love you!!!"

✪✪✪

As we were eating breakfast, I heard church bells on the far side of the pumpkin field and I knew it was the Calvary Full-Gospel Church church bus arriving with the congregation onboard. I said, "Hey, Steven, ya wanna go to church?"

He said, "Okay."

We packed up everything and got dressed (I wore my Lucky Green Dress, of course), and at nine a.m. on the dot, we walked up to the Calvary Full Gospel Church.

The bus driver was very excited to see me; he'd found my backpack and kept it in the bus under the front seat in hopes of finding me. He introduced me to everybody he came across like we were old friends and I introduced Steven to them. His name was Cider, "Though I'm liquor-free now!" he told us. There were only about twenty-five people in the congregation, but that number nearly doubled when the preacher and the choir pranced in from outside singing a great big gospel song. (Uncle Joe would've been so jealous of the Calvary Full-Gospel Choir; their choir robes had *fringe* on them!) And I bet they were every bit as good as the Austin Angels Halleluia Heaven-Bound Gospel Choir who sang on the night that I was born.

Steven had never experienced such a spectacle — by the end of the day he said his face hurt from smiling. The preacher's name was Reverend Thadius T. Harding, III. When he preached, he seemed to sing every word, and he ended almost every one with an *"uh!"* His sermon was inspired by the storm that had passed through Circleville the previous week: he titled the sermon "Finding the Silver Lining." His energy and enthusiasm were very similar to my Daddy's; I couldn't wait to tell everybody that I'd found Daddy's northern counterpart.

Just before offering-time, Reverend Harding called on Cider to introduce Steven and me to the congregation. We stood out quite a bit — not so much because of the Lucky Green Dress, like ya might be thinking. Every woman in the congregation had on her best Sunday-go-to-meetin' dress. We stood out because we were the only white folks there. Reverend Harding asked us if we had anything we'd like to share with the Brothers and Sisters gathered there and I stood up. "Steven and I just wrote what we think is a pretty good gospel song, and we thought it'd be nice to try it out."

Steven gasped audibly and a couple of hushed whispers bounced around the congregation. But then the organist, a tall, thin woman in a slightly purple wig and a blue silk dress and matching hat jumped up and said, "Let 'em sing, Reveren' Hardin', let the white boys sing!"

The little church exploded with a lot of "Yeah!"s and "Amen!"s and "Halleluia!"s. Reverend Harding called Steven and me to the front of the church.

Steven nervously took out his guitar and strummed the first chord to "Heavenly Hoedown" and the organist added some frilly organ music. Steven looked at me, frightened, so I smiled at him and counted off "Heavenly Hoedown."

By the middle of the song, the whole church was singing along, adding harmonies and variations to the tune that Steven and I hadn't even thought of! We must've sung it through a dozen times. And while we did, the offering plate was passed around.

Reverend Harding closed the service with a prayer (he blessed Steven and me in it), and then after the "Amen"s said, "How's about we go out with a little more of that song our new young Brothers just taught us?!" The organist started up and the choir members clapped their hands and started marching around the pews, singing harmonies and dancing and smiling great big smiles. Everybody in the congregation stood up and joined in behind them, including Steven and me. Reverend Harding marched everybody out of the front doors and up the street to the city park for their weekly "Food for the Soul" picnic. They had chicken and ribs and potato salad and collard greens and sweet potatoes and coleslaw and biscuits and pork 'n' beans and chocolate bundt cake with homemade vanilla ice cream and Orange Crush. Steven and I ate real food for the first time in a long time and we got so full, we felt a little sick! We told everybody the *whole* story of our journeys. They were so impressed that they took up a special little offering to help us with our "missionary work" and ended up giving us an envelope with $250 in it.

At about two-thirty p.m., Steven and I went around to every man, woman, and child at the picnic and thanked them for their kindness and told them that we had to get a move on. Reverend Harding said, "Where are y'all headin' to?" Steven and I looked at each other and admitted that we hadn't really discussed it with each other.

Steven said, "I was on my way to New York City when I ran into Jay...."

I jumped in. "We're waiting for a sign of some sort."

Reverend Harding nodded seriously, then put an arm around each of us. "Well, gentlemen, maybe the sign you're seeking is here, in this park, in our church...."

At that moment, one of the children screamed, "Look! A rainbow!" Everybody looked toward the eastern sky, and there was the most beautiful, brilliant, *fully-formed* rainbow. There was a group, "Ahhh!"

I patted Reverend Harding on the back and nodded toward the rainbow, "No sir, I think it's right there!"

Reverend Harding laughed. "I think you're right about *that*, Brother Byrd! But we're gonna pray that the Good Lord brings y'all back to Calvary again sometime, you hear me?!" Steven and I said that was fair.

Reverend Harding's wife and several other women gave us a box full of food to take with us and Reverend Harding asked Cider to take us to Hopefull, the next town over (we found out later that because of something having to do with alcohol, Cider wasn't allowed to leave the city limits). As we drove out of the picnic area, the church bells bellowing out of the loudspeaker, all of the women stood in their places and waved hands and hankies at us and blew kisses, and the children chased after the bus pushing each other and laughing wildly. None of the men other than Reverend Harding stood up, but they all smiled and nodded their heads toward us. Steven and I sat in the front seat across from Cider, and we waved back at the wonderful people.

Cider didn't talk and seemed a bit nervous for the first few minutes we were traveling, so when we went over the overpass where Steven and I had met and lived for the past week, it was almost like Cider didn't exist at all. Steven and I looked at each other and smiled; we were both happier than we'd ever been in our lives.

Suddenly, Cider said, "New York City." He kinda rolled it around in his mouth. I don't think he was saying it to us; he was just saying it.

"Back where I come from, we call New York City the Big Apple Pie!" I told him.

"Huh? Oh? The Big Apple Pie?" He thought about it then added, "Yeah, yeah, yeah...." And then he started chuckling. Steven and I looked at each other and shrugged.

Twenty miles and forty-five minutes later, the Calvary Full-Gospel Church church bus came to a grinding halt on the side of the highway in front of a small green metal sign that said:

Wellcome to Hopefull, Ohio

I figured since there was no population listed that this was a pretty small town. About fifty yards beyond the sign was a shiny aluminum and glass bus station with a huge parking lot surrounding it and a really tall carport on one side (for the buses to park under when it rained, I figured).

Steven and I sat quietly in our seats, both of us thinking about the journeys behind us and wondering about the one ahead of us. Cider leaned forward onto the oversized steering wheel, peered out the windshield and took several deep breaths and then pointed up into the sky, "Y'all see that?" Steven and I leaned forward. He was pointing at the rainbow.

"Yeah," I told Cider, "That's our sign. We're gonna follow it to the Big Apple Pie, if that's where it leads us."

Cider said, "Wouldn't a map make it a little easier?"

Steven said, "Yeah."

Cider said, "They got maps in the bus station, I'm sure of that."

Steven said, "We'll probably get a map."

"No we won't! That rainbow appeared like a sign for us to follow it. What if there are some other important places we need to go on our *way* to the Big Apple Pie?"

Cider said, "Maybe you'll find a pot of gold." Steven and Cider laughed.

"You laugh now, but you'll see."

"I ain't gonna see nothin'," Cider said as he jiggled the bus into gear, "I'm goin' back to Circleville!"

Steven and I said goodbye and gathered up our instruments, backpacks, and the box of picnic food and climbed out of the bus.

Cider grinded the gears back and forth again and again from Drive to Reverse to turn around on the narrow Route 22. It made an awful noise and we wondered why he didn't just use the big, empty bus station parking lot to turn around — he took the fact that he couldn't drive the bus out of the city limits very seriously.

When he finally got it turned around, Cider opened the side window next to the steering wheel and pressed his face into it, the way he'd done when I first met him a week earlier. His voice was raspy and different, like he'd become a carnival fortune-teller all of a sudden. "Somewhere under that rainbow is the Big Apple Pie!" He pointed at the rainbow with his wide-open eyes.

I gave him a thumbs up sign and he gave me the "OK" sign and Steven just shook his head at me. I said, "You just wait and see!"

Part Three

Somewhere Under That Rainbow

Chapter Eleven

Godspeed, My Friends

They *did* have maps at the Hopefull Bus Station, usually, but — *surprise! surprise!* — the distributor had taken them all away just the day before because of a misprint (the outside covers didn't match the inside maps). The woman was very nice about it and said they should have the new ones in any minute, with any luck. Steven thought that was pretty funny, "with any luck." After we'd left the counter and sat in a couple of chairs attached in a row, he said, "Why doesn't your Lucky Green Dress help us get the maps here?" I pointed out the huge picture window overlooking the bus station parking lot, Route 22, the mountainous hills beyond that, and the sky above it all with the brilliant rainbow stretched across it like something out of the Bible. "There's our map, Steven."

"Are you serious?" he blurted out. "After we get out of Ohio, we have to go across Pennsylvania. Do you know how *wide* Pennsylvania is? And it's covered with mountains and forests. And then there's New Jersey. Jay, if we try to walk there, it'll take us months!"

"But the rainbow. We're supposed to follow the rainbow."

"I can't believe you're really serious," Steven said, sinking into his chair. "I'm exhausted."

"Well, I am serious. I'm serious because I'm sitting here next to a man I first saw in my Daddy's tent revival and followed him cross-country to Ohio — without a map."

Steven sighed. "You followed a *cloud*."

"Exactly."

"How about if we take a bus. Maybe it's a sign that Cider brought us to a bus station. We can keep an eye out of the windows and make sure we're still following the rainbow."

"But...." It was very hard talking sense to Steven at this point.

"*Please* can we take a bus," he pleaded.

"Well, okay. But only if you promise we'll get off and follow the rainbow if it takes us off of the bus's path."

"I promise."

"Do you swear?"

"*Yes!* Cross my heart and all of that." Steven went to the window to get tickets for the next bus to the Big Apple Pie. The woman told him the next bus should be there in half an hour, and the one after that at ten p.m.

The bus station was really nice. It looked brand new or completely renovated — or never used. Everything looked like it was from the 50s, and the chrome and linoleum sparkled like it'd never been touched.

We bought a couple of eight-ounce bottles of Coca-Cola from an old-fashioned top-load Coke machine and stared out the picture window at the rainbow while we drank. Steven said, "You know, it probably won't be there tomorrow."

I said, "I think we'll have to wait and see."

We finished our Cokes and bought two more (they only cost a quarter). A Greyhound bus with "NEW YORK CITY" over its windshield slowly topped the hill and Steven asked me to hold his Coke while he went to the bathroom.

The bus pulled into the station spurting and spewing a cloud of gray smoke out of its back end. It only got halfway into the parking lot before it died completely. The driver and a couple of the male passengers quickly hopped off and tossed all of the luggage from the belly of the bus onto the pavement away from the bus. A busload of senior citizens stepped carefully off of the bus, one at a time, most of them with hands over their mouths. Most of them walked around to the highway side of the bus to gaze upon the incredible rainbow. Others just stood looking at the men tossing the luggage. I didn't see any of them come into the building. But all of a sudden, out of nowhere, a sprightly little old lady was standing next to me, her reflection looking enough like my Daddy's Momma — my Mamaw — to startle me.

I gasped and turned toward her and she was startled by my being startled! "I'm sorry, but you look just like my Mamaw."

She said, "Don't apologize, she musta been a real fox!" I smiled and she snorted and punched me in the stomach playfully. I tried not to react, but she knocked the wind out of me. She said, "Who's the sodie fer — yer feller?" I held it out to her, unable to speak. "Fer Mamaw?" I nodded and she took Steven's Coke from me and guzzled it down in one continuous swallow, which gave me time to catch my breath.

She belched long and loud, then said, "Where'd ya git that purty green dress, baldy?" I told her that my Uncle Joe gave it to me because it was his Lucky Green Dress. She said, "Well, it ain't doin' him much good now, is it?!" She snorted again and I held my stomach tight for a second, then explained to her that he passed it on to me for luck, but she already knew that. She was teasing me. She said, "My name's Leona. Don't tell me yer name 'cause I'm just awful with names and I'll forget it anyhoo!"

Steven came out of the bathroom and said, "Get your stuff, the bus is here!"

Leona said, "Are you a *bat*? That bus is on fire. It ain't goin' nowhere."

She invited me to sit down so she could "talk at me," and that's exactly what she did! Steven tried to join in on our conversation, but Leona kept her back turned toward Steven, so he wandered off to see if he could find out anything about the bus.

Leona talked and talked and talked, and the more she talked, the more she reminded me of my Mamaw. Not because of what she said, but because of *how* she said it. Mamaw always had something funny to say about any situation, and she was always doing exciting stuff.

When I was ten, eleven, and twelve years old, I got to spend two weeks out of each summer on the farm with my Mamaw and Papaw. They had a tiny little farm in a tiny little town called Big Squaw, Texas — it's not too far from Huntsville, Texas, where the big state prison is, which was where we were on our tent revival circuit at the beginning of summer each year.

Daddy thought it would do me some good to spend some time on a farm where physical labor was the routine (not that putting up and taking down the tent revival every week was a piece of cake!). But Daddy didn't know his parents as well as he thought he did. They didn't make me work at all. They just liked having me hang around, doing whatever I wanted to do. (*It's only two weeks, and he's just a child!*) I mean, I did have chores to do, but they were pretty fun.

One thing I had to do was "see to" the earthworms. Mamaw was convinced that earthworms were gonna be the future of cooking that soybeans ended up being. (I didn't know this 'til my third year there.) She even had some recipes she was perfecting. Things like "No-Oatmeal Cookies" and "Earth Burgers," stuff like that. I never tasted any of 'em, of course, and Papaw just said she was crazy. He'd say, "Old woman's just crazy, *plain and fancy*."

But, like I said, all of this information didn't come to light 'til my third year there. The first night I was there, at age ten, she took me into the back part of the barn at dusk. We had to carry flashlights because what she was about to show me was "top secret." The back room of the barn smelled like the air smells right before it's gonna rain, and there along one wall were three brand new wooden trays, about four inches deep, five feet wide and two feet across, standing up on legs that made them come right below my chest and Mamaw's waist.

On a shelf above the trays were several Mason jars with "magic liquid" in them. (I found out later that the magic liquid was really just water.) Mamaw put her flashlight under her arm, unscrewed the lid on a mason jar and carefully splashed the water over the rich black dirt that filled the trays. I watched, mesmerized, unsure what we were doing, figuring this was another part of her elaborate vegetable garden, or thinking that maybe it had something to do with the pigs she kept in a pen up by the outhouse.

"Do you see that? Do you see that?" I didn't know what I was looking for, but wanted so badly to see something that I said yes before I even did. A moment or two later, the dirt started moving, and fleshy pink *fingers* sprang through the black crumbs. I gasped and Mamaw squealed.

The next evening when my chores were done, and every evening after that for the whole of my two-week stay, Mamaw put me in charge of sprinkling the magic liquid over the "little fellas," as she called them. For those two weeks, I just stared at the earthworms as they crawled through their world. I didn't touch them. Not that I was afraid of them, I was just worried that if I made contact, the magic spell would've been broken.

But that was when I was ten.

When the time came the next summer, at age eleven, for me to spend two more weeks on the farm, I barely said hello before I was asking about the earthworms. Of course, I was put in charge of them again. This time around, I talked to the little fellas. As soon as they popped their little heads to the surface, drawn up by the magic liquid, I said, "Howdy!" and I was sure they were wiggling their little heads (or tails) at me in an earthworm sort of greeting. They weren't just the little fellas anymore, they were my little friends.

My human friends were spread out over forty some-odd different towns. I would only see them once a year for a week or sometimes for just a couple of days. Sometimes, I would arrive in a town and the friend I'd had there the year before would be gone — just up and disappeared without a word — and I'd have to start all over again with somebody new in that town. But I had a feeling that the earthworms were always gonna be there, and I believed that Mamaw was always gonna be there, too.

Mamaw and I were *best* friends. We played lots of silly games that we made up. My favorite was watching Papaw think while he was sleeping. He would always fall asleep in his old chair, and Mamaw and I would sneak up on either side of him and stare into his ears, which had unusually large canals in them, and we could actually see his brain moving in there! Mamaw said she could even see what he was dreaming, and when he woke up one time and caught us and got mad, Mamaw said he was just feeling guilty for dreaming about that other girl again! Papaw called Mamaw a fool, but he didn't deny it, so Mamaw said that meant it was true, and she started chanting, "Roy is sweet for Ozelle! Roy is sweet for Ozelle!" Papaw got so mad, he chased Mamaw out of the house and into the middle of the muddy stinky pigpen with a broom!

After that, Papaw tried to keep me busy by myself so that I wouldn't get Mamaw in trouble. One day, he told me I oughta go out and name all the earthworms. It sounded like a real good idea, but I said I thought I'd better tag them, you know, so I'd be able to remember who was who and who I'd already named. Papaw thought that was a real good idea and said I was "smarter than my britches."

He whipped out his pocket knife and cut up a piece of paper into half-inch squares, and some twine into three-inch lengths, and he sharpened a stubby little pencil and sent me on my way.

I figured they would be surprised by the earliness of my visit this day, so I took an extra moment to announce my arrival before sprinkling the magic liquid over them. When I finally did, I picked up the first worm that surfaced, and, oh, was he a big fella! To my twelve-year-old eyes, he looked to be a foot long. I let him dangle through my fingers and squirm across my palm while I decided what his name should be. A dozen names came to my mind in an instant — all of them beginning with the letter "W" — but for some reason this guy looked like a "Warren." I laid Warren down on the dirt in his box while I scratched out his name on a little piece of paper, poked a hole in one corner of the paper with the pencil tip and fed the twine through the hole, careful not to tear it.

Warren thought I was done with him and had started back down into the dirt. I pulled him up and slid the twine under him and let the name tag fall to his side. I lifted up the two ends of the twine so that Warren was saddled in the middle. Now, being that at that point I had spent my whole life in the back seat of a Rambler station wagon and never got to be a Boy Scout, I admit I'm not an award-winning knot-maker. But I had no idea that a simple three-inch piece of twice could be so dangerous. I don't know what I did wrong. I don't know what I did at all. It must've been a "slip knot" that I'd made, because I certainly did slip, and suddenly Warren was lying on the soil in front of me in two pieces.

I ran out of the barn, across the yard, and into the kitchen crying. Mamaw ran to me and hugged me into her flour-dusted apron. She held me long and hard 'til I finally gathered up enough strength to tell her what had happened, and once I did, she said, "Shoot, Jay Byrd! I tell you what, it'll take a whole lot more than a piece a'twine to kill one of those little fellas!" She took me over to the kitchen counter where she was making her "No-Oatmeal Cookies." I thought she was gonna comfort me with a cookie — and she probably *was* — but fortunately she told me what was in them before she offered one to me.

I didn't know if I should be relieved that I hadn't killed Warren or if I should be horrified that Mamaw was gonna kill him soon. She told me that sometimes she'd just about put them in the oven when she'd notice some of the cookies still movin', and she'd have to take 'em back out and chop 'em up some more!

Well, I'm getting *way* off track now!

Mamaw

Papaw said that she and me were quite a pair,
We stayed up late and hardly slept a wink;
But when Papaw fell asleep in his favorite chair,
We'd stare into his ears and watch him think!
You know, the sun was Mamaw's best friend,
She talked to him and said that he would answer;
She'd ask him what was just around the bend,
Then she'd tell me he said, "Music for the dancers."

✪✪✪

The ten o'clock bus came, but there wasn't enough room for all of us. Leona got on it. I followed her out to see her off and she offered me her seat. I told her I couldn't go anywhere without Steven and she said, "Of course not, silly me! Taa-taa!" and then she was gone.

Those of us who were left behind bedded down as best we could in the bus station with the promise of another bus to arrive in the morning. Steven and I probably would've hit the road on foot that night, but it was sprinkling, and it did so all night long. Most of the older folks drank coffee out of a 50s-style machine and sat in the chairs and tried to stay awake all night, but Steven and I were tired, so we found a corner and slept under the flourescent lights amid the chatter (and the snores of the seniors who just couldn't hold out).

The next morning, another bus came, just as planned, with plenty of room for all of us, but we didn't get on it. When I woke up, Steven was standing at the big window, gazing out at the sky. I walked over to him to get some quarters for a Coke and he said, "It's still there. I can't believe it." I looked up at the rainbow, as brilliant as ever, waiting patiently for us.

I smiled and said, "Now do you believe me?"

He said, "I guess I *have* to!"

We agreed to stay on the highway as much as possible. The box of food lasted about a week, which was just long enough, and we always managed to find a roadside rest stop or a covered picnic area to hide under each night, because each and every night it rained. But each and every day, we woke up to see the same rainbow shining in a clear blue sky, leading us along our way.

That is, until June 7 rolled around. Early the day before, we were feeling particularly confident and turned off of the highway and onto the beautiful hilly landscape. But nightfall came a lot faster than we expected it, and we were sure it was gonna rain, so we frantically chased the setting of the sun to find some sort of shelter to sleep under. All we could find was a big old oak tree on top of a hill in the middle of a pasture of sheep. I told Steven as we bedded down that my Lucky Green Dress would protect us from getting wet. I hung it on a low branch of the oak tree and it flapped in the wind as the cool breeze ahead of the rain blew through the countryside.

But it didn't rain — the Lucky Green Dress *did* protect us! It was a mixed blessing, though. I was up before Steven. I put on the Lucky Green Dress and stretched to meet another beautiful summer day. Rolling hills and old-fashioned wooden fences sectioned off pieces of land all around us. White ribbons of smoke from hidden chimneys framed the sky, making it all the more obvious. I ran down the hill a little ways so that I could see the whole sky. The rainbow was *gone*!

I woke Steven up in a panic. He came to slowly, then jumped up disoriented when I started chanting, "It's gone! It's gone!"

"*What?*"

"The rainbow! It's gone. We're lost!"

He rubbed his eyes, a little perturbed at me, and said, "Don't worry, we'll find our way somehow." He put on his glasses and looked around. "We're in Pennsylvania."

"How do you know that?"

"Look. Amish people." He pointed to a dirt road off in the distance. On the dirt road was a horse and buggy carrying five matching doll-like people, all of them dressed in black. Two of them were bigger than the other three, and these two sat in the front of the buggy and the three little ones sat behind them. Behind that horse and buggy was another horse and buggy with two large doll-like people, and four little people, and behind that one, another and another and another. Shortly, the landscape had a solid line of horses and buggies traveling across it like a parade of ants. The last horse and buggy carried just one big person, and it was bigger than the others but was piled high with wooden benches; they shone like gold in the sunlight. "Amish people live in Pennsylvania," Steven said.

I quickly ducked behind the tree and warned Steven to do the same. He laughed and said, "What are you doing?"

I whispered, "They're *witches*! They'll *get* you!"

Steven laughed at me. "Where do you get such silly ideas? Sometimes you act just like my Grandma Thayer!"

You probably guessed already that my sisters had told me lies about Amish people. Like many of the other stories my sisters told me, I had no actual knowledge of or experience with Amish people — there aren't any Amish folks in Okey-Dokey, Texas. But our Momma's great granddaddy was born into an Amish family in Pennsylvania. He ran away from home when he was a teenager, changed his name, and ended up in Louisiana, where he lived near a community of folks who practiced voodoo.

Steven told me what he knew about the Amish (*They don't believe in buttons!*) while we finished off the last of the food (two chicken legs, one dinner roll with honey, two ears of fried corn, and a mushed up pile of orange stuff in tinfoil that used to be a piece of pumpkin pie). While we both sucked at the chicken bones to get every last morsel of meat off of them, we decided that we would knock on one of those Amish folks' doors in hopes of getting directions, and possibly a hot bath and a meal.

When we got to the dirt road where the line of Amish folks with their horses and buggies had passed earlier, there was a lone horse and buggy coming up over the hill toward us with a man at the reins. I waved as the horse and buggy approached and the farmer pulled the reins and said a soft "whoa" and stopped right beside us. He was an odd-looking but handsome man, dressed in a simple black suit, boots, and a hat. His small beard outlined his jaw and made it and him look very *square*. He looked us over for a brief moment — well, he mostly looked me over, me and my Lucky Green Dress, but that's exactly what I wanted him to do, 'cause right away the magic of the Lucky Green Dress started working on him!

He smiled a friendly smile and said, "Hello. I am Jacob Yoder, a farmer up just north of Holmesville." His accent was odd, too.

I introduced Steven and me and Jacob promptly invited us to dinner and we happily accepted. We climbed aboard and sat behind Jacob and none of us said another word until we reached the Yoder Farm. Jacob stopped the buggy in front of a barn. He helped me down out of the buggy and then took the ukulele case by the handle and handed it to me.

"An instrument?"

"Yes sir, it's a baritone ukulele!"

"The children would love to hear some music, I am sure of that!"

At that moment, a pretty woman in a long black dress and a white bonnet walked out of the farmhouse next to the barn wiping her hands on a towel. Jacob introduced his wife Elizabeth to us, calling us English folks. I said, "Well, actually, I'm from Okey-Dokey, Texas, and Steven's from Kornflake, Indiana.

Elizabeth lit up at the mention of Indiana. "The Schlabachs live in Indiana!"

I said, "But Steven said you people all live in Pennsylvania." As soon as I said it, I could feel my face turning red, and I knew better than to look at Steven.

The Yoders laughed at me and Jacob said, "Do you think you are in Pennsylvania? This is Holmes County, my friends! Ohio."

Steven was embarrassed. "I'm sorry, we really just wanted to stop and see if you could give us directions back to the highway. We're on our way to New York City."

"The Big Apple Pie," I interrupted. "But the rainbow is gone."

Elizabeth didn't seem to hear me. She moved toward

Steven. "Oh, please, you must be hungry. We don't want to keep you from your journey, but please do stay through dinner at least. The children will want to have met you."

Jacob piped in, "And they play music."

Elizabeth turned back toward the house as if the matter was closed. "Oh, the children *love* music."

I looked at Steven and we shrugged and smiled at each other.

Supper was to consist of Bova Shankel (it's like a vegetable pot pie), broccoli and cauliflower salad, applesauce, and raisin and raspberry half-moons with vanilla ice cream for dessert, just about all of it raised, grown, and handmade right there on the Yoder Farm. Steven and I sat at the kitchen table drinking instant coffee and talking about dinner while Elizabeth prepared it and Jacob washed up before going to get the children from playing something called Andy-over with the neighborhood children. I think she was about to tell us what Andy-over was when two little girls came running and screaming frantically through the farmhouse into the kitchen.

"Mommy! Mommy!"

Elizabeth squatted down to them, but as soon as they caught sight of Steven and me, neither of them could speak. Elizabeth gently but anxiously shook each girl by the arm and said, "What is it, children? Heidi! Keri! Where is Jeremy?"

The older one tried to speak but looked over at me and was struck silent again. The younger one started crying.

Elizabeth looked over at us with a frustrated smile, and about that time, a man who looked a lot like Jacob arrived at the kitchen door and said softly, "Elizabeth."

She brought him in and he didn't even look at us once while they discussed what had happened. Jeremy was the oldest Yoder child; he was fourteen and had broken his arm playing Andy-over. He was at the doctor's house getting a cast put on his arm.

Jacob came into the room rubbing his hands together and

the two girls ran to him.

"Daddy! Daddy!" They both told him stuttering versions of the story the man had just told Elizabeth.

Jacob went with the man to see after Jeremy while Elizabeth and the girls and Steven and I stayed at home.

After a bowl of ice cream, the girls started warming up to us and Keri, the little one — she was five and Heidi was eight — even came over and asked about the rhinestones on my Lucky Green Dress and why I didn't have any hair. When she asked about my hair, Elizabeth called out after her, "*Keri!*" and Heidi laughed.

"That's okay, Mrs. Yoder." I told the girls the story of Cousin Mandy and the ringworms, which they loved.

Jacob returned with Jeremy, whose right arm was in a cast. Heidi and Keri ran to him and he showed them the cast and smiled at them. Jeremy looked up to his father and said, "I'm sorry," and his father patted him on the back and smiled and said, "We'll figure it out, son."

Over dinner, Heidi and Keri recounted the events of the day that led up to Jeremy breaking his arm, with differing views about certain facts. When it seemed like their conversation was moving toward a disagreement, Jacob said very quietly, "Children."

They both said, "Yes, sir," in unison and moved on to a more agreeable subject. Jeremy didn't talk much at all, he just watched and listened and smiled.

As soon as the last bite of half-moons (which are just like turnovers) was swallowed, Elizabeth stood with her plate and said, "Alright. We still have the chores to do, and we're behind schedule now."

Everybody stood and took their plates and cups to the sink. Steven and I followed suit, and Steven said, "Can we do the dishes for you?"

Elizabeth took Steven's dishes out of his hands, "Oh, no, you are our guests!"

Steven said, "Please let us help with something."

And so they did. Jacob asked if we could help Jeremy with his chores and we agreed. "The milk house has to be cleaned because the milk inspector is coming in the forenoon tomorrow."

We didn't know what that meant so we didn't think much of agreeing to do it. Jacob asked Elizabeth to gather up some work clothes that would fit us. Elizabeth sews all of the Yoder's clothes and she makes extra clothes of varying sizes to sell at the neighborhood yard sales that take place once a month. She barely glanced at us and came back with two sets of clothes that fit Steven and me perfectly.

Jeremy was our supervisor in the milk house. He didn't mind telling us what to do, but he wasn't bossy; he just knew what had to be done and he went about telling us each thing to do. He said if we worked fast enough, we'd have time to play ball at the schoolyard in the evening after family devotional. Steven said we'd have to be getting on the road that evening, and I agreed with him and told Jeremy that we weren't much at ball-playing anyway, but told him we'd still work fast so that he could go. Jeremy raised his cast toward me as a rebuttal.

Even if we had been professional ball players and even if we didn't have a journey to travel, I don't think Steven and I would've been able to play ball (or anything for that matter) that evening; we were beat by the time the milk house was clean. The Yoders seemed to take it all in stride, though. While we were doing that one job — the two of us doing the job of one fourteen year old — the girls were cleaning the guest room and folding the laundry in the basement, Jacob tilled a couple of acres for planting corn, Elizabeth put a Martin house on a pole in the yard and planted flowers around its base in a circle, *and* she was cooking all the while. As soon as the dinner dishes were washed and dried and put away, she made a batch of chocolate chip cookies and while they baked, she made some molasses cookie batter to be refrigerated and baked the next day. Oh, and did I mention that there isn't a drop of electricity on the whole farm?

Everything was planned down to the minute. When we finished cleaning the milk house, we sat with Jeremy for less than ten minutes on a broken-down old fence 'til the sun touched down on a particular hill in Mount Hope, off in the horizon and Jeremy said it was time to go in for devotional. Every Sunday evening at dusk the Yoders sit around a kerosene lamp and read passages from the Bible and talk about what they are thankful for, and then they pray holding hands. On this particular evening, they were all thankful that Jeremy wasn't hurt worse than he was.

After the devotional hour, Elizabeth sent the kids up to bathe while she went to prepare supper, telling them that we were gonna play music for them before bedtime. Heidi and Keri went running and squealing to bathe first and Jeremy went to his room to take a nap while he waited his turn for the bath.

Before Steven and I had a chance to get up from the coffee table to go change out of the borrowed clothes, Jacob reached out toward us and asked for our "kind assistance." There were several tasks around the farm that had to be done in the next week because of different inspections that were gonna take place, and most of them either required Jeremy's assistance or were the complete responsibility of Jeremy. Jacob told us that he believed we had been led there by God to help them.

Steven said, "I don't think we can stay here for a whole week."

"Oh, no. Not a week. He is just a little boy; you are both men. We can do what needs to be done in two or three days." He said that we would be clothed and fed and we would be allowed to join in the communion of his family and neighbors and he said it in the same way that Elizabeth had decided we were staying for dinner.

Of course, I kinda thought that maybe Jacob was right, maybe we *had* been led there for some reason (after all, the rainbow was gone), but I was sure Steven had his own thoughts, and I figured they didn't include us helping out on an Amish farm. So, you can just imagine how surprised I was when I turned to him and he was smiling and nodding his head.

"We can help out for a couple of days."

I tell you what, nobody'll ever be able to convince me that the Lucky Green Dress doesn't have special powers!

That first night and every night except for Tuesday night (when the children had Bible Devotion at a neighbor's house), we sang songs for the Yoders. We taught them the choruses and they joined in, timidly at first, but more and more confidently as the week went by. They also sang us some of the German songs they sing in church, and we tried to sing along, but I don't think I could tell you what the songs were.

And boy, oh, boy, did we get fed! It seems like every time we turned around, Elizabeth was setting the table for another meal, or placing snacks out on the coffee table or on a bench in the barn or wherever we were. We had spaghetti, chicken, hamburgers, hot dogs, hot ham and cheese sandwiches, meatloaf, beef with macaroni and cheese, veal sandwiches; rhubarb squares, stuffed creamed mushrooms, mashed potatoes, macaroni salad, potato salad, corn, green beans, pickles, peas, fresh garden salad; peaches and cottage cheese, apple fritters, lemon angel-food cake, apple dumplings, raspberry cheesecake, Rice Krispie treats, root-beer floats, struesel cake bars, popcorn, cookies, pie, and a different kind of bread every day. But we didn't gain a pound 'cause we worked *hard.* We milked the cows, we fed the cows, we ground up the feed, we hauled manure, we washed the milkers, we washed the dumping station, we washed the buggy *and* the horse, we washed the laundry, we ironed the clothes, planted flowers, sprayed the fields, mowed the lawn, put the hay in the barn, hunted mushrooms, put up a new fence, replaced a rotting beam in the barn, mowed the graveyard, cleaned windows (not just the Yoders, but Elizabeth's mother's, too), and we cleaned out the machinery shed. Every time we came up for air, Jacob was right there, putting us to work on another job. The days flew by and we lost all sense of purpose and where we were planning to go and all of that. Steven and I fell in love with the children and Elizabeth and Jacob made us feel like we were a part of the family.

Friday morning, June 12, we woke up at the usual time of five-fifteen a.m., but it was raining. I whispered to Steven that maybe we'd finally get some rest. Steven said, "They'll probably make us work anyway!" We laughed and then he said, "What we need to do is to get back on the road."

It was the first time I'd thought about our journey since we'd arrived. We decided that as soon as the rain stopped, we'd have to say our goodbyes and get on our way. We fell back asleep and Elizabeth let us sleep in while she and the girls cleaned the rest of the house. Jacob and Jeremy had gone into town.

The rain continued late into the afternoon, and it finally stopped while we were sitting around the living room singing church songs with the girls. We ate lunch without Jacob or Jeremy, and, after lunch, we went into the yard to help milk the cows. Steven and I promised each other that that would be our last task on the farm. We hadn't even brought ourselves to tell Elizabeth yet; in fact, we had no idea how we were gonna go about it.

But the answer came to us. When the four of us came out of the milk house the girls squealed, "Look at the rainbow!"

Elizabeth smiled and said, "That is God's promise, children."

They both nodded. "Uh-huh."

Steven was giving me a kind of odd look and I laughed at him. Elizabeth asked what was funny and I said, "Somewhere under that rainbow is the Big Apple Pie."

Elizabeth became serious. "You are leaving."

The girls screamed out, "Noooo!" and hugged our waists.

Elizabeth said, "Children."

We told her that we had to and she said she understood and said, "That will make Jacob sad."

Steven and I went out by the cornfield and sat on the fence that we had helped build and looked out at the rainbow. Steven shook his head and said, "It's weird, isn't it?"

"You mean the rainbow? I don't think it's weird at all. It's a sign."

He looked at me and chuckled. "Okay, Moses."

"*What?*"

Before long, the familiar figures of Jacob and Jeremy were coming toward us on their horse and buggy, directly under the arc of the rainbow. I said, "The best way to do it is to just tell him as soon as he gets here."

Steven agreed. And so we did.

"Jacob, do you see that rainbow in the sky," I asked.

"It is most beautiful."

"Somewhere under that rainbow is the Big Apple Pie."

Jacob shook his head slowly for a long time, then said, "I understand. We knew you would be going soon. But can your journey wait 'til tomorrow?" Come to find out, they were planning a party in our honor for that very night! We had met lots of their neighbors and friends that week and they wanted to honor us to show their appreciation.

"Well, we can't leave if y'all're gonna throw us a party!"

✪✪✪

The party was actually more like an Amish church service. It was held at the Hershberger's farmhouse. Abraham and his son Jonas had helped us help Jacob build the fence around the new part of his cornfield. We had met several of the women and children at the yard sale the day before and some of the other men at the general store. Of course, we didn't remember any of their names except for the Hershbergers. Jacob re-introduced us to everybody.

There were three ministers taking part in the service; I thought this was special for us, but Jeremy said they always have three or four ministers at church service. We sat around the Hershbergers barn on the beautiful handmade benches we had seen from the top of the hill. Everybody sang German songs — Steven and I kinda joined in — while the three ministers went up into a loft to council and pray over things. When they returned, the first minister, Brother Yutzy, told us what they had talked about upstairs (which included the arrival of the two English fellows — Steven and me), and then they prayed for us. Their praying was very simple and quiet, completely different from the way folks pray in my Daddy's tent revival! Brother Yutzy prayed and everybody agreed with him under their breath, their eyes shut tight. The service was so quiet, I could hear the soft clucking of chickens from outside, and an occasional cow or lamb noise, too.

Next, the main preacher came up. I thought his name was very appropriate: Christian Weaver. Brother Weaver made a comment that since this was a celebration of their English friends, he wouldn't preach too long of a sermon and several of the women laughed (I figured that meant Brother Weaver was long-winded like my Daddy). The sermon was taken from the thirteenth chapter of John in the New Testament of the Bible, which deals with Jesus washing the feet of his disciples and telling them to do so with their brethren. Before we knew what was happening, the people around us were preparing for a communal foot-washing, and it was mine and Steven's feet they wanted to wash! Jacob and Elizabeth took us aside and told us that some of the men in the community had had some concerns about us living with them, and the ministers felt that they should all humble themselves to us as servants in order to overcome their fears and reservations and to accept us as we were.

And so they washed our feet — about twenty times! Jacob and Elizabeth went first, I guess to ease us into the situation, then the other people we had met that week. They worked their way down through everybody who was at the party, except for the children. It was really weird, but everybody had such gentle faces, we couldn't help being drawn into it. With our feet squeaky clean and back in our boots, the third preacher, Brother Zook, appeared at the pulpit end of the barn and led everybody in another German song, and then he prayed again, and then we all went inside for the food. It was a great party; we got home at nearly eleven o'clock at night, which was really late for the Yoders and had become really late for us, too.

We left in the "forenoon" of Saturday, June 13. There was nothing emotional about our departure. We pulled them each away from their chores long enough for a quick goodbye and then Jacob took us to the end of the dirt road where we had met him, to where the dirt road came to a paved road. He told us to follow that road north for about a mile and we would likely come to the highway.

I felt like saying, "You mean just follow that rainbow?" because of course it had returned that morning to lead us on our way. But I just said, "Goodbye, Jacob."

Jacob said, "Godspeed, my friends."

Steven and I walked one direction on the paved road and Jacob went the other direction. He was on his way to his sister's farm to pick up his nephew Duane to help out on the Yoder Farm 'til Jeremy's arm got better.

Every Morning When I Rise

Sometimes I think the road I'm on is short,
And every sign is pointing to the end;
There's nothing I can do but close my eyes and wait;
At times like these, I reach for you again.

Chapter Twelve

Firecracker, Firecracker, Boom! Boom! Boom!

There's a little cheer my sisters used to chant in the back seat of the Rambler sation wagon that we were confined to for the first thirteen years of my life. It went like this:

Firecracker, firecracker, coming soon;
Firecracker, firecracker, boom! boom! boom!

It was a cheer complete with hand signals, and it took place at the beginning of a summer thunderstorm.

When the lightning flashed, Rose Anne and Deana would give each other a signal with their eyes, and they would use their most devious voices and say, "Firecracker, firecracker, coming soon...." The anticipation was awful and exciting at the same time, but finally, the thunder would sound and they would chant, "Firecracker, firecracker, boom! boom! boom!" and each "boom!" would be accented with a slug on my arm or leg from both sides.

The three of us would explode with laughter and Momma would often look back at us with an approving smile. (I guess they were happy, too, because a thunderstorm always meant a mandatory rest stop.) Over the years, though, the "boom! boom! booms!" got more and more accented, to the point where it was more a game for just the two of them than for all three of us.

The last time the complete cheer was ever chanted in the Rambler, the "booms!" were so hard that I started crying, and the next couple of times Rose Anne and Deana chanted the first line of the cheer, Daddy gave a stern, "Girls!" and that was the end of that, and the game disappeared into our history.

✪✪✪

After Steven and I left the Yoder Farm, we wandered along the highway for most of the rest of the month of June, hitchhiking a little and walking a lot. This highway was a lot smaller and less inhabited than the one that had led us to the Yoders. We barely managed to stay dry because it rained every night. Every sunset, we made ourselves a shelter out of whatever we could conjure up, slabs of rocks, moss-covered tree limbs, and, only occasionally, picnic tables.

One day, we woke up to find the rainbow way off of the highway. It seemed to be calling us — or mocking us — just beyond a thick grove of trees, much farther north than the highway seemed to be taking us. It took me a long time to convince Steven that we should leave the highway behind, again, and head off into the hills of Pennsylvania to continue following it, particularly after what had happened the last time we did that. Finally, he said, "We're not gonna stop at anybody's house, no matter *how* hungry we get." I promised.

Of course, Steven was a lot more prepared for living in the forest than I was. It gets dark under those trees way before it gets dark outside of the forest, and it gets a whole lot darker in there, too. And the noises that a forest makes are unlike any noises I'd experienced so far in my journey. Wild animals and weird wisps of wind and tree branches rubbing together. Every little noise I heard, I'd say, "What was that?" and Steven would tell me, if he could. Sometimes he didn't know, so he'd just tell me it was "a bug or something," but that only made it worse. I figured a bug would have to be pretty big to be making a noise that loud, and pretty ugly to be making such a scary noise!

We were too deep into the forest by the end of the first day to turn back — I was too proud to admit what a horrible mistake I'd made — and when we woke up the next morning, of course we couldn't see a rainbow because we couldn't see the sky because we were in the middle of a *forest*! We didn't know which way was which. Half of the time we were trying to keep going forward, and the other half of the time we were trying to find our way back the way we came in. At first, we thought things were kinda funny — "Oh, there's that boulder again!" — but we stopped seeing the humor when we saw the boulder for the *umpteenth* time.

Steven did his best to find food for us to eat, but he wasn't familiar with a lot of the things we found, so he was afraid for us to eat it. Once we saw some deers eating berries; we chased them away and ate all the berries on the bush, even though they were bitter and gave us stomach aches.

Every day was a little hotter than the day before it — which was a surprise to me, since my sisters had convinced me that it snowed all year long north of Oklahoma. There were lots of springs, so we had plenty of water to drink, but we were so hungry, the water didn't taste very good. Every day, we walked and walked and walked, hardly saying two words to each other — one look expressed all of our misery to each other. And each night, we'd plop down wherever we were as soon as the forest faded to black and just go to sleep right there, hoping we'd wake up to find ourselves at the edge of the forest.

We finally emerged from the forest on July 3. We didn't know it was July 3 until it was July 4, but that's another story. On the morning of July 3, I heard weird breathing noises in my sleep. Only they weren't in my sleep. They were *real* weird breathing noises. I sat bolt upright and discovered that we were just a few yards from a field full of camels — snorting, slobbering, heavy-breathing camels! I had gotten somewhat accustomed to strange noises in the forest, but this was completely different. And there was a bad smell, too. There was a fence about five yards from where Steven and I had plopped down, and the camels were just beyond that. I shook Steven awake and without opening his eyes he muttered, "What."

"Camels."

"What?" He sat up slowly, rubbing his eyes, put on his glasses and looked. Sure enough, there they were. Steven saw them too. They were in a large, fenced-off pasture on top of a hill. In the distance were more hills. "Camels," he repeated after me. "We must be hallucinating."

"Do you think?"

"Well, we haven't eaten in *days....*"

"I'm gonna find out." I stood up. My head spun a little, but I maintained my balance. Some of the animals took a step back, all of them kept their eyes glued on me as I inched toward them.

"Be careful."

Each step I took forward, they took a step backward as a group. When I got to the fence, I squeezed the barbed wire in my hand. "The fence is real."

Steven said, "Well, that's a relief — we must be getting *somewhere.*"

"Maybe we walked all the way to Arabia."

"We could have!" We laughed for a minute, then I started to step through the fence. The camels jumped back a little. Steven said, "What are you doing?"

"I wanna make sure we're not hallucinating."

"Be careful, Jay. I'm serious."

I boldly walked toward the camels, my hand outstretched. Just as I got to one and almost touched it, the whole lot of them scurried away. Steven screamed, "Look out!" But he was too late. A camel had snuck up behind me and stuck his head in my rear end and easily lifted me up and tossed me to the ground. The others took his cue and circled around me: I started getting a little nervous.

"Steven?"

"Yes."

"They're real."

"I see."

"And I'm trapped."

Steven told me to stay put — which was kind of a silly thing to say, since I was completely surrounded by camels now. He stood outside of the fence and started making barking noises at the camels, trying to get their attention off of me. It didn't work. He threw a stick toward me and it hit one of them on the behind, which made him very mad. He spit at me, and all of them started rocking to and fro. I screamed out, "Help!"

Steven said, "I don't know how to help!"

"I'm not hollering to you, I'm hollering to the Lord, to the Lucky Green Dress, to anybody. *Help!*"

Steven joined in, "Help!"

Suddenly, out of nowhere, there was a *Bang!* It echoed over the hills and the camels took off running in every direction. Another *Bang!* Steven called out to me, very serious now. I ran to him. We looked all around and finally spotted an old man with a long gray beard and a pointy hat running along the fence toward us, and he had a shotgun! Steven screamed, "We gotta get outta here!" He handed me my backpack and instrument over the fence, then grabbed his own and started to make his way through the barbed wire.

I said, "Aren't you going the wrong way?"

He said, "We gotta go *that* way." He pointed to the far side of the field, past a flurry of angry and scared camels. Up above it all was a glimmer of the rainbow. A chill ran down my spine. I guess we'd been going in the right direction all along. I looked toward the little old man with the gun; he was running at us. Steven was right; if we ran back into the forest, we might never find our way back again.

"Hurry!" I helped him through the fence and we shot across the hoof-beaten ground. The man didn't shoot again, but he got close enough so that we could hear his high-pitched little voice screaming angry words at us. At the bottom of the hill was a stream. We jumped over it without even slowing down, and then we came to another fence. I tried to bound over it, but one of my boot tips caught on it and I flipped in midair and fell with a thud. (It was a good thing I had on the Lucky Green Dress because the ground I landed on was soft and moist, and it didn't hurt at all.) I was so relieved, I started laughing. Steven kept yelling, "Are you alright? Are you alright?" but I couldn't answer him because I couldn't talk because I was laughing so hard.

We ran up the next hill, and there on top of it was a broken down John Deere tractor with grass and weeds growing up all around it. We ran to the other side of the tractor and fell to the ground. I rolled on my back to catch my breath while Steven watched the man jump up and down like a cartoon character on top of the hill we'd just come from.

Then a thunderous *kaboom!* sounded from the sky and the man disappeared the way he came from. Steven glanced at me, panting, and we burst out laughing, exhausted but exhilarated. We went over the episode again and again 'til our exhaustion caught up with us, then we dragged ourselves to the big back tire of the tractor and sat there with our eyes closed.

I looked up into the sky and said, "Thanks for saving us!" And as if in response, a distant thunder boom sounded.

We let our thoughts wander, not even noticing that the rainbow had faded and the sky was turning a glorious shade of greenish-gray. A summer storm was coming! A flash of lightning and boom of thunder brought me out of my dream state. I had wandered back nearly fifteen years to the backseat of the Rambler station wagon. With the next flash of lightning, I said, "Firecracker, firecracker, coming soon...." Steven opened his eyes and looked at me. "Huh?" I held up a hand and waited for the thunder, then said, "Firecracker, firecracker, boom! boom! boom!" and I slugged him on the arm three times.

"Ow! Ow! *Ow!*" I apologized and told him about my sisters' little chant. He closed his eyes again and laid his head back on the tractor tire, rubbing his arm. I looked out at the countryside before us, and two hills away was a huge glazed donut, just standing there.

"Steven, a donut."

He said, "Jay, don't even talk about food."

"No, look. A big glazed donut."

"What?" He opened his eyes. "Where?"

"There."

He saw it, too. "Oh my god, we're *definitely* hallucinating!"

A flash of lightning and crash of thunder hit somewhere very nearby, bringing Steven and me to our feet, our arm hairs standing at attention. I said, "We might as well oughta go find out!" We jumped up and started running toward the donut. In my head I imagined us in some kind of a children's storybook and I hoped that we'd be able to munch on the big donut for many days — maybe even move *into* it! When we topped the first hill, we noticed that it was raining on the donut but not on us.

Steven said, "It's gonna get all soggy! Hurry!" He ran down the hill and up the next like a madman, I followed after him as fast as I could. When we topped the next hill, the rain was coming down hard all around us and it felt great. Halfway up the next hill, just across a little highway, was a little pink and green restaurant surrounded by eighteen wheelers, with the big glazed donut on its roof and a flashing neon sign beneath it:

donut
dinette

The rain got increasingly harder as we crossed the highway, ran up the front steps of the diner and through the front door. The door slamming behind us echoed loudly through the diner where the only other sound was the sizzling bacon and eggs on the grill. The place was filled with big hairy truck drivers, and they had all stopped mid-sentence and mid-bite to turn and stare at us standing just inside the front door.

A skinny woman with a big pile of hair and lots of makeup and jewelry popped up from behind the counter holding a five-gallon jar of mayonnaise in one arm and a five-gallon jar of mustard in the other. She said, "Sorry, folks, the barn dance was *last* night!" The diner erupted with truck driver laughter. Steven and I just stood there, trying to catch our breath and dripping a big puddle of rain at the front door, not sure what to do and too delirious to do anything at all.

When the laughter died down, we realized that somebody was calling out to us. "I *said*, over here." On the far right side of the restaurant, a monstrous guy in a sleeveless Harley-Davidson Motorcycles T-shirt with tattoos on his arms hiding behind curly red hairs was skooching out of a booth, revealing the only other woman in the place besides the waitress. This woman looked just like him, complete with the sleeveless Harley-Davidson T-shirt, except that her arms weren't hairy and the hair on her head was bright green, the same color as my Lucky Green Dress! The guy motioned us over. "My old lady wants to know where you got that dress!" Everybody laughed some more, but the guy and the green-haired woman kept smiling. "I'm serious. That's our favorite color." We walked past many booths with the greasy-faced truckers looking at us out of the corners of their eyes, all the way to the back of the diner, to the smiling table.

The man squeezed into the booth next to the woman and pointed at the seats across from them. After we sat and everyone realized he wasn't gonna hurt us (I guess), the noise of the restaurant slowly returned to a normal level — clanking silverware on plates, ice water being poured, truck driver conversations, and outbursts of laughter.

The guy introduced his "old lady" to us as "Sam" and himself as "Bug."

Sam said, "His real name is Kim, but he hates it when people call him that!" Bug groaned.

I said, "Is Bug your stage name?"

He gave me an odd look. "They call me Bug because I can flip a Volkswagen Bug single-handedly. But I didn't invite you over here to talk about us. I wanna know where you got the balls to wear a dress in the Donut!"

I said, "Well, it's my Lucky Green Dress. My Uncle Joe gave it to me when I left Okey-Dokey, Texas, my hometown, to bring me luck."

"Your lucky dress, huh?"

"Yes sir."

"Well, buddy, it's your lucky day, then, 'cause we're gonna buy you guys breakfast! Whattya say to that?"

"I say, 'Where's the menu?'!"

Bug ordered for us. Waffles, western omelettes, hash browns, fresh fruit bowls, whole wheat toast, coffee, and fresh-squeezed orange juice. Bug and I talked a lot and Sam and Steven stayed quiet for the most part.

As it turned out, though, we weren't just lucky because we got a place to sit in "the Donut" (as the regulars call it), or because we got breakfast bought for us. We were also lucky because Bug and Sam were on their way to Hoboken, New Jersey. When Bug found out that we were on our way to the Big Apple Pie, he said, "If it's alright with my sweet old lady here, we'd be willing to stuff you boys into our rig and take you as far as Hoboken." Steven and I looked at each other, then Steven turned to Bug and said, "Do you have a map?" Sam laughed and said, "Don't worry, we know how to get there."

Bug said, "If you'd be willing to tough it through a little Fourth of July party with a bunch of stuffed shirts like us in a mansion overlooking New York City—"

"The Big Apple Pie," Sam corrected.

"Oh, right, the Big Apple Pie. Well, if you think you could stand to eat a bunch of hot dogs and burgers and drink some beer and pop some fireworks, well, then, we might be inclined to give you a personal escort *and* tour of New York City, the Big Apple Pie."

We said, "Yes! *Please!*"

✪✪✪

Bug and Sam's "rig" was also chartreuse green, the color of Sam's hair and the color of my Lucky Green Dress. It had two big, roomy seats up front, and a coupla half-seats behind theirs that supposedly turn into a bed, but neither of them ever sleeps back there because neither of them can sleep on their side, and that's the only way they can fit back there. Steven and I wedged ourselves into these seats. On the dashboard was a tiny copper-colored replica of the Empire State Building with a thermometer going up the front of it.

Steven found a big spiral-bound laminated road atlas on the floor between us as soon as we got in the rig. He opened it to NEW JERSEY and kept checking our progress the whole way. The drive from the Donut Dinette to Hoboken, New Jersey, is supposed to take about four hours under normal circumstances, but it rained hard the whole time we were on the road, and traffic moved very slowly, when it moved at all. Plus, there was construction all along the way, and detours because of that. It ended up taking us nearly nine hours to get there. Fortunately, we all liked each other because we were stuck with each other! Sam drove because Bug hates driving in the rain.

We told Bug and Sam our whole life story — well, I should say *I* did — and then Bug told us his and Sam's life story (well, mostly *his* life story). He was born in New Hampshire in 1961, the third child of twelve. Steven asked Bug if they were Catholic, and he said, "No, just white trash!" His father was a trucker and his mother was "a real *mother.*" They moved every six months or a year or so, leaving behind piles of unpaid bills and bounced checks. Bug has lived in every state but five: (in alphabetical order) Alaska, Florida, Hawaii, Minnesota, and Montana. He got his first job at the age of nine (he has always looked old for his age), sacking groceries at the Piggly Wiggly in Oklahoma City, Oklahoma. When he was fourteen, the law caught up with them and his father went to prison. Bug supported his family by working construction for about a year, then ran away from home so he could go back to school and be a "normal kid."

After high school, he realized that his diploma didn't do him much good, and he'd never be normal, so he started driving a truck. He saw Sam hitchhiking in Michigan and said he knew he loved her as soon as he saw that hair.

Sam was born in Detroit. Her mother died when she was seven and her father never remarried — he was far too busy being a "big shot executive" at the auto factory. She grew up in a pretty rich neighborhood, married the man her father wanted her to marry as soon as she graduated from high school. She was miserable, but it took her seven years to come to her senses and decide to leave him. One morning, she just woke up, went to the mall and had her hair dyed green, walked to the highway (her husband wouldn't let her drive) and stuck out her thumb. Bug saw her first and picked her up, even though it was against the rules of the trucking company he worked for to pick up riders.

Bug got fired, but he quickly got another job, and Sam got her commercial license, and they saved up and bought their own rig, and now they pretty much live on the road. Steven said, "Don't you ever miss having a home?" and Bug answered, "Whattya mean? We've got homes all over the country."

"Like Bob and Lonnie," Sam said as she pulled to the side of a residential road in front of a huge white two-story house. "They're gonna love you guys!"

Bug looked at his watch. "Nine-fifteen; what a trip."

Lonnie came around the side of the house with two cups of beer. "That horrible rain...I figured you'd be needing these! — Oh, you brought friends! Great! I'll get more beers!" Sam hugged Lonnie then introduced us and we all went around the house to the backyard where three grills were smoking under a little hut and Lonnie's "old man" Bob was standing over them with a silly chef's hat on grilling hamburgers and hot dogs. He was big and hairy and in silhouette looked just like Bug.

"How do ya like your burgers?"

Bug yelled out, "In a hurry!"

"Well, they're ready now, then!"

A refrigerated truck with Budweiser logos on it was parked at the garage and it had spigots all around that served up ice cold beer. Lonnie went to get us beers when another man who looked a lot like Bug and Bob and a woman appeared on the second floor deck. The woman called back into the house, "They're right, it stopped raining." She leaned over the railing toward us, "Lonnie? Bob? The radio says they're gonna do it now while the rain's stopped."

"Quick! Get upstairs," Lonnie called out, "Sam, get upstairs! Boys! Get upstairs. You, too, man in the dress!" We all rushed into the house and up the stairs and out onto the deck, which was now filled with about fifty people, a hodge-podge of beards and bellies and black T-shirts and tie-dye and tattoos. We had no idea where we were going in such a rush, but when we looked out over the railing, the Big Apple Pie was right there in front of us, like a huge postcard, only it was *real* and it was right there in front of us! It was the most incredible, dazzling thing I've ever seen in all my life. On both ends of this picture were bridges with big swooping drapes of lights, and directly in front of us a crowd of big buildings, the biggest buildings either of us had ever seen, and in the middle of them all, was the mother of skyscrapers, the Empire State Building! For a brief moment, I couldn't breathe.

"Oh my god, Steven, look!" Steven and I pushed our way to the front of the deck, and no sooner had we laid our hands on the wooden railing than a burst of fireworks shot up into the sky behind the Big Apple Pie, behind the Empire State Building. We all gasped uncontrollably, then let out a group "Oooh!" Then another flash of fireworks. "Ohhh!" And another. "Aaah!" We all laughed at ourselves, but none of us seemed to care how silly we sounded. Lonnie started hopping up and down and moaning like she was crying, "I love it! I love it! I love it!"

Every color and style of twinkling, glittering, shiny explosions littered the sky, each of them bigger and better and more exciting than the last. Once, there was a set of three smaller explosions right in a row, and Steven leaned toward me and said, "Firecracker, firecracker, boom! boom! boom!" and he hit me in the arm. I hit him back and we laughed wildly, and I thought I was gonna cry. We were there! We had made it to the Big Apple Pie!

Well, almost.

First, we had to wait for Bug and Sam to finish enjoying Bob and Lonnie's Fourth of July party. Right after the fireworks display, everybody went back downstairs to fill up their plates and cups, but Steven and I spent most of the party out on the deck, gazing across the river at the Big Apple Pie.

Steven did go inside once to use the bathroom, and when he came back out, he said, "Did you notice?"

"Notice what?" I said.

"Their whole house is done up in rainbows."

✪✪✪

A while later, when we went back inside, a little guy — a junior version of all the others — said, "Hey, there's the dude in the dress! Let's hear a song, guys!" Somebody else said, "They play songs?" Another said, "Just what this party needs, a band!" Lonnie came over and said, "How do you guys feel about playing for your dinner?" So we did.

I think we had sung four or five songs for them when suddenly, out of nowhere, the little guy came running into the room in one of Lonnie's lacy nightgowns with nothing on underneath. Lonnie jumped up and screamed, "Hollis, I'm gonna kick your retarded butt! Take my gown off!" He farted and everybody moaned. Lonnie sat back down. "Forget it, you can have it now."

He jumped up and down, "I wanna sing a song! I wanna sing a song!"

"Shut up and sing your stupid song."

Hollis cleared his throat, hummed a note and sang, "Start

spreading the news / I'm leaving today; / I'm gonna be a part of it, / New York, New York...." Bug pushed his way into the middle of the room and put a big arm around the little guy and joined in. "These little town blues / Are fading away; / We'll make a brand new start of it, / New York, New York!" Then everybody stood up and closed in and sang together (or tried to, anyway!):

I want to wake up in the city that never sleeps,
To find I'm king of the hill, top of the heap!

Then they all mumbled to a stop because none of them knew any more of the words to the song. Steven and I started clapping, and they all joined us.

Bug hollered out, "Whattya say we take you guys to the Big Apple Pie?" Everybody cheered. At first Steven and I thought they were *all* gonna go with us, and we weren't sure how we felt about that — I mean, they were nice and all, but they were getting kinda rowdy.

Fortunately, they just wanted to see us off. Lonnie passed out sparklers to everybody as we climbed up into the truck. Bug told Sam that he'd taken the trailer off of the rig, which pleased her. She was also pleased that it'd stopped raining because she hates driving in the Big Apple Pie as much as Bug hates driving in the rain.

Bug started up the truck and everybody lit their sparklers and waved them at us as we headed down the road toward the Big Apple Pie.

The Place That Used To Be My Home

I'm lost here.
Maybe I have two hometowns;
Feels like I have none.
It took so long to get here,
I just can't bear to run.
There's not one square foot in this big city
That I can call my own;
And I gave up every claim I had to the place
That used to be my home.

Chapter Thirteen

We're Not Superstitious....

We're not superstitious, but my Daddy says that Uncle Joe is and has been since he was a kid. Uncle Joe refused to turn thirteen. He skipped the age of thirteen because he was afraid something terrible would happen to him that year. So, he's a year older than anybody else his age! We're not superstitious, but why take chances?

God Bless New York City (My Big Apple Pie)

Well, God bless New York City, my Big Apple Pie,
Bless all them blarin' sirens that make my eardrums cry;
Bless all them cabs on concrete slabs that'll kill me by-an'-by,
Oh, God bless New York City, my Big Apple Pie.

Well, Kornflake is my hometown, I miss it, yes I do,
In fact, I'd prob'ly run away if I wasn't here with you;
'Cause nights in New York City, ya can't even see the stars,
Unless ya go out drinkin' an' see 'em in the bars.

Well, God bless New York City, my Big Apple Pie,
From Wall Street up thru Harlem an' the boroughs far an' wide;
Bless all them guys with switchblade knives that'll kill me by-an'-by,
Oh, God bless New York City, my Big Apple Pie.

Chapter Fourteen

The Big Apple Pie

Something you might not know about the Big Apple Pie is that you have to *pay* to get in — just like an amusement park! They have big walls of ticket booths at every entrance that you have to drive through, whether you're entering by tunnel or bridge, and if you don't pay the admission price, they won't let you in. They don't worry about people sneaking in, either, because the Big Apple Pie is an island! Well, Manhattan is an island, and that's where all of the big buildings are, and that's where all of the people are, and that's where we wanted to be.

Bug said the best way to come into the Big Apple Pie is through a tunnel. Sam said she hated the tunnel, but it was faster than the bridge and it was getting late. The wall of ticket booths had a sign on the top half that stretched across the whole street:

HOLLAND TUNNEL

We were as excited and exhausted as if we were waiting in line to get on a roller coaster. As soon as we paid our admission and got past the ticket lady, there were hardly any cars and the tunnel was wide open. Bug "put the pedal to the metal," as the truckers say, and sped through the tunnel at about a hundred miles an hour. Steven and I gripped the dashboard and leaned forward. Sam kept her eyes covered the whole time we zipped past zillions of bathroom tiles and flourescent lights. "This is the part I hate! This is the part I hate!" she kept screaming. I glanced at Bug to see if he was as scared as the rest of us, but the grin on his face made me decide that either he knew what he was doing or he was insane and any minute we were gonna crash into the wall and the Hudson River was gonna come gushing in on us and everybody was gonna drown — except me, because I'd already be dead, because my head would've smashed into the dashboard and the little Empire State Building thermometer would've gone up through my chin and into my brain —

Oh, my lord, what was I thinking?

I leaned back away from the dashboard and right about that time, we exploded out of the Holland Tunnel and into the greatest city in the world. Even with my limited experience of the world and the cities of the world, much less the *great* cities of the world, I knew that this was definitely *the* greatest city in the world.

The exit road from the Holland Tunnel curls around in a big circle this way, and then that, and then suddenly, you're in China — or that's what it seems like. All the signs are written in Chinese characters — even the McDonald's sign! Sam told us it was Chinatown.

From there, Bug drove us up First Avenue, by the United Nations Buildings where the President of the United States and all the important people from all around the world have meetings; we went up to Harlem, we drove by a jazz club called Birdland where Bug said "all the greats have played"; we drove through Central Park — it's as full of big green trees and grassy hills as you please, and it's right in the middle of the Big Apple Pie. We went up and down the avenues, north and south, across the streets, east and west — they're all numbers — everybody was honking and yelling and running red lights (especially the taxi cab drivers). The buildings were so tall that they disappeared into the night sky like country roads; the lights were so bright, people were wearing sunglasses! Bug would say, "There's the Chrysler Building," and we'd look one way, then Sam would say, "Oh, that's the Citicorp Building, I think," and we'd look the other way; then Bug called out, "Look, *Cats*!" and Sam called out, "*The Phantom of the Opera*!" Most of the landmarks they called out didn't mean much to Steven or me, but they were Big Apple Pie landmarks, so we were impressed. Rockefeller Center is where they tape TV shows that are seen all over the country. St. Patrick's Cathedral is a really, really big church. The Intrepid Museum is an old ship that they turned into a museum. The New York Public Library is the biggest library I think I'd ever want to see and it has two life-size cement lions guarding its front steps.

But Bug said he saved the best for last. It was the Empire State Building, a landmark we were very familiar with, and not just because of the thermometer on Bug and Sam's dashboard. For this building, we actually parked the truck and got out. We got there just in time to be in the last group of people to go up (I'm glad I had on my Lucky Green Dress!). We waited in line to get on an elevator; then we got off and had to wait in line for another elevator. When they built the Empire State Building, I guess they couldn't make one-hundred-and-two-story elevators!

When we walked out onto the observation deck, the Big Apple Pie was literally under our feet. We wandered around speechless, looking at the view from every side again and again. It took a while to get right up to the edge because there were so many people, but we managed it. Bug said, "You guys go wander off on your own, we're gonna go to our favorite corner and smooch a little!"

Up above, the building's needle poked up through the clear night sky — we read on a little plaque that the builders of the Empire State Building planned to fly blimps right up to that needle, park 'em, and the people were gonna climb off of the blimp and down a ladder onto the building. That sounded pretty exciting to me, but Steven said he had to stop thinking about it or he'd throw up!

People all around us were talking in all kinds of different languages and taking lots of pictures. But they weren't just taking pictures of the Big Apple Pie, they were taking pictures of *us*, too! Steven pointed out a couple of kids secretly taking a picture of Sam (with her bright green hair) and big old, loveable Bug in his Harley-Davidson Motorcycles T-shirt, going at it behind some kind of electrical machinery, and while we were spying on them, a woman came up and asked in broken English if her husband could take a picture of me and my friend and "the pretty man-dress"!

When the bulb flashed, it caught Bug's attention and he and Sam came running over and he asked the people to take a picture of *all* of us.

The man took another picture, nervously, as if following a command. Bug said, "And another one for the boys!" He turned to Steven and me, "We'll give 'em our addresses and they'll send us a copy!" Steven and I nodded and smiled and the flash went off, but we weren't really looking at the picture-taker.

Bug walked briskly toward the man as soon as the third picture was taken and, frightened, the man held his camera out to Bug (I think he thought Bug was gonna take it). Sam went to try to help Bug communicate with the foreigners and Steven and I stayed behind looking at each other, our smiles faded.

Steven said, "Are you thinking what I'm thinking?"

"I don't know, what're ya thinkin'?"

"That we don't have an address to give them."

"I guess if they just sent 'em in care of the Big Apple Pie, we might not get 'em, huh?" Steven laughed and we looked out at the Big Apple Pie. "I guess we'd better find an address, then," I said, searching the buildings below us.

But then I saw a landmark we hadn't seen in our tour. Actually, it was two identical buildings down at the southern tip of the island, towering over everything around them. "Hey, what are those?"

A man with funny plaid shorts, white socks up to his knees and a feather in his Robin Hood hat leaned over toward us and said, "Dem's da Twin Towers One and Two. Da Werld Trade Center. A hunerd-and-ten stories apiece, dey are. Da foundations are twenty-and-tree miles deep apiece. T'were da tallest buildin's in da werld fer only a short piece; just until da Sears Tyer in Chicago was completed. Da Twin Towers house four-hunerd-and-eighteen thou', and six-hunerd square miles of office space; da entrance lobby is seven stories high. Dare are a total of twenty-and-tree express and seventy-and-two udder elevators and forty-and-tree thou', and six-hunerd windows in da towers. Dare are two observation decks: an enclosed one on da hunerd-and-sevend fleur and an open deck on da roof of da Number Two, and dare's a lovely restaurant dat goes 'round and around on da top fleur of da Number One."

I thanked the man. He said, "Fer sure, and could I teck a picture of ya in da bright grin holiday dress?"

"Sure!" The man took a picture of us, then quickly disappeared into the thick crowd.

Sam appeared and said, "Hey, guys, they're closing up shop. I guess it's time to go."

Bug and Sam held our place in the elevator line while we bought about five of every different design of postcard they had in the souvenir shop and a couple souvenir writing pens. They also had the little copper landmark replicas with thermometers on them — like Bug's Empire State Building — but they also had replicas of the Statue of Liberty, the UN Building, and the Twin Towers. We bought one of the Twin Towers thermometers to give Bug and Sam to add to their collection.

At street level, we suddenly felt a lot smaller than we did on top of the Empire State Building. When we were back in the truck, I asked Bug and Sam if they ever went up on top of the Twin Towers and Bug said, "Naw. I don't care much for them modern skyscrapers; I really only like the Art Deco ones, the Empire State Building, the Chrysler Building, those are the ones that really count." Steven and I looked at each other, both of us thinking about the little keepsake we'd gotten for them. At the corner of Thirty-Ninth Street and Ninth Avenue, Bug pulled over and said, "Well guys, here's a cheap place to bed down."

Steven and I strained to see out of the truck window and I read, "Street Lucky's Hotel." Bug and Sam burst out laughing, and Steven and I thought they were playing some kind of a joke on us, and so we laughed with them.

Sam said, "Silly! Read that sign again."

"Street — "

Sam cut me off, "No, that's S-t. That stands for 'saint,' too."

"Oh, '*Saint* Lucky's Hotel.'" Bug and Sam burst out laughing again.

"Not 'Saint Lucky's,' silly, 'Saint Lucy's'! It's St. Lucy's Hotel."

Bug said, "I wouldn't suggest you wear your dress," he chuckled, "I don't think you'd wanna get lucky in there!"

I didn't think much of what Bug said, but I took him at his word and changed into the clothes Elizabeth Yoder had given me back on the Amish farm, then I put the Lucky Green Dress in the dress bag that Ruther Jean had given me back in Beaumont, Texas, and slipped it in my backpack. The little brown paper sack with the Twin Towers thermometer rubbed against my hand. I took it out and handed it to Sam. "We bought this for y'all, as a little thank you gift, so you'd always remember us, but then you said ya don't like the Twin Towers."

Sam opened it and said, "Oh, Bug, look, it's *another* thermometer!" She stood it next to the Empire State Building on the dashboard and they sat quietly looking at it for a moment, then burst out laughing.

"*What?*"

"I always hated that little Empire State Building thermometer," Bug started, continuing to laugh, "It doesn't tell the right temperature, and it drives me crazy. But I couldn't get it off without tearing out the whole dash 'cause I used Super Glue to put it on!"

"I'm sorry," I said.

Sam said, "Don't apologize. It's not your fault — it's very sweet!"

"Listen, guys, we don't need some little New York souvenir to make us remember you. You think we're gonna forget you that easy?" He took the thermometer from the dashboard and held it out to us. "*You* keep it as a reminder of Sam and me — the two ugly old truckers who brought you the last mile to the Big Apple Pie!"

Steven took it and said, "You aren't ugly!" He hugged Bug, then Sam, and then I hugged the two of them, and then they opened their doors and we all got out. Bug took out his wallet and gave Steven a fifty-dollar bill. "Maybe you have money, maybe you don't. Now you have that."

"Thanks Bug." Steven sounded like he was starting to get choked up. "Will we ever see you again?"

"When you boys get famous, and we see you singing on TV or somewhere, we're gonna come hunt you down and get that fifty bucks back!"

"It's a deal!"

We all hugged again, then Steven and I climbed the steps of St. Lucy's and stopped at the door and waved goodbye one last time.

✪✪✪

We decided that St. Lucy's was only religious in name as soon as we entered. At the front desk was a man with a white and tan polka-dot shirt on. At least, I thought it was polka-dots. When we got close to him, I realized that the polka-dots were actually stains, like coffee stains, but they were all over the shirt. His hair was dark black but patchy, and greased to his scalp in such a way that you could very easily make out the shape of his head, which was kind of weird-shaped. Steven and I stood at the desk while he stared down at what might've been called "the books" — green ledger paper with lots of lines and lots of scribbled pencil markings all over it. Numbers, lots of tiny numbers.

We waited patiently for him to look up at us, but he never did. We shuffled a bit — mistakenly thinking that might get his attention — and cleared our throats; that amused us for some reason and we started laughing. The man came out of an apparent deep sleep, flung his head up, and his glasses flew off his face and landed on the floor between Steven and me. We both bent down to pick them up and almost hit heads and came up laughing, Steven holding the glasses out to the man. He wasn't very amused by any of it.

"*What* can I do for you?" He slid the thick lenses back on his face. "I said, What can I do for you?"

Steven jumped in, "We'd like a room. For the night."

"*Rooms*," the man spat back, "No doubles." He had on a little red bow tie that was smudged black on one side. We filled out the forms, paid what seemed like a ridiculously small amount of money for two rooms. (I can't remember exactly, but it was something like twelve dollars each, which seemed really cheap to us.) He kicked off of his desk and rolled in his chair across the floor of his small area to get the keys out of a tall cabinet. I noticed that he had on dress shoes and no socks, and his pants were worn so thin, you could see his knees. I felt sorry for him, mean as he was. He gave me two keys and said, "Third floor. There's the stairs."

At the top of the first flight of stairs, I stopped and held out my two fists, each with a key in it. Steven pointed at one and I gave him that key, then we walked up two more flights. We searched the doors and found Steven's room first. There were lots of locks on the door, but the key only fit one of them, and, fortunately, that was the only one that was locked! The door creaked open and Steven slid his hand in slightly, feeling for the light switch, but not finding one. When he brought his hand back out, the palm was almost entirely black

— just from rubbing the wall a little bit. I was glad I hadn't worn my Lucky Green Dress in here, it would've gotten filthy.

I started to move on to find my room, but Steven said, "Wait! Don't leave me alone!"

I said, "You mean to tell me that you can sleep out in the middle of the woods with all the wild animals and the noises and who knows what, but a little hotel room *scares* you?" He held out his blackened hand in his defense. "Oh, alright!" I pushed the door wide open and tried to see the wall next to the door frame using the light from the hallway.

Steven said, "Maybe there's a string." I walked into the room; Steven stayed behind but called out, "Be careful!"

I found a string hanging from the ceiling in the middle of the room. *Click!* The single bulb twenty feet up or so, on the ceiling, barely brightened the room, but it revealed the tiny lamp on the tiny table next to the tiny bed. I turned that on and we were able to see the room in all it's, uh, glory.

At least the sheets were clean.

I decided to get on to my room because I suddenly felt very weary (heightened by the fact that I didn't have a big, cozy bed to fall into). I joked to Steven, "Be sure and use all the locks on the door. They must be there for a reason."

He said, "Don't worry, I will."

In my room, with the overhead and bedside lights on, I got a better look at my "arrangements" (as my Nana would call them). The bed wasn't really a bed at all, it was a cot with a thin wafer of a mattress on it, and it was about a foot shorter than me. The closet had no door on it, but the doorway was draped with lots of cobwebs. At the foot of the bed, wedged into the corner, was a tiny triangular sink. It had a steady stream of water trickling out of one of the two spouts that followed a bright orange trail of rust that stained the whole bottom half of the sink. At the head of the bed was a weird heavy metal contraption that I decided was an antique heater (don't worry, it wasn't on!), and above it was a huge window, so caked with dirt that no light could get in or out.

I dug through my backpack, trying to find something to clean the window with and came across all of the discarded pieces of paper from my names-and-numbers necklace. I went through them one at a time to find the ones that contained names and numbers of folks I didn't meet on my journey. I wet them in the sink, one at a time, and went to work on one of the many little window panes. After I'd used up all the usable pieces of paper, I had one clean window pane that looked at a brick wall no more than five feet away! There was a little bit of bluish light shining between my window and the brick wall, and I decided that it was moonlight, and somehow felt like my effort wasn't completely in vain.

Now, I was exhausted. I wanted a hot shower, and I needed to go to the bathroom. But neither of those things existed in my room. I opened my door and looked both ways down the hall. Nothing but doors with numbers or letters on them, none of them a bathroom, as far as I could tell.

I laid on the bed and went through the names and numbers of the folks I had met on my journey. Then I got a great idea. I took out my half of the postcards I'd gotten on the top of the Empire State Building and I wrote every one of them and everybody in my family a note. I sat the Twin Towers thermometer on the window sill and pretended it was my view and wrote the same thing to everybody:

> Howdy! Wish you were here and all that! I'm lying on my very own bed in the very middle of the Big Apple Pie! My best friend in the whole world, Steven Cheslik-DeMeyer, from Kornflake, Indiana, got a room of his own!
>
> Right now, I'm looking at the Twin Towers, the two tallest buildings in the Big Apple Pie — taller, even, than the Empire State Bldg,

which I stood on top of today. Just like King Kong!

Tomorrow, I'm gonna work on conquering this big ol' city, the greatest city in the world! The Big Apple Pie! Love you! Miss you! Wish you were here — but I'm glad I am at the very least!!!

Love, James Dean Jay Byrd

I fell asleep in the middle of postcard number twenty-five, or something like that, and I had a really neat dream:

Steven and I were sitting in lawn chairs eating apple pie a la mode — like my Aunt Konk makes, only bigger and with real apples — in front of our cute little trailerhome (a mini-version of the Nicki 2000). The yard was manicured perfectly with Astro-turf and egg-carton tulips. Next to us, behind a little wooden fence (like the ones in Circleville, Ohio) were two horses; one of them was the humongous brilliant pink horse that I'd ridden in Paris, Tennessee. He still had on the silver-colored saddle and the sequin-encrusted hooves — but the crown on his head was made out of real gold with real gems! The other horse was an Appaloosa, white with black polka-dots, and had a beautiful, silky tail with a pretty bow tied at the top. Steven and I finished eating our pie and got on the horses (he got on the Appaloosa and said, "This is my favorite horse!") and then a cloud came out of the sky and our horses hopped up on it. While we rode on the cloud up into the sky, Steven played his guitar and I was singing a song about Steven and me and our

> *magical flying horses. I looked down at our little trailerhome, growing smaller and smaller below us, and realized it was sitting on top of the Twin Towers — we lived on top of the Twin Towers!*
>
> *Up, up, up we floated on our cloud. Eventually, we couldn't see the Twin Towers anymore, or even the Big Apple Pie for that matter, but we didn't seem to care. Before too long, we could see the whole United States of America — there was Texas and Indiana, and all of the states — and everybody was standing in their backyards, and they were all singing along!*
>
> *As we floated farther and farther out, we could see all of the foreign countries of the world, and everybody was standing around their little foreign houses, and they were all singing along in their own languages!*
>
> *And then there was a bright flash of light and everybody started clapping and cheering.*

When I woke up, it took me a minute to remember where I was. I scribbled the words to the song in my dream, and just as I was writing the name of the song at the top of the page — "My Man, Our Horses, And Me" — a bright light hit my face. It was a happy little sunbeam that'd found my one clean windowpane. It was morning and I was in the Big Apple Pie! I had woken up in the city that never sleeps. I hoped it wasn't also "the city that never goes to the bathroom," 'cause I sure needed to!

I poked my head out of my room and looked both ways. Steven was standing at the end of the hall. I called out to him, "Good morning!"

His sleepy face brightened up when he saw me. "Good morning!" He was standing outside of a door that had the letters "WC" on it.

"What's that," I asked.

"It's the bathroom."

"Why does it say 'WC'?"

"I don't know. A man told me this was the bathroom. I *hope* it's the bathroom!"

I said, "Well, maybe it's the name of the person who owns it."

"That would be kind of weird."

"Maybe W.C. Fields owns it," I guessed.

Steven laughed. "I don't think so."

"Well, it's gotta mean something."

"Yeah."

Just about that time, an old, old man opened the 'WC' door wearing nothing but a little white towel and said, "'Water closet. It stands for 'water closet.' Now, would you two cackling hens shut the hell up?" He ambled down the hall.

"But, Mister, this is the city that never sleeps!" I called after him.

He cursed at me as he slammed the door to his room and Steven said, "Maybe that's why he's in such a bad mood!"

✪✪✪

While we showered and shaved, I sang "My Man, Our Horses, And Me" to Steven and he came up with a harmony part. We decided unanimously that I should wear the Lucky Green Dress on this, our first day in the Big Apple Pie. The man at the front desk was the same man who was there the night before. He didn't even look up when I asked him where the post office was; he just pointed over his head, "Thirty-third and Eighth Ave." I pulled out of my backpack the pants and shirt that Elizabeth Yoder made and laid them on top of the desk. "These clothes don't really fit me; do you think you could find somebody who might be able to use them...." He *shooshed* me without looking up, but when we went out the front door, I looked back and the clothes were no longer there.

Steven said, "That was a very sweet thing of you to do."

"Did you see his *pants*? I hope he didn't think I was being rude."

"It doesn't matter what he thinks, I think it was very sweet."

"I'm gonna make the Big Apple Pie a better place to live!"

Steven laughed, "If you wanna make it better, you can start with those rooms!"

"Whattya mean? My room was really nice! Wasn't your room alright? I don't remember!"

We went one block over and one block up and came to a restaurant called the Eighth Avenue Deli. We ate pancakes and scrambled eggs and something we'd never heard of before: "home fries." The waitress, who was old enough to be our grandmother, but not nearly sweet enough, told us they were "just like hash browns," and because that's what we both wanted, we believed her. But they weren't *anything* like hash browns. They were chunky and hard on the outside and soft on the inside and had bell peppers cooked into them. We put lots of ketchup on them, and they weren't too bad; and the pancakes and scrambled eggs were perfect.

After we finished eating, we finished writing postcards to our families and friends back in Texas and Indiana — Steven had gotten the same idea as I had the night before, but all of his postcards were personalized, so he didn't get as many written.

We walked another block over and another block up and came to the post office. The main branch of the United States Post Office is a big, imposing building that covers a whole city block. Bug had driven us past it, but he didn't point it out, he was too busy pointing out Madison Square Garden, which is right across the street. The stairs across the front of the post office are a block wide, and at the top of them are these huge columns that hold up an enormous marble banner across the width of the building with a message etched in it in one massive line:

So *that's* what Carl the mailman was talking about!

I was reading the sign as I walked up the steps, and suddenly I fell down right on top of a lady who had been sitting on the steps reading.

"Hey — *hey!!!*" she screamed. I jumped up, apologizing. But then she noticed my Lucky Green Dress and her face lit up. She was dressed in a white denim pantsuit with colorful western scenes across the front, around the hat and on the boots, all done up in sequins! "Hey, now! That shore is a purty, purty dress yew gawt on thar, cowgerl!" Steven laughed nervously and gave me a funny look as he sat the guitar and ukulele on a step and started picking up the postcards I'd spilled all over the steps when I fell. She had the most peculiar accent either one of us had ever heard; Steven couldn't understand a word she said.

I said, "Where are you from?"

She motioned to Steven, then to the instruments, and said, "Care to accomp'ny me, cowboy?" Steven just looked at her, not even aware she was talking to him. She shrugged and sang, keeping rhythm by slapping on her thighs:

All my life, I been a cowgerl,
Roamin' across the rusty range;
When the fellers an' the fillies ask me, 'How gerl?'
I swaller a gob a'spit an' this I sang....

Sangin' yay-tee yay-tee heedle hay-hay.
Sangin' yay-tee yay-tee heedle-hee.
Sangin' yay-tee yay-tee heedle hay-hay.
It don't mean much to them, but it means a lot to me!

Her voice was pretty — but *loud* — and everybody was staring at us. She sure didn't seem to care. Steven held up the handful of postcards and said, "We need to go in."

I apologized again and told the lady that we had to go mail our mail and she said, "Awrighty! But yowl come on back now, ya heah? Yowl come an' sit an' chat a while with li'l ol' Mizz Alison. Awrightay? Ya heah me?"

I said, "Yes...ma'am," and Steven just stared, unable to say anything. We walked up the stairs — being very careful about where we stepped this time — and into the beautiful marble lobby of the main branch of the United States Post Office.

It was Sunday, but the post office was as busy as it could be. It took us a while to find the slots where you put the letters in, but we finally did, and as we dropped our mail in, one postcard at a time, a young woman standing behind us waiting her turn for the slots said, "That was Miss Alison, wasn't it??"

"Do what?"

"Your friend out there. Wasn't that Miss Alison? *The* Miss Alison?"

Steven said, "She's not our friend."

I said, "Whattya mean, *the* Miss Alison?"

"What do *you* mean? She's *famous*! She's like a big star down in the Village."

I said, "Famous?!"

"Yeah, I swear!"

"Wow! What does she do?"

"She's a cabaret star. A singer. She's just great! She's like Patsy Cline, but she's *alive*. I just saw her show last Friday night. You have to go see her!" She looked down at my Lucky Green Dress. "I thought for sure you were her friend, the way you're dressed!" She dropped her letters in the slot. "Oh well, bye-bye!" Steven and I watched her walk away and disappear out a side door.

Steven said, "Look, we can sneak out the side door!"

"Sneak out? Steven...it's *the* Miss Alison."

"Are you serious? We don't know any Miss Alison! She could be a serial killer."

"A serial killer?! You're *crazy!* Besides, even if she is a serial killer or anything, we've got my Lucky Green Dress to protect us." I started walking toward the front doors and Steven followed behind.

"Your dress is gonna protect us and *I'm* crazy?"

I pushed through one of the revolving doors at the top of the staircase on Eighth Avenue and headed down toward Miss Alison who had returned to reading her book.

I plopped down beside her and said, "So, you're *the* Miss Alison."

"Ohhh! Yowl came-did back!"

"Yes ma'am. You're the first famous person we've met in the Big Apple Pie! I mean, you're not Dolly Parton or anything, but that woman up there said you were somebody."

"Aw, shucks, I ain't no-wire near as faymiss as Dally Part'n. I'm just li'l ol' Mizz Alison, tha's all!" She pulled a couple of glossy handbills out of her huge saddlebag purse and handed them to Steven and me. "Heahs ma caw-erd!"

I said, "Thanky!"

"Wait a minute," she said in a completely different voice, "Where are you from?

"Okey-Dokey, Texas."

"Texas! Well, you sure don't talk like no Texan!"

"Well, I talk like I talk, that's all."

"That was better," she said.

"What?"

She opened up a book and pointed at some foreign-looking word: *Texxis.*

I took the book from her. "What is this?" It was called *How Tuh Tawk Texxin.* It had little caricatures of silly hick people with cowboy hats on, saying things like "Haowday, yowl!"

"I don't talk like this. I can't even pronounce these words."

She yanked the book out of my hands and said, "Ya mean I spent" (she looked at the back of the book) " — three-dollars and ninety-five cents plus tax on this and it's worthless?" She started moaning and crying and carrying on, and everybody stared at us again. Steven started making face signals to me that I could tell meant "Let's get out of here!" but I was enjoying myself.

Miss Alison noticed Steven's face gestures and said to him, "You think I'm loopy, don't you?" Steven laughed nervously. She patted the stair beside her and said, "Sit down, let Miss Alison tell you her story." Steven shrugged and started to protest. Miss Alison spat out, "*Sit!*" and Steven did.

Miss Alison was born Alison White in a little town *north* of the Big Apple Pie called Bridgeport, Connecticut. Miss Alison was her stage name (remember Ruther Beaucoup?), and her pretend hometown was a fictional town called Rio Big, Texas, "Because *everything's* big in Texas!" When she was seven, her Aunt Prissy went to Texas on a business trip and came back with a full cowgirl outfit and fake Shetland pony for Miss Alison. Her folks could hardly get her out of that outfit or off of that horse for months without her throwing a fit. In the end, one of the pony's legs fell off and her father said he had to take it out back and shoot it. She pointed out that the picture on the handbill she had given us pictured her on her horse, named "Glue Baby" after the fact (for comic effect). "So, yeah, I'm kind of scarred for life," she said, "But I make a good living out of it! And what are you boys here in New York City for — to get famous like the rest of us?"

I said, "Well, I don't know, I just followed a vision out of my Daddy's tent revival and it turned out to be Steven, and he was just searching the country looking for a place to write songs when he saved my life in Circleville, Ohio, and we started singing together and followed a rainbow all the way here to the Big Apple Pie."

"The what?"

"The Big Apple Pie. That's what we call it back in Okey-Dokey, Texas!"

"Are you serious?"

"Yeah. We know it's called the Big Apple, I guess, but that's just what we've always called it!"

Miss Alison smiled at Steven. "And where are you from?"

Steven paused a little too long, so I jumped in, "He's from Indiana. Kornflake, Indiana. His family owns a popcorn farm there!"

She said to Steven, "Does he ever let you talk?"

"Not much. Usually, I have to write a song to get a word in edgewise!"

"So, let's hear it."

"What?"

"A song. It looks like you've got your instruments. Let's hear a song."

"Here?" Steven and I asked in unison.

"You need a stage and a microphone?" We didn't answer. Miss Alison snapped her fingers and pointed at our instrument cases, so we took out our guitar and ukulele and sang "My Family Tree." Miss Alison clapped and cheered for us. "Oh, my *god*, you boys are really good! Sing another one!"

I told her a little about the Queen of the Rodeo Contest in Paris, Tennessee, and then we sang "(I Am The) Queen Of The Rodeo," and this time when we finished, five other people had made their way to a piece of stairway a few steps up from Miss Alison. When we finished singing that, all of 'em clapped. Miss Alison turned around and invited them all to come sit closer for the concert. We sang "My Man, Our Horses, And Me," "Are You On The Top 40 Of Your Lord?" and "Doggone Happy," and even the Loretta Lynn song, "You Ain't Woman Enough To Take My Man." By the end of each song, there were more people standing around, and they all kept clapping for us.

But then a security guard came out of the post office and chased everybody away. Steven went to put his guitar away, but his case was littered with coins and dollar bills. "What's this?"

Miss Alison laughed. "My friends, you have just busked."

I asked, "Is it legal?"

"Only if you're good!" She wrapped her arms into ours and we walked down the post office stairs together. "And yowl are really, really good!"

"Miss Alison," I said.

"Yes, hun?"

"It's not *yowl*...it's 'y'all.' Like ball."

"That's what I said, 'yowl.'"

"No, '*y'all.*'"

She tried again, "'Y'all'?"

"Right!"

"So, where do *y'all* wanna go now?"

I said, "Well, we're living at St. Lucky's Hotel."

Miss Alison said, "I've never heard of it. Does it have any stars?"

I said, "Just Steven and me!"

She laughed, "Now you're talking!"

Steven said, "It's really called St. Lucy's."

"St. Lucy's? Eww! You aren't really living at St. Lucy's?"

"Yeah."

Miss Alison shook her head violently, "Do you know what kind of people live in St. Lucy's? —Well, never mind."

Steven said, "It's the only place we have."

"Why don't *y'all* come stay the night with me in Queens," she offered.

"You're not a serial killer, are you, Miss Alison?"

Steven jumped in, "*Jay!*"

"Well, we have to get it out of the way."

"No, but I played one on TV once!"

✪✪✪

Miss Alison's apartment is big and cozy and decorated from top to bottom like an old Western movie set, complete with wagon wheel chandeliers and an "authentic" outhouse door with a moon-shaped cut-out on the bathroom. She even has a pet rabbit named Li'l Roy that she dresses up in a cowboy hat, leather vest, and pistols, and makes him dance and "lip-sync" to Roy Rogers records.

The most prominent thing in Miss Alison's apartment, though, is a very modern big-screen TV. A really big big-screen TV. Miss Alison loves to shop but hates to go shopping, so she goes home-shopping on cable television. The last thing she bought in a store was the big-screen TV, and she says she hasn't regretted it once. She got the TV so she could get a better look at items on the home-shopping channels before buying them. And boy, does she have a collection of stuff! Particularly kitchen stuff. Her kitchen is stocked with every kinda gadget you can imagine (and some you could *never* imagine), and with them she made us a feast.

Fat-Free Fast-Fried Free Range Chicken, Homespun™ Pasta Happies, U-Bake-It™ Rye Bread, Crisp 'n' Lite™ Vegetable Medleys (made in her Crisp 'n' Lite™ freeze-dryer), and Sunshine Tea. For dessert, we had Presto™ Pastry Cakes with Food Lab™ Home-Cultured Blackberry Yogurt Topping. It was all very odd and kinda space-age, but tasty.

For the rest of the day, we told each other about ourselves, from beginning to present-day, Li'l Roy was forced out of a deep sleep for another performance, and Miss Alison made us sing "My Man, Our Horses, And Me" again into the phone for a friend of hers.

That night, we took a taxicab from Miss Alison's apartment in Queens, over the Queensboro Bridge and down Fifth Avenue. We ended up in the Village, also known as Greenwich Village, at a tiny little two-story building with a little bar on the street level where a bunch of guys were standing around another guy who was sitting at a piano, all of them singing "New York, New York" (the song everybody at Bob and Lonnie's in New Jersey were trying to sing), and a few people were sitting at little tables drinking bright colored drinks with paper fruit and umbrellas on toothpicks in them. Steven said it was *surreal*, but what I thought he said was that it was "so real" and I embarrassed myself when Miss Alison asked what he said and I told her, "He said they're so real."

She said, "No, not really!"

She told us to hang out downstairs 'til she came and got us. She went upstairs to get ready for her show. We were very excited about getting to see a New York show one day after we'd arrived, and we found ourselves singing along with the piano singers. A very bleary-eyed man sitting at the bar shouted out to me, "Hhhoney, yyyou lossst yer wwwig." And then everybody stopped and looked at us.

I said, "I don't have a wig." They all burst out laughing.

The piano player said, "Yeah, but can ya sing?"

"Miss Alison seems to think so!"

They all said "*Wooaah!*" and the piano player said, "Then c'mon over here, Missy, and show us what you can do!"

The guys standing around the piano sat down and the piano player said, "So. What songs do ya know?"

"Well, we've only written a few so far." Everybody laughed.

"Anything *we* might know?" the piano player asked.

"Well, I don't know," I said, "We've got one called 'Queen Of The Rodeo' — about the contest in Paris, Tennessee" (laughter), "and 'My Family Tree' — which is all about Steven's granddaddy" (laughter), "and 'Doggone Happy,' which isn't really about anything at all; it's just about being happy" (more laughs). "Is there anything I could say that wouldn't make y'all laugh?"

The piano player said, "Oh, don't mind them." (But he was laughing, too!) He said, "It means they like you. You're workin' that accent, aren't ya?"

"Huh?"

"Do you know any covers?"

"Any what?"

Steven jumped in, "We know 'You Ain't Woman Enough To Take My Man' by Loretta Lynn." Everybody roared.

The piano player stood up and dug through a pile of songbooks on his piano. "You won't believe this, but I think I might, just — yes!" He had a songbook titled *Country Gold.* He looked at the Table of Contents page, and, sure enough, there it was. He asked Steven what key we sing it in and Steven told him "G" and somebody in the audience said, "Oh, gee whiz!" and everybody laughed some more. The piano player said, "Alright, now, Clarence, let's give 'em a chance — there'll be plenty of time to behead them later...!"

The piano player played and Steven and I sang, and the little audience continued laughing, but it was different somehow — like they'd stopped laughing *at* us and were laughing along with the song. When we were done, they all applauded and cheered and yelled out, "Yee-*haw!* Encore!"

The piano player thumbed through his books and said, "How about 'Stand By Your Man'? Tammy Wynette?"

I said, "Yeah, I think I know that. Steven?"

"Sure."

And so we sang "Stand By Your Man," and we only had to look at the words in the songbook a couple of times. By the middle of the song, Miss Alison had slipped halfway down the staircase that led upstairs to the cabaret theater, and she was watching us sing. When we were done, everybody cheered again, including Miss Alison. When the cheering died down, she called across the room, "Who's your agent, boys?!"

"What?"

The piano player said, "Do these belong to you?"

"Not yet, but I'm working on it! Get 'em to sing 'My Man, Our Horses, And Me' for ya."

Steven said, "He doesn't know any of our songs." Everybody laughed. "And we don't have our instruments."

About that time, a young guy ran down the stairs past

Miss Alison and pushed his way onto the piano bench. "Step aside, Missy!" He played a pretty little intro then started playing a horse-trottin' kinda rhythm and whispered, "'My Man, Our Horses, And Me'!" We sang it and he followed along very nicely. The folks sitting at the tables paid attention to us like never before when we sang that song, and then, when we were finished, they stood and applauded.

Miss Alison said, "One song and y'all get a standing ovation? I'm scared a'you boys!"

✪✪✪

We sat right up front for Miss Alison's show, which was called "Miss *ME!*" It started at eight-fifteen that night and lasted an hour. She sang about a dozen songs — songs by Roy Rogers and Cole Porter and Patsy Cline and even Willie Nelson, and she talked between a lot of the songs about being "raised up" in Rio Big, Texas. She was really good and the little cabaret theater was as packed as it could be (more packed than it legally should've been) with very appreciative people.

The big surprise of the night, though, was the way Miss Alison closed her show. "*Y'all* know as well as I dew that this big ol' city, this big ol' New Yoke City, it's a big ol' town. It's a whole heckuva lot bigger than my li'l ol' hometown a'Rio Big, Texxis. An', ya know, I'm always suh-prized by tha kindsa folks ya run into in this big ol' impersonal New Yoke City. But folks, I'd like fer *y'all* ta meet a coupla special folks I met up with jus' recently. Jus' this mornin', 'smatter a'fact. — Bobby, could ya dew me a fayvah, honey, an' turn up tha houselights. The — Bobby. The houselights, Bobby. Are ya back thar, Bobby?!" She held her hand up to shade the spotlights from her eyes and looked toward the back of the house. "*Bobby!*" Finally, the guy in the back of the room jumped up — everybody was watching him — and turned on the houselights.

"Ladies an' gents, this is James Dean Jay Byrd in his Lucky

Green Dress and Mr. Steven Cheslik-DeMeyer!" The audience clapped politely, Steven and I stood briefly, embarrassed a little bit, then sat back down.

The piano player stopped, then did a piano roll from the bottom keys all the way up to the top. He hit the highest note of the piano and waited for his cue. And Miss Alison gave it to him. "This is a li'l ol' song written by these fellers right 'cheer; it's called 'My Man, Our Horses, And Me.'" That's right, she sang our song! In front of all those people. And they loved it! And then she sang it through again, saying, "Now, I want all of *y'all* to join me at this go 'round, alrighty?!" And they did! I'm not lying. It's like she had practiced the song with the whole audience while Steven and I weren't looking, because everybody sang along. It turns out, she *had* practiced the song with her piano player — that's why he knew it so well when he played it for us at the piano bar downstairs.

It was so exciting that both Steven and I got teary-eyed, and then, when we saw each other trying not to cry, we started laughing, and that made it harder to keep from crying!

After the show, Miss Alison introduced us to Collette, the owner of the cabaret. Collette said, "Miss Alison tells me you're getting your act together. Be sure to call me first when you're ready to do a show, I'd be happy to have you guys here at Collette's." Then she gave us her business card!

Miss Alison said, "Call them 'Y'ALL.'"

Collette said, "Y'ALL. I like that!"

✪✪✪

For the next couple of days, Miss Alison was off from work and rehearsals, and we kind of lived the life of stars, or so we thought, playing with Li'l Roy, watching the home-shopping channels on TV and eating funny foods. But then on Wednesday, Miss Alison left while we were still asleep and returned as we were waking up with a box of donuts, a set of keys to her apartment and a stack of newspapers.

"It happens to the best of us, fellas," she said, "But I think it's time y'all got jobs." We apologized for not doing it sooner and she said, "No, no, that's not what I'm talking about at all. It wasn't time yesterday, or Monday, but today, it's time. I've got a rehearsal so I'm gonna run. Take your time, eat the donuts, drink some coffee, look through the papers and see what you can find. — But don't go gettin' *careers*, 'cause y'all are gonna be big stars real soon, y'hear?!"

Steven and I said, "Yes, Miss Alison!"

She laughed. "That's the way I like to hear y'all talkin'!" She threw the new set of apartment keys on the table next to the donuts. "So you won't think I'm holding you prisoner! But don't get lost!" And then she was gone.

Steven and I quickly made up the couch and took showers and got fully dressed before we even started the coffee. We felt guilty, even though Miss Alison said not to, and we were anxious to go through the want ads and get a job and make her proud.

We started to get a little discouraged going through the want-ads, though. Everything required some kind of experience, which we didn't have. But then, finally, in the last paper in the stack, I stumbled onto the perfect ad:

> REVIVAL THEATER Looking for counter help. Several positions available. No exper. nec. No phone calls; just come in Thu., 11-3. 55 W. 82nd St.

I read it to Steven. "I think 'no exper. nec.' stands for 'no experience necessary.'"

Steven said, "Could be."

I said, "We could both get a job there, and I could help you out with the stuff you don't know. We should do it."

"Sounds good to me."

We spent the rest of the day cleaning Miss Alison's apartment (and washing our dirty clothes in her machine). In the process, we came across the fifty-dollar bill Bug had given us in a pair of Steven's overalls, so we took it down to Miss Alison's neighborhood grocery store (what they call a convenience store back in Texas and Indiana) and bought as many groceries as we could.

That night, Miss Alison came home very exhausted, which made us happy, because she let us cook some "normal" Midwestern and Southwestern food — Armadillo Eggs (a jalapeño appetizer), Chicken-Broccoli Divan, Potatoes Delmonico, Green Beans Empress, and Ruth's Texas Dirt Cake for dessert. Needing the recipes gave us a good excuse to call our families, not that we really needed an excuse!

Miss Alison took a long, hot bath and Steven cooked (I chopped and cleaned things for him). While we ate dinner, Miss Alison slowly started noticing that everything in her apartment was clean. First, she noticed Li'l Roy's cage, then she noticed everything else.

"Your mamas sure did raise y'all right!"

✪✪✪

The next afternoon, Miss Alison gave us directions to the Revival Theater on Eighty-Second Street. But as we approached the building, something seemed not quite right to me. For one thing, it looked like a movie theater and not a church at all. It even had a movie theater marquis out front:

NOW SHOWING:
PINK FLAMINGO'S
FEMALE TROUBLE
TWO BY JOHN WALTERS

I thought, well, maybe somebody turned an old movie theater into a revival church — that's certainly what my Daddy did with a circus tent. And "John Walters" was probably the preacher, and "Pink Flamingo's Female Trouble Two" was probably the name of this week's sermon. I mean, we *were* in the Big Apple Pie, after all.

We went in the glass door and there on our left were candy and popcorn cases filled with candy and popcorn! "Look!"

Steven shook his head at the bin of bright yellow popcorn, "It looks *awful*!"

"Do you think they serve it during church?"

"Church? What are you talking about?"

"Can I help you guys?" A good-looking middle-aged man with long straight hair and huge, bushy sideburns was standing behind us.

"We're here about the jobs," Steven said.

"Ah, but, I thought it was something else," I stammered.

"Counter help?" the man continued.

"Yeah," Steven answered.

"You have any experience?"

"No sir," I replied.

"Well, don't worry," he said, "A monkey could do it. It's just a matter of how much the big monkey likes the little monkeys! The pay's not much, but there's free movies and candy!" Steven and I didn't move. "I'll get the apps."

He went through a door on the far side of the lobby. Steven smirked. "You didn't really think this was a *church*, did you?"

"What was I supposed to think? That's what the ad said: 'Revival Theater.'"

"They show old movies at revival theaters."

The man returned and gave us each a piece of paper with writing on one side and two chewed-up pencils. "Knock yourselves out, fellas. Let me know when you're done. The name's Lloyd Miller. Lloyd."

"Steven Cheslik-DeMeyer."

"Jay Byrd — um, James Dean Jay Byrd."

"James Dean? After the actor?"

"No sir, not exactly."

"We had a James Dean Festival in June!" He turned and walked back into the office.

I looked down at the application in my hand. I wondered why I hadn't worn my Lucky Green Dress today (other than the fact that it was still wet from being washed). There were the usual lines for name, address, and all that, and we put in Miss Alison's address and phone number; but just below that, it had a box we were supposed to fill in with "Work Experience" and, below that, three lines for "References."

We didn't want Lloyd to think we were as new to the city and as inexperienced as we were, so we tried to fill up the Work Experience section as completely as possible. I wrote:

> April 1992 to Present - miscellaneous odd jobs, Eastern US
> 1980-1992 - sales, Okey-Dokey Mobile Madness, Okey-Dokey, TX
> 1970-1980 - construction, tent revivals, East Texas

and Steven's looked like this:

> I don't have a lot of experience in this particular field, but I have worked for most of my life on a popcorn farm doing assorted hard work, from planting and harvesting, to fence building and various homecrafts.

To fill up the lines in the References section of the application, we both put Miss Alison first, our parents second and each other third. When we were finished, we took a deep breath, smiled nervously at each other and tapped on Lloyd's office door.

"'S'open!"

The first thing that caught our attention as we opened Lloyd's office door was a baritone ukulele hanging on the wall behind him. The office itself was small and cluttered with film reel tins and movie books, magazines, newspapers and posters, popcorn buckets and Coca-Cola cups.

"Oh, wow, a ukulele!" I blurted out.

"My Uncle Floyd passed that down to me after the accident. Bowling. He lost an arm. I tried playing it a couple of times, but I never got the hang of it. I like the way it looks, though, so I hung it up on the wall to remind me never to go bowling!" He laughed, but I think it was the truth.

"I've got one almost just exactly like it," I said.

"No kiddin'?"

"No kiddin'! It was given to me by my grandmother's aunt's boyfriend, or something like that. Ollie Biddle."

"You play it?" Lloyd asked.

"Not much yet. Steven's teaching me. We write songs and sing and stuff."

"With a baritone uke? What kinda music?"

I looked at Steven. He said, "I play guitar. It's kind of old-timey string band style music. It's just the two of us, guitar and ukulele and we sing harmonies."

"No kiddin'!" He stood up, took the ukulele off the wall and held it toward me, "Let's hear it!" I took it and gave it to Steven.

"Why don't we try 'Calypso,' Steven said, so we did.

Afterwards, Lloyd said, "Excellent, just excellent. You got anything else? We sang "My Mama Likes The Feel Of Cottage Cheese." "Good stuff," he said. "You ever hear of WTCG AM-520?"

"No, what is it?"

"Nobody listens to the radio anymore."

"Well, we just got into town a couple days ago." That slipped out; I wasn't gonna say that.

"Really? I've got a little program on this little radio station WTCG every Friday night twelve to six a.m. Good hours, huh?" Steven and I nodded — we weren't sure if they were good hours or not, but if he thought they were, we weren't gonna disagree. "The good thing about 'em is I can do whatever I want to. I like to do some live stuff, whenever I can find somebody willing to play on AM radio. Would you guys be interested in coming in tomorrow night, just for the hell of it? Bring your guitar and your ukulele, and sing a couple of songs?"

"Sure!"

We were all three so excited about the radio thing that we almost forgot about the jobs. We were saying "thank you" and "goodbye" and all that and we were just about to head out the door when Lloyd said, "*Oh!* Did you guys wanna work here or what? It's fifty bucks a shift, under the table."

Steven and I both said, "Sure!" It sounded like a lot of money at the time, but even still, Lloyd could've said it was ten bucks a shift and we would've jumped at it.

✪✪✪

The next day, we worked from four to midnight. I wore my Lucky Green Dress. We got there at three-thirty and the only person there was a stringy-haired girl named Peg. The first thing she said was, "Oh, like I really dig your dress, man! It's *sooo* green and sparkly!" Lloyd wasn't there, but Peg said he told her to take care of us. She said, "Just do what I do, but better, because you're new!" We scooped popcorn, poured cokes, served candy, took money, swept the lobby while the movie was playing, and picked up the litter from the theater between movies. It was pretty easy and we both liked Peg a lot.

Lloyd told Peg to make sure we left at midnight on the dot, even though a movie was still playing, and she gave us the directions for getting to the WTCG station, which entailed taking a subway train and a bus way downtown. The studio where Lloyd was doing his show was on the top floor of a very old-looking building; the elevator chains rattled all the way up the nineteen floors.

When we stepped off of the elevator, we could hear Lloyd's voice booming out of a speaker high up on the wall. A door on one side of the room had a dim red box above it with the words "ON AIR" flashing on and off. Steven pointed at the sign and we didn't say a word.

We couldn't see him, but Lloyd could see us from the studio, and he was very excited. "This is your white trash country gospel connection friends, and tonight, we have quite a surprise for you — and, let me tell you, it's a surprise to me, too! We have a couple of live guests tonight, and one of them is wearing a *Barbie* dress! It's the most beautiful dress I think I've ever seen — and he looks so beautiful in it! It's green and glittery and lacy. It's a dress very similar to what my girlfriend Kathy wore to our senior dinner back about fifteen years ago. But it's very exciting, and we're gonna have to get the scoop on *that*! And let me tell you, folks, these guys are kind of the shining example — the sparkling, shining example of what this radio show is all about, because their music is *very* what I would call 'white trash country gospel.' I hope they don't mind me saying that. We'll ask 'em what they think when I get them in the studio in just a minute because I mean it as a compliment! But right now, let's hear a song by good old Merle Haggard. Perfect for the occasion, it's called 'Shopping for Dresses'!"

The song came on then faded right back out and the "ON AIR" light went out and Lloyd came out of the studio. "What's *this*?"

"Oh, you haven't seen it yet!"

"I should say not; I think I'd remember something like that."

"It's my Lucky Green Dress. My Uncle Joe gave it to me when I left home, as a good luck charm."

"Well, I'm charmed! Come on in, guys. Don't tell me any

more; we'll do it on the air, so it'll be fresh!" He gave us headphones and sat us down in front of two big microphones across from his chair. We put the headphones on but the Merle Haggard song was so loud in them that we had to take them back off. Lloyd flipped a switch or two and the song disappeared and his voice came through the headphones. "Can you hear me?"

"Yeah."

"One more thing before we go on the air. What do you call yourselves, Steven and Jay Byrd? Jay Byrd and Steven?"

"We call ourselves 'Y'ALL.'"

"That's perfect!"

When Merle's song was done, Lloyd came on the air, and said "Howdy, friends, we've got a couple of fellers in the studio tonight — and I dare say they're gonna be famous real soon — they call themselves 'Y'ALL'! Say howdy, Y'ALL!"

"Howdy!"

Lloyd asked us lots of questions and then asked us to sing a song. We had just finished writing "God Bless New York City (My Big Apple Pie)," and we were very excited about it, so that's what we sang.

When we finished singing it Lloyd started cussing. We thought we'd done something terribly wrong. He quickly put a record on the turntable and glared up at us. "What's wrong, Lloyd?"

"The phones are completely lit up! Ten lines — all lit up!" What did he mean? What had we done? Frantically, he picked up the receiver and said "WTCG, please hold. WTCG, please hold...." He did that ten times, then he went back to the first one. "WTCG AM-520, thanks for holding. Lloyd Miller at your service. That's right, it was live! They're sitting right here, ma'am, that's what 'live' means! — I'll tell 'em! I don't know, I'll ask 'em." He pushed another button. "WTCG AM-520, thanks for holding. Lloyd Miller at your service!" He played two more records before he was done answering calls. Thirty calls came through after that one song. That seemed like a lot of phone calls to us; Lloyd said it was "a whole helluva lot."

"Just about every one of 'em asked if Y'ALL are coming back again. After this record, I'm gonna announce that you'll be here every Friday night at midnight and then you're gonna sing another song. Okey-doke?"

Steven and I looked at each other. We were baffled. We didn't know what to say. We didn't say anything. The record ended, Lloyd went back on the air and announced us again and we sang "My Man, Our Horses, And Me," and before the song was even over, the phones lit up again!

We were regular guests on Lloyd Miller's Friday show — what he called "The Midnight Shack" — every Friday in July and August. We changed our schedule at the Eighty-Second (that's what we called the theater) so that we could see Miss Alison's show once a week on the way to *our* show. We took a subway train from Miss Alison's apartment in Queens to Collette's Cabaret in Greenwich Village. After Miss Alison's show, we'd go have dinner with her at a diner around the corner, then we'd take a bus down to WTCG and sing on the radio. Every week, people called up the station while we were there — some had just discovered us, others were "old fans" from our first appearance. The old fans would call in requests. We tried to write a song a week so we could have something new to sing each time.

Our appearances on the Midnight Shack got longer and longer. The first night we were there, we were back at Miss Alison's apartment by one-thirty a.m.; by the end of August, we were never in the radio station for less than three or four hours, and sometimes we'd stay the whole six hours and go eat breakfast with Lloyd. We would sing a song or two, talk with Lloyd on the air, sing another song or two, Lloyd would play some records, we would answer some phone calls on the air, we'd sing another, and then, suddenly, it'd be three or four a.m., or even later!

We felt like we were famous, but still, hardly anybody knew

us — the Big Apple Pie has more than seven million people in it, and we had reached barely more than a hundred, according to Lloyd. But then, on August 21, a guy named Blair called up to tell us he'd been listening to us since the beginning of July and he was planning an "event" on August 31 in the upstairs lounge of his restaurant, a place called the Flamingo. He said he'd love it if "Y'ALL" could make a public appearance there. He even said he'd pay us: one hundred dollars! Our first professional performance!

That night, I had my Twin Towers dream again (for the umpteenth time) — the one where Steven and I live on top of the Twin Towers. We told Miss Alison about the phone call the night before and she said, "I know, I heard him! That's great news. I told y'all, Y'ALL are gonna be big stars real soon. Miss Alison's gonna be coming to sleep on *your* couch!" We told her that would be fine by us, anytime!

"I had the Twin Towers dream again."

"Oh, that's a good sign," Miss Alison said.

"Do ya think? Should we ask 'em if we can move up there now?"

"May*be!*" The next thing Miss Alison did is something we'll never forget as long as we live. She offered to help us put a show together, "If you're looking for that kind of help."

"Really?"

"Of course! It'll be great!"

Miss Alison had us make a list of all the songs we'd written, and she helped us pick and choose and put them together in an order that would make for a good show. She also said we had to work on some stories.

"Stories?" Steven and I asked.

"Yeah, you know, introductions. You've seen me do it a hundred times."

"We don't know any stories," I explained to Miss Alison.

"Didn't you tell me you were born in a broom closet and that your Daddy's a tent revivalist?"

"Yeah."

"Honey, y'all have *stories*!"

So Miss Alison went and bought a dozen double-dipped chocolate donuts and we sat around the box eating them and talking about what songs we oughta sing and what stories we oughta tell in our show.

When we figured all of that out, more or less, Miss Alison said that the show had to have a beginning, a middle and an end. Of course, that seems pretty obvious now, but it was a real education for us — we'd never created a "show" before. It wasn't as easy as all that, though; we talked for *hours*, we even bickered a little bit, but fortunately, the donut shop was close by and open all night long. Three dozen donuts later, we had a show!

✪✪✪

For the next nine days, we practiced our show over and over and over again until we had it memorized (more or less), and Miss Alison gave us directions on how to make it better, and she helped us make the songs come alive when we sang them — by looking at each other at certain times and doing other things like smiling at the audience or looking off thoughtfully. Stuff like that.

To give us a taste of being onstage in front of an audience with bright lights on us and microphones in front of us, Miss Alison rearranged her own show a little bit to give us an opportunity to sing a couple of songs in it every night. And afterwards, she would tell her audience about our upcoming show at the Flamingo, and she would tell them they *had* to go, or else she would "spank them!" That next Friday, when we went to do Lloyd's radio show, Lloyd "demanded" that his loyal listeners attend our show, which was coming up the following Monday.

Miss Alison also paid to have handbills made. We put some at Collette's and the other cabarets and cafes and theaters and bars in the Village, and we put some at the Flamingo — and we even went up to Times Square on Sunday the thirtieth and passed them out to the tourists!

Before we knew what had happened, Monday, August 31, eight p.m. had rolled around, and the upstairs lounge of the Flamingo was packed. *Packed!*

Our dressing room was the outside balcony of the upstairs lounge, which you got to by going through a glass door behind a curtain at the back of the stage. The balcony hung over the sidewalk and the front awning of the Flamingo. A railing with flower boxes on it hid us from the cars passing by on the avenue and the folks on the sidewalk, but, unless we stayed squatted down, our heads poked over the top. Once in a while, we'd forget and stand up for a second, but somebody would yell out, "Hey, look!" and we'd duck back down. We could see the swarm of people in the lounge through the fancy drapes hanging in front of the glass door that opened to the balcony, but they couldn't see us.

Before anybody arrived, we had put a sign on the best chair in the front row that said:

LOVINGLY RESERVED
for
MISS ALISON

We peeked out one last time and Lloyd Miller was sitting in her chair! We panicked. We didn't wanna be rude to him, but we didn't want him to sit in Miss Alison's chair. But seconds later, the glass door opened and delivered Miss Alison to us.

"That's Lloyd in your chair," I said, "We can ask him to move."

"He's cute, huh?" She winked at us. "Too bad nobody came, huh?" she said.

"What?"

She did a little happy dance, "Oh my *god*, it's great! There must be two hundred people in there."

"Two hundred people?" My knees got wobbly.

Miss Alison said, "Don't forget to breathe, take your time, and whatever you do, don't forget to relax your butt, relax your butt, relax your butt!" She jiggled my behind.

"Miss Alison," I exclaimed, "Is this necessary *right now?*"

"Listen to you, how tense you are! *Relax your butt!*"

"Okay, okay." I relaxed my butt.

"It's time, Y'ALL! Have fun! Wait for your cue."

She went out onto the little stage. Everybody clapped feverishly, and I swear I could feel the balcony shaking. When the applause finally died down, Miss Alison waited a moment, then said, "Ladies and gentlemen, friends and family, Y'ALL!"

Steven and I gave each other a quick peck, then ran out onto the stage. Everybody clapped and whistled and hooted and hollered and "oohed" and "ahhed" as we made our way to the stage. When they calmed down and we looked out into the room, we saw lots and lots of warm, smiling faces, all of them anticipating what we were gonna do. Steven and I both stared out like deer stuck in the headlights, our minds blank. Miss Alison cleared her throat, and I came out of it and said, "Howdy, we're Y'ALL!" and Steven started playing, and we were off and running.

They really seemed to enjoy our songs — I swear I think I even saw a couple of people mouthing along with the words (they must've heard us on the radio!), and one woman had tears streaming down her face as we sang "Does It Feel Like Home?" I think they enjoyed the stories I told them about us, too.

We sang "My Man, Our Horses, And Me" twice, the way Miss Alison did in her show, and I invited the audience to sing along with me the second time through and they did! Everybody sang along and swayed back and forth and smiled at us. Lloyd had an arm around Miss Alison and he was swaying her back and forth with him, singing along.

Without thinking about it, I did a little yodel at the end

of the song, and Steven instinctively played along. The audience screamed and pounded the floor.

We said "Goodnight, y'all," and ran off the stage, past the curtain, through the glass door and out onto the balcony. The audience went wild. They were still clapping and hollering and stomping the ground and their chairs when we got outside, and once we were out there, they started chanting "Y'ALL! Y'ALL! Y'ALL! Y'ALL!"

I looked at Steven, "What are we supposed to do now?!"

He said, "I don't know! I think they want an encore!"

"Maybe Miss Alison will tell us what to do." We peeked through the drapes into the room. Everybody was standing, jumping, clapping, cheering; everybody but Miss Alison. She was hunched over in her seat, bawling like a baby!

The chanting slowly turned into "ENCORE! ENCORE! ENCORE! ENCORE!"

We didn't have any more songs prepared. But they kept cheering, so we went out on the stage and stood there 'til the craziness finally died down. I said, "Thank you all so much, but we don't know any more songs!" A few folks let out moans of disappointment. I looked over at Miss Alison; she had sat up and was drying her face and at the same time mouthing something to me, but I couldn't figure it out.

"What?" She mouthed it again and I shrugged, then she muttered something, but still I couldn't figure it out. "What?"

"'You Ain't Woman Enough To Take My Man'!" she yelled. Some of the other people in the audience had apparently heard us sing it before, because they started chanting "YOU AIN'T WOMAN! YOU AIN'T WOMAN! YOU AIN'T WOMAN!"

So we sang "You Ain't Woman Enough To Take My Man." We thanked them and thanked Loretta Lynn for writing such a great song, then ran out to the balcony again. But they weren't done with us. The craziness started up again and continued until we went back out again and sang "Stand By Your Man."

Miss Alison followed us out onto the balcony after that

song and told us not to go back out. "You wanna leave 'em wanting more!"

Steven said, "Don't worry, we don't have any more!"

When we finally went out, people stood in line and asked us to autograph their programs! They wanted our *autographs!* We were *famous!*

By midnight, the Flamingo was finally settled back down. There were only a few folks still standing around and they weren't standing around us, so we relaxed. Miss Alison gave us both big hugs that lasted way too long, and when she came up from both of us, she was crying. She said, "I'm just so proud of you both, I can't even tell you! You were *excellent* tonight!" She pulled us both into her and the three of us stood in a huddle and cried like babies!

We took a taxicab home that night; Miss Alison didn't want anybody to see us all puffy-eyed and teary. As we were crossing over the Queensboro Bridge, I said, "Someday, we'll be ridin' over this bridge in a limousine!" and Miss Alison started crying again.

Epilogue

Y'know how sometimes, time goes by really fast and other times, it just kinda ticks by? Well, for the five years following that night at the Flamingo, time started speeding up, and it kept up its steadily quickening pace, faster and faster. Faster and faster and faster things happened for us. We did a cabaret show at Collette's, we performed several more times at the Flamingo and once in a while on WTCG AM-520 (until it went off the air). We performed in clubs and cabarets and restaurants and theaters and bars and coffeehouses and bookstores and festivals all over the Big Apple Pie and all over the state of New York, and Pennsylvania and Connecticut, and all over the United States of America, and even in Canada! We performed on FM radio stations and on neighborhood public access cable television shows and on nationally broadcast public television and nationally syndicated commercial TV. And we made records and CDs and cassettes and music videos.

But then one morning, about five years after that exciting *first* night at the Flamingo, I woke up after having my Twin Towers dream again. I looked out of our windows, and I didn't see any big ol' buildings poking up through the sky, and I didn't see any cabs on concrete slabs or, thankfully, any guys with switchblade knives....I looked at Steven, awake but still in bed. He said, "What's wrong?"

I didn't answer him. I got out of bed and sat down at the table and started writing.

> *I was born in Okey-Dokey, Texas, which is the southeast point of the equilateral triangle created by it, Houston and Galveston....*

Steven said, "What are you doing?"

"I don't know. Writing."

"What are you writing?"

"I'm scared we're gonna forget it all."

He said, "*What?*"

"Where are we?"

"I don't know. Tennessee someplace." He reached over and pulled the map off of the front seat.

"I had the Twin Towers dream again."

"Hmm." He was busy looking at the map. Steven loves maps.

"Y'know, we never did go up on top of the Twin Towers, did we?"

"No. But I don't think they'd really let us put a trailer up there!"

"Well, I don't know. If we had enough money, they might."

"We don't have enough money!"

"Not yet." I continued writing.

I left when I was twenty-four, led by a vision.

I stopped. "We never even went up on top of the Twin Towers."

"Yeah, I know."

"To see if we even like the view."

Steven was up and starting to cook breakfast. "The *what?*"

"The view! What if we don't even like the view?"

He took a carton of eggs out of the fridge. "I don't even know what you're talking about anymore."

"The view! The *view!* What if we don't like the view? What if we do get enough money to live on top of the Twin Towers and we don't like the view?"

Steven shook his head. "I think you've finally lost your mind, Jay Byrd. Scrambled or over easy?"

I got in the driver's seat and started up the Winnebago. "You better make 'em scrambled."

"Where are we going?"
"I wanna check out the view!"

✪✪✪

I was born in Okey-Dokey, Texas, the southeast point of the equilateral triangle created by it, Houston and Galveston. Steven was born on a popcorn farm, in Kornflake, Indiana, but New York City, the Big Apple Pie, is what we call home now.

So, we're watching the sunset for the umpteenth time here. One-hundred-and-ten stories up in the air. You can really experience the sun setting from a hundred and ten stories in the air. I don't know if we'll ever have enough money to even ask how much it'd cost to put our trailerhome on top of the Twin Towers and live here, but if and when that time comes, we've seen the view and we love it!

My Man, Our Horses, and Me

THE END

Index of Songs

If you'd like another copy of *The Good Book* for a friend, or if you want to check out other merchandise at the Y'ALL Country Store — or simply to find out when Y'ALL will be performing in your neck of the woods, visit "The World of Y'ALL" on the Internet at www.luckygreendress.com.

To get a free subscription to *the little Y'ALL newsletter*, Y'ALL's seasonal publication, send your name and address to Y'ALL, PO Box 24903, Nashville, TN 37202-4903. Or email your information to: bedazzled@luckygreendress.com.

And, if you write a book report (no less than a paragraph, but as long as you want), and send it to the address above , you'll receive a bumper sticker stating "I Read the Good Book: the true story of Y'ALL" (while supplies last).